THE APPREHENSION OF BEAUTY

THE APPREHENSION OF BEAUTY

The Role of Aesthetic Conflict in Development, Art, and Violence

Donald Meltzer
and
Meg Harris Williams

Published for
The Harris Meltzer Trust
by

KARNAC

To
Our Own and All
Ordinary Beautiful Devoted Mothers
We Dedicate This Book

And that same day, too, gazing far down from the boat's side into the same golden sea, Starbuck lowly murmured: "Loveliness unfathomable, as ever lover saw in his young bride's eyes! Tell me not of thy teeth-tiered sharks, and thy kidnapping cannibals ways. Let faith oust fact; let fancy oust memory; I love deep down and do believe."

And Stubb, fish-like, with sparkling scales, leaped up in the same golden light: "I am Stubb, and Stubb has his history; but here Stubb takes oaths that he has always been jolly."

Ch. CXIV–"The Gilder"
in *Moby Dick*, by Herman Melville

CONTENTS

ACKNOWLEDGEMENTS

The authors would like to thank the fellow contributors to this book; these are the psychoanalytic colleagues who have presented their intimate experiences to teaching seminars in the form of clinical material: Giuliana Fortunato of Milan, Romana Negri of Bergamo, Marja Schulman of Helsinki, Sveien Haugsjerd of Oslo; Giuditta Alberio of Novara, and the staff of Pietro Pfanner from the University of Pisa (Calambrone). They also wish to thank Ann Stokes and Lawrence Gowing for permission to reprint the dialogue between Donald Meltzer and Adrian Stokes.

I would like to thank Maria Rhode and the *Journal of Child Psychotherapy* for permission to reprint her review of the original (1988) edition of the book here as an Afterword and Ian Craine for preparing an index for the present edition.

Meg Harris Williams

ABOUT THE AUTHORS

Donald Meltzer (1923–2004) is widely known as a psychoanalyst and teacher throughout Europe and South America. He is the author of many works on psychoanalytic theory and practice, including *The Psychoanalytical Process, Sexual States of Mind, Explorations in Autism, The Kleinian Development, Dream Life, Studies in Extended Metapsychology, and The Claustrum*, all published by Clunie Press (Karnac Books).

Meg Harris Williams (1951–) is a writer and artist with a lifelong psychoanalytic education, and stepdaughter of Donald Meltzer. Her books include *Inspiration in Milton and Keats, A Strange Way of Killing, The Chamber of Maiden Thought* (with Margot Waddell), *A Trial of Faith, Five Tales from Shakespeare* (for children), and *The Vale of Soul-making*.

FOREWORD

On the original publication of this book in 1988 Donald Meltzer wrote:

This volume has grown over the years almost as a family project of Martha Harris, her two daughters Meg and Morag, and her husband, Donald Meltzer. It therefore has its roots in English literature and its branches waving wildly about in psychoanalysis. It is earnestly hoped that it will reveal more problems than it will solve. Its roots in English literature—Shakespeare, Milton, Wordsworth, Keats, Coleridge and Blake—are as strong as the psychoanalytical branching from Freud, Klein and Bion. Its philosophical soil is certainly Plato, Russell, Whitehead, Wittgenstein, Langer, Cassirer and, in aesthetics, Adrian Stokes.

The fundamental thesis of aesthetic conflict over the obtrusive outside and the enigmatic inside of the object is traced into various dimensions: development of the personality, violence as an interpersonal and social phenomenon, and art as an active and receptive undertaking. While it is, from the clinical sense, a sequel to [Donald Meltzer's] *Studies in Extended Metapsychology*, it also goes some distance towards uniting the Kleinian source with its later tributaries, thus mapping out a current of clinical and theoretical progress that is certainly accelerating.

Donald Meltzer died in 2004. During the preceding years his conviction was reinforced that *The Apprehension of Beauty*, together with its later partner *The Claustrum*, represented his core philosophy—the philosophy toward which his other books and theories had always been striving. Despite, or perhaps because of, its many `wild roots' in other genres of thinking (literary, psychoanalytic, philosophical) he felt it to be his own, original philosophy of mind—it was *what he really meant*. *Beauty* is by no means a perfectly crafted book; by contrast with *The Claustrum*, it is idiosyncratic, untidy, some would say unstructured; and it was written under the distressing circumstances of my mother (Martha Harris)'s accident and prolonged illness. Yet it was his own interpretation of Kleinianism and its inherent implications. It might be inferred that it was his wife's illness and disability that pressurized him into saying what he really meant: he was saying it on her behalf also. For during his later years he came increasingly to see himself as a 'Kleinian,' not in the standard kosher or dogmatic sense, but rather, as regards his personal affirmation of the overriding influence of Mrs Klein as teacher and analyst on his personal ideas and development. This was an internal relationship that became increasingly dominant and clear to himself in Meltzer's last years; he is a son of Klein, but a sibling of Bion, in terms of the internal family; and the clinical implications of this predominance of Klein, as regards his approach to psychoanalytic material whether in the consulting room or in supervision, are far-reaching, and show clearly in this book. Meanwhile, outside clinical psychoanalysis itself, *The Apprehension of Beauty* with its central concept of the 'aesthetic conflict' is probably the book of Meltzer's which has to date borne the most fruitful practical repercussions in the related fields of education, neurophysiology, and literary and cultural studies.

Meg Harris Williams, November 2004

INTRODUCTION

From its medical parentage Psycho-analysis has always had a deeply biological orientation to the concept of Mind. It took Freud forty years to loosen the equation of mind and brain, at least to the extent that their unity could be brought into question. But it was necessary for the findings of anthropologists to indicate that there was a great difference between World and Culture. The baby relates himself to the world and only slowly, in the way that Wordsworth eloquently bemoaned, does the culture impinge on him to constrict his sensibilities. It is not without justice that psychoanalysis has been accused of representing the narrow values of the middle-class or bourgeoisie, sprinkled with bits of Jewish xenophobia. The tendency of psychoanalysis as a social organization has been to see itself, in Bion's terms, as a Basic Assumption Fight-flight Group, always in the process of fragmenting itself while waiting for the next messiah. The quest for respectability and the unmentionable economic factors in the lives of its practitioners have always served to tighten the hold of this organizational level on the so-called training. Since any organization must select its candidates for obedience rather than creativity, the policy to train practitioners rather than educating interested people has always been followed. The result has been a rapid spread, but, like an oil-slick, very thin. Its guild structure has always been the 'enemy of promise', claiming a non-existent monopoly of its all too public 'mysteries'. On the other hand the work-group functions have continued to make progress over nearly a century. Their development has remained largely unknown to the critics of psychoanalysis who seem, almost to a man, to be content with reading early Freud.

Yet the main line of advance, from Freud through Abraham to Melanie Klein and Bion, has been widely borrowed without acknowledgement. The progress in method and model of the mind has been steady, and the clinical achievements have gradually widened and become more impressive. Consequently the reputation of psychoanalysis as an art has unostentatiously brightened while its claims to scientific status have slipped into irrelevance. This paradoxical situation reflects the disappointment widely felt in the consequences of explanatory and experimental science, with its shibboleths of health and wealth.

This book is meant, therefore, to give voice to a process that has been taking place all along but which has been disguised by a splitting process. On the model of pure and applied mathematics, psychoanalysis divided itself into pure and applied: the latter operating through the 'Imago Groups' which formed at various times and in various places, finally incarnating themselves as the section on Applied Analysis of various Societies. But, as with all such splitting processes, the defence against depressive pain—in this case mourning for the defunct dream of respectability—was evident. It is not possible for an art form, however precise its descriptive methods or systematic its collation of findings, to be respectable. The reason is clear. An art form must be highly individual and its oeuvres unrepeatable. Its arbiter of value, whether applied to the individual analysis of a patient or to a contribution to its literature, must be aesthetic, and its impact must therefore vary with the receptiveness of its recipient. There can be no arguing, only evocation.

The authors of this book have been bound together by analytic and family ties for nearly thirty years and have had a great influence on one another's thinking and sensibilities. It seemed appropriate that this should be a joint venture, interdigitating clinical psychoanalysis and literary criticism in defiance of the splitting tendency. It is intended as a celebration of the beauty of the method which Freud discovered and developed, a method that enables two people to have the most interesting conversation in the world, hour by hour, for years, and to relinquish it with regret owing to the imperative of psychic reality. In doing this, in celebrating the beauty of the method, we are, in fact, celebrating the beauty of the method by which the mind—as a phenomenon made possible by the giant computer of the brain—operates upon the emotional experiences of our lives to give them a representation through symbol formation that makes thinking about these experiences possible. And it is clearly this 'thinking about' which generates the 'learning from experience' whose consequence is the structural alterations and reorganizations by which the mind grows. This 'growth,' in complexity, integration and richness, would seem, judging by the innate open-endedness of the system, to have no finite boundaries. The history of our truly great creative men and women bears witness to this through their works. It is, after all, not only the poets, but the handful of creative people of each era who are Shelley's 'unacknowledged legislators of the world'.

It seems somehow fitting that the mind should discover its own beauty only after it has discovered the beauty of nature and of man's works that bear witness and extol it. In this respect the growth of the individual's aesthetic awareness mirrors the evolution of the race, in its transformation of weapons into tools, in its gradual move from anthropomorphism to understanding nature, in its even slower development from possession and exploitation to responsibility for the world. I can remember well how at the age of eight, against a background of awe at the beauty of horses and trees, the beauty of man's works burst upon me during travels with my parents circuiting the Mediterranean. To breathe life and beauty into stone seemed to me then the highest possible aspiration. Perhaps it still does, although music and poetry seem more impossible.

In a certain sense, psychoanalysis discovers that creativity is, for the self, impossible. The muse, inspiration, Milton's 'unpremeditated verse', all creation of beauty comes as in a dream and is a function of the internal objects, of the lares and penates of the individual artist-scientist. 'Who am I to be a poet seeing how great a thing it is?' Keats wrote to his friend Reynolds. That some of the greatest creators have also been mad at times bears the most impressive testimony to the lack of unity of the mind, but also to the ferocity of its struggle against the internal and external forces of philistinism, minus K.

That is the theme of this book: the struggle in the individual between aesthetic sensibilities and the forces of philistinism, puritanism, cynicism and perversity. James, a little boy of seven years, in the fourth year of his therapy at the Tavistock Clinic with Marja Schulman of Helsinki (previously briefly reported in *Dream Life*) had developed considerably from the state of nearly mute autism, but at great emotional expense to his succession of young and unusually lovely young therapists. His post-autistic state was severely obsessional (much in the manner of Mrs. Hoxter's 'Piffie' reported in *Explorations in Autism*.) This took the form of endless drawings meant to represent the route from James's home to the clinic. Eventually a repetitive item, a volcano, became the focus of interest, not because of its outpourings of lava (as in the usual small child's representation of the breast-with-a-hole) but by virtue of its continual emission of threatening noises.

Over a period of months it gradually became clear that these threats had something to do with wastefulness: James's wasting of time, of toys that he destroyed and discarded, of the felt-tip pens he dismantled,—perhaps of his therapist's patience and good-will. Certainly he seemed to waste her thoughts and words to which he paid no heed as he relentlessly pursued his own researches. But one item of value about her he did acknowledge, her beauty, to which an ingenious and varied seduction was directed. He begged her to take off her clothes, he wished to see and suck her breasts; she was forbidden to have other babies or children in therapy, and only grudgingly allowed the possibility of a husband.

Quite an astonishing equipment of cynicism and devious use of language was brought to bear on the inference that he was wasting the felt-tip pens in particular. Waste was a meaningless concept; at what moment could a felt-tip pen be said to cease to exist? When its casing was broken? When its felt was pulled out? Or only when the ink was washed from the felt with water? Or only when it was ground to bits underfoot? If one shred of felt-tip-pennishness could be demonstrated, then nothing had been destroyed or wasted, only the form had been changed, a kind of Law of the Conservation of Felt-tip-pennishness. But James's ingenuity was matched by his therapist's delineation of his confusion between words and objects, of his misuse of ambiguity, of his denial of intentionality, and finally his denial of psychic reality vis à vis herself and his internal objects. This seemed eventually to carry the day and the concept of waste became established. Henceforth the wasting of time, materials, ideas, patience and possibly love had to be reckoned with. But the idea of sparing her was not acceptable. Two alternatives were fielded: one was the aim of so controlling and tyrannizing that the termination of the therapy could never be brought about; the other was a plan to construct a substitute object with all the necessary qualities but which, being his own creation, could reasonably be said to be his absolute possession.

The implementation of the first of these, which took the form of obscene abuse and threats of an ingeniously gory quality, was felt to be impeded by the presence of his father in the waiting room, where he might be able to overhear. So it was necessary for James to construct a device, to obviate this danger of interference. This he fashioned from the plastic strips which held the wall-protection formica in place, and the screws, the former being the cables and the latter the filters of his device. Its function was both to filter out the obscenities from his language and also to change the musical quality to a loving murmur for transmission to the waiting room. This all had a somewhat charmingly imaginative play-acting quality.

But the process of constructing his own alternative object had no such abstract aspect, for James began to turn up session after session with bits of old machinery scavenged during trips with his father to a neighbouring rubbish tip. There were parts of an old piano, of TV sets, radiograms and record players. Clearly, as with the grumbling volcano, the most important attribute of his agglomerated object was to be the sound that it made, a 'singing-machine' to parallel his 'P.A. System'.

Over the next year a subtle metamorphosis took place. The 'PA System' was discarded as the abuse and tyranny turned into pleading and boasting, pleading to be allowed to see and suck the therapist's breasts and boasting that he would be able to have and feed a baby himself some day. And the 'singing machine' was discarded for a less delusional device, again being constructed, at home this time, with his father's help. It was a periscope. The trouble was this: their house was almost high enough to see the dome of St. Paul's. Symbol formation was slowly making headway against tenacious concreteness.

It was the experience over the years of seeing the evolution of personality structure in arrested development of autistic children such as Marja Schulman's James, Doreen Weddell's Barry (*Explorations in Autism*) or Diomira Petrelli's Francesco (*Studies in Extended Metapsychology*) that hardened to conviction the long held suspicion that aesthetic considerations played an important role in development. When Francesco entered the room for his first session and stopped in astonishment before Diomira Petrelli and murmured 'Are you a woman—or a flower?' one could catch a glimpse of the reaction of the newborn to the first sight of its mother and of her breast. The formulation of the aesthetic conflict followed easily and almost immediately opened a new way of approaching developmental conflicts, for it placed the turmoil over the present object in a fugue relation to those already extensively studied about the absent object. In between these two areas of conflict it was then possible to insert Bion's vision of 'the absent object as a present persecutor', that is, the space where the object used to be as a ghost of its former existence.

Formulation of the aesthetic conflict as an inside-outside problem, as a conflict between what could be perceived and what could only be construed, led directly to the problem of violence as violation: violation of the privacy of internal spaces and their representations. The integrating force of this view of violence made itself felt over the whole range of violations, physical and mental, of individual against individual, groups against individuals and group against group. The previously formulated distinction between group and gang (*Sexual States of Mind* and *Studies in Extended Metapyschology*) was given a new sharpness of import with respect to internal as well as to external organization, especially regarding sexual crimes and sexual perversions.

Finally it became clear, mainly through Meg Harris Williams' work, that the application to literary criticism and the differentiation of true and false art found a new language in this spatial dimension. If we claim that the formulation goes beyond 'what oft was thought but ne'er so well expressed', we hope to be forgiven for hubris.

1   The Apprehension of Beauty*

It became a fundamental tenet of Melanie Klein's views on infantile development that the accomplishment of a satisfactory splitting-and-idealization of self and object was a primary requirement for healthy development. By means of this mechanism, in her view, it becomes possible for an idealized part of the infantile self to ally itself with an idealized object, in the first instance the mother's breast, as the bulwark against persecutory anxiety and confusion. The confusion particularly between good and bad in self and objects is, by this means, separated in a categorical way: exaggerated and rigid, it is true, but affording a working basis for the task of gradual reintegration of the split-off aspects in the course of development, as the values of the paranoid-schizoid position are gradually replaced by those of the depressive position, with the relinquishment of egocentricity in favour of concern for the welfare of the loved objects of psychic and external reality. This gradual shift in values has a sweeping effect upon judgement and the estimation in which are held the various attributes of human nature. Thus goodness, beauty, strength, and generosity replace in esteem the initial enthralment to size, power, success, and sensuality.

But the mode of operation of this primal mechanism of splitting-and-idealization has remained elusive and mysterious, the more so as we have become increasingly aware of the major part played by both inadequate and excessive use of it in the genesis of mental illness. Over and over again we find that the borderline, psychotic, or psychopathic patient has a fundamental defect in the differentiation of good and bad, being unable to make the distinction, or making it with rigidity bound to descriptive criteria which mock the very purpose of the operation, or even holds them in quite an inverted relation to one another. As the ubiquity of this defect in the more psychotic portion of the personality more and more pressed itself upon me in clinical experience, the more I also became aware of its conjunction with another serious defect: namely the failure of apprehension of beauty through emotional response to its

*This paper was originally published in 1973 and provided the title for a collection of Donald Meltzer's papers published in Italy.

1

perception. I noticed that whereas the more healthy of my patients recognized beauty as a *donné* without uncertainty through a powerful emotional reaction, the more ill were very dependent upon social cues, formal qualities and intellectual criteria. Often their judgement appeared sound, and in some instances even served as the basis for successful careers where aesthetic judgement was quite central. Nonetheless it was clear that, due to the lack of direct and immediate emotional response, they were deprived both of confidence in their judgement and of sincerity in their interest.

Two pieces of clinical material, some five years apart in my experience but bound together by a curious coincidence of content, have both consolidated this juxtaposition of which I speak and carried me some distance toward the solution of this interesting problem. One of them comes from a rather healthy patient with neurotic problems related to the early loss of his father, and rather late in his analysis, while the second comes from a patient suffering from bouts of depression with anorexia nervosa, very early in her analysis. I will describe and discuss them separately and then examine their relation to one another and to the problem in hand. Both center around a single dream.

The first patient became aware that circumstance was going to oblige him to cut short his analysis, more a matter for sadness than anxiety as he was feeling quite thoroughly relieved of the symptoms for which he had originally come. In this mood he became quite acutely aware, one weekend, of the beauty of the autumnal countryside and its link with his age, which was approximately that of his father at the time of his death, and with the age he estimated the analyst to be. Sunday night he dreamed that *he was driving along the road in his new car, with which he felt very pleased, but was startled to see a bald man lying on the verge. As he drew closer he saw to his horror that the man appeared to have a branch of autumn beech leaves protruding from his chest. As the man seemed alive, my patient jumped from his car to go to his assistance, intending to draw the branch forth from the chest immediately. But to his surprise the man, despite his showing every sign of great distress, stopped him from doing so, saying, 'No, call Dr. S* (a woman analyst whose paper on aesthetics my patient had recently come across), *we must first determine where the branch came from.'*

Needless to say, the analyst is bald. This intelligent patient

2

had come to understand the part which scrutiny of the counter-transference plays in the method of psychoanalysis. He felt that the analyst by this means understood the nature of his pain — about his father's death, about the premature end of his analysis, about ageing, the beauty of nature, and the beauty of analytical method. Thus the branch of autumnal beech leaves expressed the quality of my patient's pain linked with the perception of beauty, of its being and ceasing to be and ever renewing itself. He was struggling to hold together within himself the joy and the pain of the truth about living and not living things, of the frailty and the feebleness of life forces pitted against the malignant, which so often seemed to be favored by the great random factor. In other words he was seeming to shift his perception of beauty from the idealized good object to the struggle itself, thus including the malign and the random, along with the good, as participants in the drama, and thus in his love of the world.

My second patient was a young woman whose cachexia due to repeated and worsening bouts of depression and anorexia was hidden by her fashionable waifish beauty and masses of fine brown hair. From the outset of the analysis it was clear that an intelligent and sensitive but fragile adult self, identified with her paternal object, was being constantly overwhelmed by the primitive struggle between the tiny girl and an internal witch mother. In this struggle ravishment by beauty and reduction to helpless dependence were the prelude to being devoured. She could at times be so confused over the externalization of this conflict that she had to rush in panic to hide herself in bed, sleeping curled up completely covered. A few days before this material to be presented, she had had just such a panic at the dinner table when the sensation of the fat from a morsel of duck in her mouth struck terror in her connected with a recent horrifying dream image of *a seagull, denuded of feathers, flapping its stumpy wings helplessly while being swarmed over by bees.* It was just so that she herself felt often when her three little boys competed so fiercely for a place on her lap.

Some weeks following this dream image and panic one of the boys had bitten her on the finger in such an encounter and to her surprise had brought from her a torrent of tears which lasted all afternoon, in lieu of her usual flash of rage. It was at a

3

weekend following some days of complaining about the previous month's bill, and how long was the analysis going to last, and wouldn't twice a week be enough, and mightn't she grow helplessly dependent, etc. The retreat to bed lasted three days, involved missing the first two sessions of the week, and was accompanied by rather usual getting-dressed-in-mummy's clothes type of dreams. The interpretation of the transference situation on the Wednesday brought very evident relief and the patient launched upon a rhapsody about the beauty of the huge copper beech which stood outside her bedroom window. Its leaves had just broken out and, with the morning sun shining through them, suffused an exquisite pinky, gold glow, yet they were not yet developed enough to hide the structure of the tree and the 'skeleton' of its branches. But she then remembered another dream, not from the weekend but from the night before, in which *she had been riding on the upper deck of a bus, sitting on the nearside. As the bus brushed against the branches of a copper beech, they seemed to threaten to come in the patient's window and attack her face.*

Several items of history and circumstance are important to the understanding of this dream. In the first place the house in which she lives is owned by her mother and let to the young couple. Its beauty and indeed grandeur is closely linked in her mind to her mother's beauty, vitality, and social position. While the patient's hair is brown, her mother's is apparently rich auburn. It was only in the following session (when I see the patient quite early in the morning) that the sun streaming in suddenly lit up a bright red area in the patient's hair. When I commented on it she laughed, saying, 'Oh, that belongs to some oriental nun, I suppose.' It was in fact a hair piece, somewhat faded from its original color, which she had been wearing the last few days, although she has in fact masses of hair of her own. The other item: In her adolescence, in a fit of jealous rage with a boyfriend, she had attacked and in fact lacerated his face with her nails. She felt ashamed and afraid that this witch-like violence in her nature could erupt on the children. Like the upper deck of the bus and her bedroom, the consulting room is also on the first floor above the ground.

I was deeply impressed by the degree and severity of the splitting-and-idealization presented by this material and by the evident role played by projective identification and confusion of identity in its perpetuation. Clearly an experience of the apprehension of beauty has been split into its joyous and terrifying components, one experienced in her waking state toward the tree outside her bedroom window, the other reserved for her dream of the tree outside the bus window. In all three locations, house, bus, and consulting room, a payment relationship is involved. In the joyous aspect of the experience, she pays tribute to the beauty of her object freely and is perhaps troubled only by the inadequacy of her language to do justice to the grandeur of her object. In the persecutory component of the experience she feels the beauty to be merely a screen for the greedy and cruel fingers of the witch-mother reaching into her to snatch away her vitality and scratch away her beauty. The redness of the bus, the hair, the beech leaves in the sun and the blood from her boyfriend's wounds seem to swim together and reveal the image of a tiny girl carried in mother's arms, close to the breast, perhaps with masses of auburn hair tumbling over the baby's face as the mother bends to kiss her. How could a mother guess the link between the baby's chortle and cooing with delight in the day and screaming beyond comfort in the night? But the hair of the 'oriental nun' reveals a most important item in the configuration for it shows the contrast between the narcissistic pull of destructiveness and the object-related thrust of love. Note that the mingling of the two types of hair, the patient's own and the hairpiece implies the reverse of the image of herself in the bus, namely red hair among the brown as against a brown-haired passenger in a red bus, which in turn contrasts with copper beech leaves trying to get into the red bus. The point I am making is that the persecutor is a *narcissistic object*, that is, one compounded of an object and a part of the self. What is not clear to the patient, and I think we must not assume that it is clear to ourselves either, is whether the destructive bit of her self has invaded the split-off bad bit of her object, or vice versa. I can conceive of the possibility that this differentiation could be of immense prognostic importance.

How now shall we relate these two pieces of clinical material to one another and to our problem concerning beauty and primal splitting-and-idealization? In the first patient's material we see something of the pain and work which is necessary, in the course of development, to bring together the two sides of the primal split, under the economic principle and consequent values of the depressive position. In the second material we see something of the primitive terror and confusion which has been segregated off from the joy in order to make the relation to the external mother feasible for the fragile ego of the baby, and in order for it to be able to feed and survive. But does the material tell us anything about how the splitting-and-idealization comes about, say, whether as an active or passive process, or whether as a purposeful or accidental one, whether guided by external wisdom and tenderness or imposed by fortuitous triviality, etc. Clearly it tells us nothing definitive of this mysterious matter, but I think it gives some very enticing hints.

I think that the material in both instances suggests that the apprehension of beauty contains in its very nature the apprehension of the possibility of its destruction. In Bion's terms, the present object is seen to contain the shadow of the absent-object-present-as-a-persecutor. The beech tree in the spring reveals the skeleton of the beech tree in the winter, and the autumnal branch in the heart contains the recollection of the death of the father and the prediction of the death of pyschoanalysis. What the fragile ego of the child cannot sustain and is riven by, the lifetime of development strives to restore, so that the beauty of the object may be looked upon directly, without doing 'damage to the soul,' as Socrates feared.

2 Aesthetic Conflict: Its Place in the Developmental Process

The evolution of the Model of the Mind which underlies the observation and thoughts of psycho-analysts has been a quiet and covert one in many respects but its nodal points are clearly marked by the progression Freud-Abraham-Klein-Bion. What began as a hydrostatic model for the distribution of psychic energy in the spirit of nineteenth century physics, gradually shifted its analogy. The emergence of the genetic aspect brought forth the archeological metaphor; the replacement of topography by structural imagery introduced a social comparison (the Ego serving three masters); the replacement of 'mechanism' by 'unconscious phantasy', the insistence on the 'concreteness of psychic reality' and the introduction of an 'epistemophilic' instinct to replace Freud's 'sexual researches of children', shifted the biological model of the evolution of the individual mind from a Darwinian to a Lamarckian basis. By 1945 the Kleinian model had achieved this modification of the evolutionary simile of ontogeny recapitulating phylogeny, on the basis of a strengthened position for identification processes and thus of a view of development which emphasised relationship with objects rather than anything equivalent to survival of the fittest. Melanie Klein's 1946 paper 'Notes on Some Schizoid Mechanisms', which introduced the ideas of projective identification and splitting processes, shattered the assumption of unity of the mind, which Freud had already begun to do in his paper 'Splitting of the Ego in the Service of Defence'; it furthermore opened up a multiplication of the 'worlds' of mental life in a way that even the 'concreteness of psychic reality' had not envisaged. The Bionic transformation, which divides mental life into the symbolic and nonsymbolic areas (alpha-function and beta elements), and places its emphasis on the mind as an instrument for thinking about emotional experiences, has only began to be felt in the consulting rooms. But Bion's firm relegation of creative thought to the unconscious dream process, and his limitation of consciousness to the 'organ for the perception of

7

psychic qualities', must in time give a decisive blow to the equation of 'reason' with consciousness and profoundly alter our view of how our lives are lived. Freud's model becomes severely modified: the Ego becomes the horse, shying at every unknown object in its path, always wanting to follow in the way it has gone before; while the unconscious internal objects become the rider directing it relentlessly towards new developmental experiences. How profoundly, accordingly, does our view of the psycho-analytical process change under this model; yet in a way we seem to return full circle to Freud's early view of resistance and compulsion to repeat, merely changing the venue of these anti-developmental forces from the repressed unconscious to the the conservative conscious mind.

This Bionic shift in the Model of the Mind must cause us to rethink the whole problem of mental pain and the developmental process from infancy. We cannot take the newborn child as a *tabula rasa* but must consider the possibility that emotional experiences, their symbolic representation in dream thought, and their impact on the structuring of the personality, may commence in utero. It requires no great stretching of the imagination to conceive of the latter months of intrauterine life, malgré the findings of neuroanatomists about myelinisation, as being fraught with emotionality. Nor is it beyond us to imagine the auditory aspects of intrauterine life, coupled to kinaesthesia, as capable of symbolic representation in the song-and-dance genre (Susanne Langer) of symbolic forms (Cassirer). It is a small step from such speculation to an 'emotional' rather than a 'traumatic' idea of the impact of the birth process and the first encounter with the world 'outside'. At the present time such speculations may seem to be beyond verification by observation, but perhaps some of the ultra-sound (ecographic) observations of foetal life followed after birth by infant observation and later by psycho-analysis may in time bring these fanciful ideas into more authenticated form.

But both psycho-analysis and infant observation already afford rich data for moulding these speculations into a form which can modify our image of development and mental life in the Bionic vein. It has probably escaped no-one's attention that the percentage of 'beautiful' mothers recorded in the course of psycho-analysis far exceeds the national average and that this appellation clearly refers back to childhood impressions often completely out of keeping with later more objective judgements by the patients of their middle-aged parent. We will start here.

First I should like to introduce a piece of clinical material as an anchorage for further discussion and exploration. An ageing poet had entered analysis owing to the repeated failure of his love relationships to endure and deepen into marriage, for he greatly desired children as well as the stable companionship of a woman. The loss of his mother in latency had been followed by an estrangement from his father due to the extreme and probably paranoid jealousy of the step-mother who entered into his life within two years of the mother's death. Herself a widow with children, the step-mother could not bear to share her home with another woman's children and had them all sent off to boarding schools. Dread of a woman's jealousy and possessiveness had wrecked most of the patient's intimate relationships: sometimes jealousy rooted in the partner, sometimes in her mother, and sometimes provoked by the patient's enduring and close friendships with former partners or with the wives of his brothers or close friends. Being a very attractive and able figure, it was by no means merely his phantasy that these women might have preferred him to the spouses who variously deserted and disappointed them.

During the first year of analysis the holiday breaks had not seemed to touch our poet for he had used them to undertake rather exciting trips which he had dutifully postponed to accommodate the analytic schedule. But there was evidence that the approaching Christmas, the fourth break, was beginning to rattle him a little as it drew nearer. Gardens of great beauty began to appear in his dreams along with buried hostility to an older brother whose behaviour with girls, and later with women, he considered ruthless and destructive. In the penultimate week before the break he announced in passing something about which I had heard nothing previously: that he had been overtaken by his collecting impulse. This had taken various forms since puberty, starting with stamps, then prints, antiquarian books, etc., — each of brief but intense duration. This time it was commemorative medals, the production of which had apparently started in the seventeenth century, and examples of which — being without great monetary value —

9

could chiefly be found in junk shops. It had been inspired by a friend whose collection he had just seen. Somehow it seemed to link with his being drawn into a marital conflict between very close friends, both of whom used him as confidant. Sensing a move closely bound up with known devices by means of which he distanced himself from the grief of his mother's sudden death, I tried to investigate this phenomenon minutely for it seemed likely that it was being invoked to abort the impact of the approaching break in analysis. The patient took umbrage at my interest, which, I fear, was a little heavy-handed and perhaps needlessly urgent.

However the urgency bore immediate fruit in dreams. To the first session of the following week, the ultimate, he brought the following two dreams:

> He awoke in a little VW as if from a drunken sleep (he had drunk a little the night before and does not own a car) to find that it was precariously perched on a cliff edge in Devon, and if he leaned forward the car tipped further quite dangerously while it did the opposite if he leaned back (we both immediately thought of 'The Gold Rush'). Then he had arrived at the hotel owned by Jean Shrimpton to meet his friends but found the man without his wife, accompanied by another friend's girlfriend. Then he was in a garden accompanied by the couple's children and trying to climb a wall to get out. But the wall had an overhang (sic!) which made this impossible. However the woman then called him to come inside and suggested that he might like to trim the neighbour's hedge. But he demurred.

We discussed various aspects of the dream: the hangover from the last week's terminal session; the starvation of the frozen 'Gold Rush' type; the fact that his friend's wife was a beauty of the Jean Shrimpton type, and also his way of presenting himself as the 'good' man to women disappointed in their husbands. I suggested that this was perhaps his real 'collection'.

In the second dream:

> He had been invited by another friend to remodel his mother's garden, which was already quite well planted with clumps of bamboo, clumps of Jerusalem artichokes and something that looked like a shrub of Ragged Robin. Then they went into the house in order that the friend might show the patient his 'collection' which was housed in a vertical

multi-sided revolving showcase. In the first section were the commemor-
ative medals of which he had spoken in the earlier session; in the next
section there were small delicate glass phials labelled 'poison' (he had
recently heard of a new perfume called by that name) *while in*
the third section there were fragments of Roman glass, beautiful in their
irridescence. One flattened flask was so lovely he felt that it must be
made of some precious stone. But to his surprise further rotation did not
bring the return of the medals but something quite different.

We only touched lightly on the bamboo (caning at school),
Jerusalem artichokes (famous for inducing flatus), and the
Ragged Robin as an idealisation of his mode of ultra-casual
dress and the homeless existence after his father's remarriage.
What mainly engaged our attention was that the 'collection'
showcase was a distorted version of a kaleidoscope. Did he
collect 'broken' women in lieu of being broken-hearted at his
mother's death? An unexpected association seemed to confirm
this. Several days before, he had by chance encountered the
clergyman who had delivered the oration at his mother's
funeral, which he and his siblings had not attended, all being
away at school. This man, he discovered, had been a friend of
his mother's in her university days and waxed quite lyrical
about her great beauty, charm, vivacity and intelligence. Her
qualities of character the patient had never forgotten, but her
great beauty came as a surprise. Were then the phials of poison/
perfume little funerary tear vessels of Roman fame? Had he
obviated the grief of mourning by constructing a kaleidoscopic
image of his mother's character out of fragments of memory,
thus replacing a more primal concept of her physical beauty by
a more sophisticated one of the fineness of her personality?

Some material from the weeks prior to these events would
seem to lend force to this suggestion. During the previous
month I had been hearing, en passant, of pregnant women,
breast-feeding women and women yearning for babies in the
face of their mates' reluctance. One evening at a dinner party he
had been offended, not on his own account but for the violation
of the baby's privacy, when a woman fed her baby at the breast
at the dinner table. That night he dreamed:

While standing on a tube platform with a male friend he noticed two
girls with a man. One of them seemed to be offering her magnificent

11

breasts for the man's admiration in a way that made the patient laugh.

It was not at all clear what his laugh had meant; certainly not derision, for the girl's attitude seemed so innocent. Perhaps he had laughed in the dream from pure joy and admiration. A second dream that night presented three rather static images contrasting with the 'magnificent breasts':

The first image was an aerial view of the countryside, the receding flood waters leaving behind the hedgerows piled up mud in which dead bodies could be seen (like scenes from the recent Colombian disaster). *In the second image a film set had been constructed in a squash court consisting of a grassy hill on which a couple of stone armchairs rested; in the third he was surprised at how tatty the décor of the opera seemed until a young girl pulled a lever to show him the two magnificent monsters that leaped from two great boxes on the stage* (they were like the 'wonderful' monsters drawn by Sendak in *Where the Wild Things Are.*).

In summary I suggested that these images could be condensed into a single statement of the disastrous effect upon him of suddenly seeing his mother's breasts emerge from her brassière (the hedgerows — squash court — boxes) to feed his baby sister, a 'monstrous' thing for her to do right in front of him at the age of four.

In the light of the later material I am inclined to make two further connections: first of all, between the stone armchairs and the flask that was so beautiful he thought it must be made of precious stone rather than glass; and secondly between the dead bodies in the mud behind the hedgerows and the collection of commemorative medals (perhaps showing draped and undraped figures in bronze?).

I propose now to leave this splendid material hovering in the background, to be referred back to as I proceed to the main body of the exposition. The psycho-analytical stance regarding emotions or affects has probably been severely hampered by Freud's early neurophysiological model, in which quantities of excitation of the mental apparatus were seen to be apprehended subjectively as emotions. On the other hand Freud clearly espoused Darwin's attitude that emotions are experienced as the consequence of the perception of one's own social behaviour, with affective display being a relic of primitive modes of social communication. The paradoxicality of embracing both views was lessened by the separating-off of mental pain under the general rubric of 'anxiety', again viewed as a quantitative representation of dammed up impulse. The essential failure to distinguish between the experience of emotion and the display of emotional states placed the theory of the meaning of emotions in a kind of conceptual limbo. Even Melanie Klein's more detailed dissection and differentiation of emotions failed to correct this. The classical juxtaposition of emotion and reason, with its implied denigratory contrasting of female and male mentality, akin to primitive/civilised and infantile/adult, failed to find any correction until Bion's Theory of Thinking.

In many ways the object-relations direction set by Abraham in his 'Short Study of the Libido', with its exciting delineation of part-object and whole-object relationships, mapped the perimeter of a territory it failed to explore. The objects were left with their anatomical state as their substantiating feature, while the meaning of this fragmentation remained largely unnoticed in theory although under continuous exploration in the consulting room. In the clinical material it was probably clear to most workers that the partial anatomical reference was the consequence of a limitation in meaning: that partial objects had been deprived of their essential mentality, their capacity for feeling and thought and judgement, while retaining their formal and sensual features. They could be used, valued, feared, placated but they could not be loved and admired, protected and served. Only the fetishist, with his partial (or even more dismantled) object, could succeed in caricaturing the passions which whole objects could arouse.

It was perfectly natural for Melanie Klein, therefore, working on the assumption of unity of the mind and Darwinian expectation of evolution of the individual from simplicity to complexity, to place her formulation of the paranoid-schizoid position in chronological primacy. The 'red in tooth and claw' implication of the equation of immaturity with primitiveness saw no need to think twice. Pain and persecution could simply be taken as synonymous. But the 1946 paper on schizoid mechanisms changed all that. The gross simplification of mental life

13

presented by psycho-analytical theory could hardly even be taken as a skeletal structure upon which phenomenological flesh derived from the consulting room could be hung. A far more complex model was required to describe the follies, inconsistencies and astonishing self-ignorance of human beings. It was no longer sufficient to cleave to a medical model that could assume that the absence of disease constituted mental health, as if the mind functioned by a physiology and embryology directly analogous to the body. It became necessary to take into account the whole spectrum, like the Rat man's father declaring of his enraged child that he would grow up either to be a great man or a great criminal.

Outside the invisible walls of psycho-analytical thought it is probably generally accepted, again unthinkingly I would say, that the brain is a giant computer and that the mind is the brain, any other description being mere metaphor. But of course that is exactly the point: the mind is the metaphor-generating function which uses the great computer to write its poetry and paint its pictures of a world scintillating with meaning. And meaning is in the first instance the fundamental manifestation of the passions of intimate relationship with the beauty of the world.

Once one has taken on board Bion's description of 'an emotional experience' as the primary developmental event, it becomes clear that his 'empty' concepts of alpha-function and beta-elements make, essentially, a distinction between symbol formation and thought on the one hand, and a computation using signs and simple modes of extrapolation from past experience and received ideas, on the other. The creation of idiosyncratic symbols as opposed to the manipulation of conventional signs, marks the watershed between growth of the personality and adaptation. The tension between the two is the essence of what Freud labelled as 'resistance to enquiry'. Bion's distinction between 'learning from experience' and 'learning about' the world is precise. It is likewise marked by the distinction we make between narcissistic forms of identification (projective and adhesive) which produce an immediate and somewhat delusive alteration in the sense of identity, and the introjective process by which our internal objects are modified, setting up gradients of aspiration for the growth of the self.

14

Our lives are greatly occupied by relationships which are not intimate. Rousseau's *Social Contract* well describes the way in which we move about the world, using the lubrication of manner and custom, of conformity and social invisibility to minimize the friction and thus the wear and tear on our psyche-soma. And it is probably in this area that the majority of psychosomatic dislocations take place. The 'hostages to fate' aspect of our posture towards the casual world of teeming humanity, where 'everything threatens the head that I love', intimidates us beyond our wildest imaginings. We strive to create, through our apparent docility to the requirements of the community, a private space in which to enjoy the usufruct of our inheritance without 'let or hindrance'. These manoeuvres create the social armour which Wilhelm Reich described so wonderfully. But we are confronted with the problem of removing it when 'at home' and donning it again in time to sally forth. We dread to send our little children naked into the world of the nursery and the school, and, later, to see them swallowed up by the great combine harvester of the adolescent community.

Of the people who do not manage the enclosure of this space of privacy and intimacy, two distinct classes, at the antipodes of the body of the community, can be distinguished. The first of these, comprising the mentally and socially ill, are cut off from intimacy by the severity of their delusional ideas: either from living in states of projective identification, or from a gross failure of development of the personality, or from such perseverance in infantile modes of relationship that intimacy of an adult sort cannot develop. The second class are the artists, whose pained perception of the inhumanities daily in force about them, juxtaposed to a vision of the beauty of the world being vandalised by these primitive social processes, forbids them to squander the huge blocks of life-time required for adaptation. If lucky they are spared by the community from total neglect or persecution, but at the expense of having their work appropriated and misused, ridiculed and imitated, all at the same time. The recent vogue in literary criticism is a precise example of acting-out ambivalence and hostility towards the artists. At best they are treated as members of the amusement industry.

The huge majority of caring parents, seeing all about them

15

the misery of maladaptation, cannot help being primarily concerned, in their methods of upbringing, with armouring their children against the inhumanities inflicted on both the poorly adapted and on those whose naked sensitivity makes them vulnerable to the grossness of inconsiderate behaviour in casual and contractual relations. Similarly our schools cannot resist the pressure from parents and government alike to direct their efforts toward producing employable grown-ups. One must see the facts without seeming to pretend that any alternative is close at hand. We wish to prepare our children for the beauties of intimacy but our anxieties for their survival overcome our judgement so that we find ourselves joining in the training process, knowing quite well that it will dampen their thirst for knowledge and constrict their openness to the beauties to which they stand heir.

Although this process reaches its climax in the establishment of the so-called latency period, close observation of family life and of the mother-infant relationship reveals evidence of its early commencement. No event of adult life is so calculated to arouse our awe of the beauty and our wonder at the intricate workings of what we call Nature (since we hesitate nowadays to cite first causes), as the events of procreation. No flower or bird of gorgeous plumage imposes upon us the mystery of the aesthetic experience like the sight of a young mother with her baby at the breast. We enter such a nursery as we would a cathedral or the great forests of the Pacific coast, noiselessly, bareheaded. Winnicott's stirring little radio talks of many years ago on 'The Ordinary Devoted Mother and her Baby' could just as well have spoken of the 'ordinary beautiful devoted mother and her ordinary beautiful baby'. He was right to use that word 'ordinary', with its overtones of regularity and custom, rather than the statistical 'average'. The aesthetic experience of the mother with her baby is ordinary, regular, customary, for it has millennia behind it, since man first saw the world 'as' beautiful. And we know this goes back at least to the last glaciation.

Correspondingly it is only the limitations in our ability to identify with the baby that leaves him, in our thoughts, denuded of mentality. This ordinary beautiful baby does come trailing Wordsworthian clouds of glory in his openness to the apprehension of the world about him, if not the wisdom that can

16

make him 'father to the man' (although, to do Wordsworth justice, his 'little philosopher' is five years, and not five days, old). Proto-aesthetic experiences can well be imagined to have commenced in utero: 'rocked in the cradle of the deep' of his mother's graceful walk; lulled by the music of her voice set against the syncopation of his own heart-beat and hers; responding in dance like a little seal, playful as a puppy. But moments of anxiety, short of foetal distress, may also attack the foetus: maternal anxiety may also transmit itself through heart-beat, rigidity, trembling, jarring movements; perhaps a coital activity may be disturbing rather than enjoyable, perhaps again dependent on the quality of maternal emotion; maternal fatigue may transmit itself by loss of postural tone and graceless move-ment. Perhaps above all the foetus may feel his growth as the narrowing of his home in typical claustrophobic fashion and deduce that life exists beyond its familiar bounds, a shocking idea to a natural flat-earther. Imagination is a foraging impulse; it will find food for thought in the desert.

How, then, may the bombardment of colour, form and patterned sound of such augmented intensity as greets the new-born, impinge upon his mind? This we must ask the moment we consider that the baby's mind may already have begun its functions of imaginatively and thoughtfully exploring the world of its emotional interest. The great variety of demeanour and behaviour of the newborn is too obvious for anyone seeing them in the mass, as in an obstetrical department, to ignore; but of course this has always been ascribed to variation in constitution, or temperament, or differing degrees of foetal distress during birth, etc. The making of such ascriptions has neither descriptive nor explanatory power and merely dismisses the problem. Certainly it is no more speculative to say that babies experience the birth process and the first encounters with the world of intense sensa with differing attitudes, ranging from complete aversion to ecstatic wonder at the 'brave new world'. Two great allegories that define these two poles of birth experience, namely Harold Pinter's *Birthday Party* and Shakespeare's *The Tempest*, both define with great clarity the baby's relation to the placenta and its transformations. Our poet's kaleidoscope-collection cabinet inside the house is an attacked placental image just as the three images of the next

17

dream reveal the jealously attacked 'magnificent breasts'. Bion's paper on 'The Imaginary Twin' (*Second Thoughts*, Heinemann, London 1970) pursues this same theme of the imagery of the placenta; but only in his last work, the trilogy *A Memoir of the Future*, does he discuss the implications of prenatal mental life and the role that the cut-off pre-natal parts of the personality play in later psychopathology.

This type of imaginative conjecture cannot aspire to any status other than that of being credible, or at least as credible as such unimaginative formulations as 'constitution', 'heredity', or 'just like his father was as a baby'. At any rate for our purpose here it is quite sufficient to establish credibility as a basis for interest in the wider speculation for which, however, we do have evidence that is more than merely suggestive. Since this wider speculation is the heart of the matter of this book it needs a small preamble of its own in the context of the history of psycho-analytical ideas.

Although it may not have found its official statement until 'The Ego and The Id', from at least the time of 'Little Hans' Freud was aware that mental pain and mental − that is, intrapsychic — conflict were absolutely bound together. Such was Freud's Darwinian bias towards action as the ultimate goal of mental functioning that varieties of mental pain, generally lumped together as 'anxiety', including even the grief of mourning, needed to be given a heuristic value as 'signal' of some danger. I say even the grief of mourning for his emphasis is upon this emotion as a signal that hopes and aspirations connected with the lost one require to be relinquished in the 'work' of mourning.

There is a subtle though immensely significant change in attitude towards mental pain in the work of Melanie Klein. Its most obvious item is the classification of mental pains into persecutory and depressive, but this represents an expansion and clarification of Freud rather than a fundamental change in attitude. It is true that her classification somehow carries the implication that persecutory pain is 'bad' and depressive pain 'good' because they have reference to regressive and progressive developmental trends respectively. But the more important alteration, growing out of her forward-looking, developmental orientation, as compared to Freud's essentially backwards-looking, psychopathological interest, is her insistence that a certain level of mental pain, different though it is for different people, is essential for development of the personality. It is true that she assumed that the basic developmental schema was inbuilt, either by genetics, pre-history, social process or internal logic, but she saw clearly that an optimal level of anxiety favoured developmental conflict and its resolution, while both too much and too little of such pain favoured stagnation or regression.

Important as these differences from Freud may be, the basic area of agreement was there: that mental pain was in one way or another related to frustration of impulse life. Only in the 1957 book, *Envy and Gratitude*, did she break with this blanket assertion. Envy of the good object for possession of its good attributes was established, yet even here it was hedged about with such ideas as 'the breast that feeds itself', circling back to the thesis of frustration. This ambiguity seemed resolved by Bion in *Learning from Experience*, when he described emotions as 'links' and threw over the traditional dualities of love and hate in favour of a more complex and philosophically far more penetrating confrontation. First of all he extended the range of passionate links to include, along with loving and hating, knowing (L, H, and K links). But further in the tradition of Milton, Blake and Coleridge, he made the imaginative leap of confronting positive with negative emotional links: love (L) with anti-love (minus L), hate with anti-hate (minus H) and thirst for knowing with philistinism (K with minus K). Moreover he demonstrated how intertwined are the positive links with one another, as did Blake in 'The Marriage of Heaven and Hell'. Likewise for the negative ones — Coleridge's 'foul fiend'. This immediately threw a brilliant light on hypocrisy, for instance, for may not anti-hate parade as love, and may not philistinism present itself as the guardian of scientific truth? Wordsworth says much the same thing, that 'hating falsehood is not the same as loving truth'.

But even Bion did not depart from the fundamental link of mental pain and frustration until Chapter 10 of *Attention and Interpretation* (1970), where he introduced the idea of 'catastrophic change', a concept he later greatly expanded in *A Memoir of the Future*, especially in the third book, *The Dawn of*

19

Oblivion. Throughout his work he had cleaved to the Keatsian formulation, 'beauty is truth, truth beauty'; but only in these last works did he begin to spell out its implications. It is the 'new idea' which impinges on the mind as a catastrophe for, in order to be assimilated, this sets in flux the entire cognitive structure. This view, which Darwin stated and Freud so stirringly enlarged, while not difficult to grasp in the intellectual aspect they expound, challenges imagination at the emotive level. If we follow Bion's thought closely we see that the new idea presents itself as an 'emotional experience' of the beauty of the world and its wondrous organisation, descriptively closer to the noumenon, to Hamlet's 'heart of mystery'.

The vista opened by Bion's formulation on mental pain and mental pleasure implies that the intrinsic conflict of both the positive and negative emotional links, surrounding desire and interest, is always present and that, therefore, at the passionate level – which is the level at which dream life pursues its course — pleasure and pain are inextricably bound together. But this essential conflict, (from whose matrix the 'learning from experience' evolves to produce structural change as opposed to augmented information,) must find its symbolic representation (alpha function) in order to become available for dream thoughts, transformation into verbal language (or other symbolic forms, as in the arts) and elaboration through abstraction, condensation, generalisation and other instruments of sophisticated thinking. [These processes have been discussed at greater length by Bion and by the author in *Dream Life* (Clunie Press, 1983)]. Toleration of this conflict, which is the heart of the matter of ego strength, resides in the capacity that Bion, after Keats, has called 'negative capability': the ability to remain in uncertainty without irritably reaching after fact and reason (see Keat's Letter to his brothers George and Tom, April, 1817).

In the struggle against the cynical power of the negative links this capacity to tolerate uncertainty, not knowing, the 'cloud of unknowing', is constantly called upon in the passion of intimate relations and is at the heart of the matter of aesthetic conflict. Traditionally it has been shelved in the form of the concept of 'first causes', which has never proved satisfactory because of the problem of 'free will'. Moses could talk directly with God but his followers had to have faith in him, which repeatedly disintegrated and had to be renewed by miracle or affliction.

'The spirit of the LORD was upon him and he did prophesy' sufficed for the prophets but eventually it was necessary for God himself to become incarnate in Jesus to be convincing — to some — part of the time. Kierkegaard's 'leap in the dark' expresses the difficulty. How does the baby ever manage it? In terms of external reality, where Plato's ideal forms are continually set aside by the great random factor, neither the baby nor the adult ever does manage it. But fortunately the evolution of mind had not stopped at living in the outside world. The human mind constructs an inner world where meaning is displayed figuratively and justice prevails. 'Let faith oust fact; let fancy oust memory; I love deep down and do believe'.

And so our imaginative conjecture posits that every baby 'knows' from experience that his mother has an 'inside' world, a world where he has dwelled and from whence he has been expelled or escaped, depending on his point of view. The 'evidence', if it will be admitted as such, is overwhelmingly in favour of the expulsion theory. But perhaps people in whom the denial of psychic reality is dominant may disagree. Freud's early view of the unconscious, and perhaps his later views of the superego, suggest that he too might have preferred the escape theory. Only in the paper 'On Fetishism' did he seem to allow for the concreteness of the world of phantasy of the inside of the body, of child and mother alike.

If we may turn back to my poet's material, the friend's wife who invites him to enter from the walled garden and to 'trim the neighbour's hedge' is not merely inviting him to a coitus in revenge for her husband's infidelity; she is also the mother inviting him to explore her inner world in compensation for the father's closeness to the older sister (and later his intimidation by his second wife). There, inside, he finds the deadness of the collection, the fragmentation representing the mother's death, on the one hand, and his jealous attacks on her consequent to seeing his baby sister fed at the breast. The collection, like the kaleidoscope, idealises the fragmentation of her beauty, which he cannot remember.

At last we have arrived at the core of our discourse. I will try to state the thesis precisely, then to pursue its implications. The

21

ordinary beautiful devoted mother presents to her ordinary beautiful baby a complex object of overwhelming interest, both sensual and infra-sensual. Her outward beauty, concentrated as it must be in her breast and her face, complicated in each case by her nipples and her eyes, bombards him with an emotional experience of a passionate quality, the result of his being able to see these objects as 'beautiful'. But the meaning of his mother's behaviour, of the appearance and disappearance of the breast and of the light in her eyes, of a face over which emotions pass like the shadows of clouds over the landscape, are unknown to him. He has, after all, come into a strange country where he knows neither the language nor the customary non-verbal cues and communications. The mother is enigmatic to him; she wears the Gioconda smile most of the time, and the music of her voice keeps shifting from major to minor key. Like 'K' (Kafka's, not Bion's), he must wait for decisions from the 'castle' of his mother's inner world. He is naturally on guard against unbridled optimism and trust, for has he not already had one dubious experience at her hands, from which he either escaped or was expelled — or perhaps he, rather than his mother, was 'delivered' from the danger! Even at the moments of most satisfactory communication, nipple in mouth, she gives an ambiguous message, for although she takes the gnawing away from inside she gives a bursting thing which he must expel himself. Truly she giveth and she taketh away, both of good and bad things. He cannot tell whether she is Beatrice or his Belle Dame Sans Merci. This is the aesthetic conflict, which can be most precisely stated in terms of the aesthetic impact of the outside of the 'beautiful' mother, available to the senses, and the enigmatic inside which must be construed by creative imagination. Everything in art and literature, every analysis, testifies to its perseverance through life. But what is its role in development and in the structure of psychopathology? For it is the human condition. What man knows the heart of his beloved, or his child, or his analysand, as well as he knows the heart of his enemy?

It is more than analogical to say that analysts have the same type of aesthetic conflict in their love affair with the psycho-analytical method and its framework of theory of the personality and therapeutic process. Clearly the method, with its intimacy, privacy, ethics, attentiveness, forbearance, non-judgemental stance, its continuity, open-endedness, implicit readiness for sacrifice on the analyst's part, commitment to recognise errors, sense of responsibility towards the patient and his family — all of which is embodied in the dedication to scrutinise the trans-ference-counter-transference process — all of these facets, bound together by systematic effort, make the method un-equivocally an aesthetic object. But within the method is the theory by which it is practised, and this theory is notoriously open to suspicion; among the list of often mutually exclusive accusations which have been levelled against it, one may include those of being reductionist, bourgeois, cynical, simplistic, hypocritical, unscientific, messianic, satanic, anti-Christian, paternalistic, mechanistic, sexist, anti-sexual, amoral, moralistic. Every one of these slanders — for in the gross they are slanders — has a grain of truth in it. And yet the analysts of today may be laying the foundations of a science of great grandeur in the future, in the way that the alchemist laid the groundwork for modern chemistry and its astonishing accomplishments.

This may seem a harsh judgement, but the facts are there. Compared to the complexity of what transpires in our consul-ting rooms, our descriptions of them are fairy tales both in their simplicity and crudeness. Take the clinical material I have reported as a background to discussion: it is just a story of my memory of my impression. No amount of tape recording or video filming will help, because the heart of the matter of what transpired between my poet and myself was ineffable, infra-sensual, in the air, and furthermore so complicated that my feeble organ of consciousness can at best notice its grossest land-marks, such as what we call dreams and associations.

The history of the theory of the psycho-analytical method reads like a fairy story indeed, like a logical extension of 'The Emperor's New Clothes'. Once upon a time there was an Emperor whose name was Freud and his patients defrauded him by clothing him in transference so that he believed that he was good and handsome and wise. But then a child called Dora laughed at him and he realised that he was just naked Freud. But then a great man, Freud, understood that the clothing of the transference had its own psychic reality and that accepting his nakedness beneath it gave him a strange beauty and power to heal his patients' minds. But later on others discovered that wearing this clothing of the transference did really effect some developmental change in wisdom and benevolence (recognition of the countertransference); while failure to remember the nakedness underneath bred grandiosity, complacency, greed. Still later it was discovered that this recognised fiction of their relationship also enabled both partners to use their minds for thinking to a degree that neither was able to do by himself (Bion). But then it began to become clear that in fact they were not using their minds, their minds were using them. Some time later . . .

The point that I am trying to make is that our theories are essentially retrospective. We gradually become aware of what we have been doing, of what has been happening in our consulting rooms, and we try, using the grossly unsatisfactory medium of language, *faute de mieux*, to describe it. But to our dismay it always sounds as if we were explaining, not just describing. And then we begin to believe our language of 'because' and forget what hindsights we are expressing and we fall into militant elitist groups using the same words, and consequently became easy prey for our critics, the fashionable exponents and enemies of psychoanalysis. Our academicism makes us vulnerable.

Furthermore the teaching of psycho-analysis has taken an institutional form which has perpetuated these élitist groupings and created what Bion would call the Fight-Flight Basic Assumption mentality between groups and a Dependency BA mentality within each. To make matters worse, the publishing of scientific findings has resided within these institutions, in collusion with a ruthlessly capitalist book-publishing community. Consequently the shibboleth significance of jargon words has tended to replace their clinical descriptive meaning as derived from the aesthetic quality of the method. No outsider reading this literature (viz., my own clinical material) could ever guess the beauty of the method. It may reveal something of the beauty of the working of the mind but nothing of the aesthetic of the method by which this is made manifest.

It is my distinct impression that this poisoned atmosphere of institutionalised psycho-analysis has bred a certain shyness about speaking of love in the transference and countertransference, for fear of appearing sentimental or of colluding in the covert aggression of the erotic transference. The term 'good' has come to mean little other than 'gratifying', while 'truth' has lost its intentional quality and has been replaced by 'verisimilitude' or a purely technical meaning something akin to 'accurate', or perhaps 'similar' in its geometric sense. Of course there is always the danger of the sharp edge of psycho-analytic instruments being blunted by the rubbery qualities of Humanism (what Meg Harris Williams calls 'Softhumanism') and Sociological Relativism. The absence of the vocabulary of aesthetics in the literature of psycho-analysis, at least in its theoretical vocabulary, is nowhere more stunningly illustrated than in Melanie Klein's *Narrative of a Child Analysis*. The terse and even harsh language of her theories, and their preponderant concern with the phenomenology of the paranoid-schizoid position, stands in astonishing contrast to the emotional, and certainly at times passionate, climate of her relationship to Richard and of his overwhelming preoccupation with the vulnerability of the beauty of the world to Hitler's destructiveness and his own.

Thus it is that the literature of psycho-analysis, anxious for medical and scientific respectability, has also gone along unthinkingly with certain cultural preconceptions about babies. Everyone is agreed that mental life, in all its richness of emotionality, thought, judgment and decision, must start at some time. Systematic observation of the mother-infant relationship, as developed by Esther Bick and practised in the training of child psychotherapists at the Tavistock Clinic from as early as 1950, reveals unmistakeably the meaningfulness of what to casual observation seem to be the random patterns of the baby's activities. These early patterns, watched through their evolution in the first two years of life, tell a story of character development and lend emphasis to the importance of the matrix of relationship and communication between mother and infant from the very first moments of post-natal life. Similarly the impact of interferences such as prematurity, incubation, early separations, failures of breast feeding, physical illness in mother or baby reveal themselves in character development as unmistakeably as the 'shakes' in a piece of

25

timber mark early periods of drought.

It is necessary to plead for this recognition because the period of maximal beatification between mother and baby arises very early, soon to be clouded by varying degrees of post-partum depression in the mother and, as I am asserting, the baby's reaction against the aesthetic impact. The picture of madonna-and-child is not always very enduring, but it is deeply convincing. One can see its power repeated in later years when a grandmother holds her distressed grandchild, waiting for its mother to return to feed it; thirty years drop from her visage as the bliss of success in calming the child spreads through her being. It is this moment when the ordinary beautiful devoted mother holds her ordinary beautiful baby and they are lost in the aesthetic impact of one another that I wish to establish in all its power — and all its afterimage of pain. 'Isn't it a pity that they have to grow up!' What congruent shaft of pain goes through the baby?

> Why did I laugh tonight? No voice will tell:
>   No god, no Demon of severe response,
> Deigns to reply from Heaven or from Hell.
>   Then to my human heart I turn at once —
> Heart! thou and I are here and alone;
>   Say, wherefore did I laugh! O mortal pain!
> O Darkness! Darkness! ever must I moan,
>   To question Heaven and Hell and Heart in vain.
> Why did I laugh? I know this being's lease
>   My fancy to its utmost blisses spreads;
> Yet could I on this very midnight cease,
>   And the world's gaudy ensigns see in shreds.
> Verse, fame, and Beauty are intense indeed,
>   But Death intenser — Death is Life's high meed.
>   (John Keats)

I think Melanie Klein was wrong to assume that the paranoid-schizoid position in object relations was anterior to the depressive position. This preconception coloured her language and distorted her thought about the processes of development. The depressive position was 'reached', or 'attained' or 'achieved' by three months, she thought; and the evidence for it was a noticeable change in the baby's eyes. But this entailed a tragic view of the depressive position, a relic of the 'romantic agony' which plays such a role in Freud's thought about the Oedipus Complex. It stands human values on its head, looking back at the relinquished object instead of forward to development and the possibility of an enriched object which the very relinquishment makes attainable. It has, as it were, a linear structure of possession and loss, rather than a complex image capable of gathering both past and future into the immediacy of a present experience. Bion has seen it more correctly in his little formula Ps↔D as the repeated oscillation in integration and values that must be traversed with every 'catastrophic change' throughout life.

Keats' poem might appear, on a superficial reading, to be an expression of the 'romantic agony'. Indeed he had to explain to his friends, who were alarmed at his poem, that he was not extolling death but rather the way in which the idea of death is central to the experience of life and beauty, as he explained shortly after:

> She dwells with Beauty — Beauty that must die;
>   And Joy, whose hand is ever at his lips
> Bidding adieu . . .
>   ('Ode on Melancholy')

The tragic element in the aesthetic experience resides, not in the transience, but in the enigmatic quality of the object: 'Joy, whose hand is ever at his lips/ Bidding adieu.' Is it a truthful object that is always reminding the lover of the transience, or a tantalising one, like La Belle Dame? The aesthetic conflict is different from the romantic agony in this respect: that its central experience of pain resides in uncertainty, tending towards distrust, verging on suspicion. The lover is naked as Othello to the whisperings of Iago, but is rescued by the quest for knowledge, the K-link, the desire to know rather than to possess the object of desire. The K-link points to the value of the desire as itself the stimulus to knowledge, not merely as a yearning for gratification and control over the object. *Desire makes it possible, even essential, to give the object its freedom.*

In my experience this is the heart of the essential shift manifest in the threshold phenomena between Ps and D. It is true, as

27

Melanie Klein spelled out, that the shift involves the transformation from self-interest in safety and comfort to concern for the welfare of the loved object. But that does not describe the modus operandi of the shift. For in the interplay of joy and pain, engendering the love (L) and hate (H) links of ambivalence, it is the quest for understanding (K-link) that rescues the relationship from impasse. This is the point at which Negative Capability exerts itself, where Beauty and Truth meet. Consider our poet's delicately balanced 'Gold Rush' state of mind, awakening from a drunken state in his VW (?fuckwagon, masturbation chamber?) Why did he laugh when he saw the 'magnificent breasts' so innocently offered in the dream, as with the woman feeding her baby at the dinner table? Joy and outrage seem to have been placed in conflict, depending on whether he was identifying with the baby or seeing it as his baby sister, as evidence of the parental sexuality, or of his mother's insensitivity? Or cruelty? Or flamboyant exhibitionism? How quickly he was tipped over into seeing the breast as full of dead babies (the bodies in the mud) or as exhibitionist and hard (the film-set hill with the stone armchairs) or as tatty with child-frightening nipples (the monsters from *Where the Wild Things Are*).

If, in fact, for the ordinary beautiful baby with his ordinary devoted beautiful mother, this aesthetic impact is what greets his emergence into the world outside the womb, then the aesthetic conflict and the depressive position would be primary for development, and the paranoid-schizoid secondary — the consequence of his closing down his perceptual apertures against the dazzle of the sunrise. In Plato's terms he would hasten back into the cave. But such metaphors tell us nothing of how it happens. Perhaps Wordworth's 'getting and spending / we lay waste our powers' can give us a hint if we apply it to the transactions of infancy and early childhood. Who, after all, is more materialistic than the small child? And the 'Gold Rush' implications of our poet's dream? There was a moving little scene in that masterpiece of the screen *The Treasure of Sierra Madre*, when the old prospector, Walter Huston, insists against the opposition of the greedy and paranoid Humphrey Bogart, that, having been allowed to remove a fortune in gold from the mountain's interior, they must, in gratitude, repair her wound

28

by returning all the rubble from which the gold had been extracted.

There could well be countless babies who do not have ordinary devoted beautiful mothers who see them as ordinary beautiful babies, and who are not greeted by the dazzle of the sunrise. Yet I cannot claim with conviction that I have ever seen one in my consulting room. Not even in my extensive experience of schizophrenic patients and psychotic children have I failed to find evidence of their having been touched by the beauty — and recoiled wildly from it, as they do again and again in the course of analysis. There is much evidence (cf. Spitz) to suggest that being thus untouched is not compatible with survival, or at least with the survival of the mind.

As an addendum to existing theory this book is a piece of hindsight. I feel confident that in our consulting rooms, whether consciously or not, depending largely on the random factor of the training group and its particular chauvinist jargon, psychoanalysts in general, for at least the last thirty years, have been treating the phenomena which Melanie Klein labelled as paranoid-schizoid and depressive positions in the way I am describing. The psychopathology which we study and allege to treat has its primary basis in the flight from the pain of the aesthetic conflict. The impact of separation, of deprivation — emotional and physical, of physical illness, of oedipal conflict — pregenital and genital, of chance events, of seductions and brutality, of indulgence and over-protection, of family disintegration, of the death of parents or siblings — all of these derive the core of their significance for the developmental process from their contribution as aspects of the underlying, fundamental process of avoidance of the impact of the beauty of the world, and of passionate intimacy with another human being. It is necessary for our understanding of our patients, for a sympathetic view of the hardness, coldness and brutality that repeatedly bursts through in the transference and countertransference, to recognize that conflict about the *present* object is prior in significance to the host of anxieties over the *absent* object.

To end this and to illustrate what is meant by 'wildly recoil from the impact of the aesthetic of the object', I offer some material from the analysis of a psychotic young woman.

Siegrie is now 30 years old and has been an acute or ambulatory paranoid schizophrenic patient under care of the community since the age of 17 when, while in Uganda with her family, during a period of political turmoil, she became paranoid and deluded towards her mother. She saw her as extremely beautiful with lights shining from her eyes, felt that she was feeding her LSD with the food and that she was intending to make her into a homosexual. At times of acute breakdown she has fits of religious delirium, is violent and requires locked-ward care and heavy medication. Siegrie has had analytic therapy for five years with the Director of the ward for research on psychotherapy of the psychoses in a large, old-fashioned and rather splendid hospital outside Oslo.

The most significant features and events of her history are these: she was the first child, conceived before marriage, of a student couple, the father remaining at University to take his degree during the patient's first half year of life. At 14 months, when the father was planning to take the family to the USA where he was to study for a higher degree, the mother decided to go back to work to save money for the trip and she placed Siegrie in a Salvation Army Children's Home where she remained for four or five months until severe bladder and respiratory illness made it necessary that she be returned to the mother. While in the USA she started to stray away from home almost as soon as she could walk and she showed a distinct preference for the company of a neighbouring family. Siegrie's family returned to Norway when the patient was three, the mother then being pregnant with a boy who died three months after birth. There was no apparent cause of death which was put down as a 'cot death'. A brother was born when Seigrie was five and a sister when she was ten. When she was fifteen the family went to Uganda where the father took a temporary teaching post, and while there the patient was converted to an American Pentecostal Church, much against the parents' wishes.

Following her first breakdown, ending soon after her repatriation, the patient finished her secondary schooling but subsequent breakdowns prevented her from acquiring any higher education or following any form of vocational training although she is an intelligent girl and is also, apparently, artistically gifted. She is attractive in appearance although somewhat plump.

The therapy has been conducted three times weekly, with the patient seated opposite the therapist; the patient has only recently consented to use the couch but still finds this disturbing after only a few minutes on each occasion. She knows the therapist's wife who was a nurse on the ward before marriage and Siegrie knows that the couple now have two children. During periods of remission she lives in a hostel connected with the hospital with three other ex-patients, all women; the hostel is unstaffed although monitored by hospital personnel.

While the therapy has made quite steady progress in lessening the frequency and duration of acute attacks of paranoid delusion and agitated confusional states, the therapist feels that it has plateaued to a supportive relationship which neither of them is willing to run the risk of intensifying by increased frequency, or use of the couch, deeper and more conflictual interpretations, etc. The patient's family also seems to prefer to play-it-safe, being friendly but keeping their distance socially. The patient went on holiday to the Mediterranean last summer with the whole family and this went reasonably well. But the mother will not give the patient a flat in the house which she owns where both the brother and sister have flats. She receives her at most once a week for Sunday lunch. In fact the patient prefers telephone contact to visits.

The two dreams that I wish to report and discuss come from the period after the summer break. At the time the general feeling was that the fire was starting to burn and that another breakdown was not far away, ostensibly springing up over the issue of the flat but also clearly arising over analytic issues between patient and analyst, each feeling that the other was holding back, settling in, keeping things comfortable. The analyst increasingly felt parasitized and was impatient for Siegrie to get on with her education.

In the first dream

> the patient was in her hostel with her companions and someone said that there was not enough light. So Siegrie climbed up into the loft to open a window. But outside on the roof was a horde of homosexual women led by a very beautiful woman, who wanted to get in but the patient hurriedly closed the window. Then there was a knock at the front door, and when Siegrie opened it, once more there was the beautiful woman

and her horde. So Siegrie invited them in. One of them had very short hair and surgical tape on her head. This woman said that she had had a brain operation for a sex change and that the patient could have one too. But at this point the beautiful woman leader looked fat and ugly and so Siegrie refused the offer.

In the second dream

Siegrie was in the bath and was having a pleasant telephone conversation with the favourite of her several boy friends and she felt a stirring of genital desire or excitement.

Siegrie is still a virgin, finding it impossible to have intercourse although fond of boys, and she is attractive to them; she is able to be affectionate and fairly erotic with the one on the telephone. There does not seem to be any tincture of homosexuality in her relations with her three house-mates. That seems almost entirely reserved for her delusional states.

I wish to approach this material from the viewpoint of the light it throws on the problem of intolerance to aesthetic impact.

The dreams can be read as follows:

When the newborn Siegrie first opens her eyes and sees the beauty of her mother's face and all the parts of her body the impact is overwhelming, enveloping, invasive, stirring powerful tendencies towards surrender. From this she can withdraw by closing her eyes but she is unable to close her genital area from being stirred into excitement indistinguishable from having a full rectum. But the impact is far less compelling to surrender (her word) since the element of beauty has vanished.

It is better, as the second dream declares, to stay in the warm waters inside mother and just commune by auditory means with a less beautiful, though also frightening object like a father. In fact Siegrie is far more comfortable with her steady, reasonable and unemotional father and would rather telephone than visit her mother.

The fight-for-the-flat that took shape in subsequent months parallels and, to some extent, replaces the fight over the use of the couch and encounter with the maternal transference. Historically it would seem that the four or five months in the Salavation Army Home was a threat to her life more from change of geography than from the separation from her mother as an external object. Changes of geography such as the trips to the USA and Uganda have similarly unhinged Siegrie. Through painting, where she can as yet only produce very faint, gossamer-like figures, she seems to be trying to accustom herself to see the beauty of humans and of the world but one feels that it will need to be worked out at the storm centre of the transference before she can emerge into emotional and intimate contact with another human being, using her eyes and containing her passions.

3   On First Impressions

Our growing respect for the unconscious mind as the locus of creative thought has not yet encompassed the vital question of its role in discrimination and judgement. While we are ready to accept that the massive equipment of this unconscious mind may put before us its imaginative conjectures, in as many forms and from as many points of view as it is capable, we are still prone to reserve for the function of consciousness (which, after all, we feel more to our credit and for which we are therefore more ready to accept responsibility) those finer functions which have to do with the correspondence of the hypothesis of meaning or significance to the observed phenomena which it is meant to cover or explain.

William Hazlitt ('On the Knowledge of Character') wrote: 'First impressions are often the truest, as we find (not infrequently) to our cost, when we have been wheedled out of them by plausible professions or studied actions. A man's look is the work of years, it is stamped on his countenance by the events of his whole life, nay, more, by the hand of nature, and it is not to be got rid of easily.' Hazlitt seems often to be speaking of initial displeasure, but his own madness of infatuation for his landlord's daughter reported in 'Liber Amoris' commenced with a powerful first impression which subsequent events suggest may have been quite mistaken.

Similarly in describing the first meeting between Bouvard and Pécuchet, Flaubert writes: 'Thus their meeting was important enough to be an adventure. They had at once become attracted by secret fibres. Besides, how can sympathies by explained? Why does some peculiarity, some imperfection, which would be indifferent or odious in one, seem enchanting in another? What is called the thunderbolt of love at first sight is true of all the passions.'

It has often been said that by the age of forty a person has the face he deserves, leaving to the bloom of youth and the unlined face of early maturity a greater power of dissimilation. But this tends to describe the erosions induced by habitual attitudes and states of mind — a person's character, in short. And that may usually mean his social character, the face he shows to the world, the summation of his relations at a casual or contractual rather than at an intimate level. The first impressions with which we are most deeply concerned here, are those relating to some prospective intimacy. These are the passionate potentialities which Flaubert believes to be subject to the 'thunderbolt of love at first sight'. The implication of 'hate at first sight' is unavoidable, as well.

The problem, as defined for us by Hazlitt and Flaubert, would seem to have two distinct dimensions: one relating to the adequacy of the evidence presented to 'first sight', and the other to the origins of special, passionate 'sympathies' (or antipathies). Experience of life tells us that a third dimension must be included in our research: namely, the conditions under which we are able, in fact, to notice the first impression, the impact made upon our minds by an initial encounter with a 'stranger'. I put this word in quotation marks to call to notice the overtone of meaning implicit in the concept. Suspicion, prejudice, aversion; these postures of unfriendliness cannot be denied, and yet we are seldom aware of them because we seldom, in fact, encounter 'strangers'. Our daily lives are so hedged about with the landscape of our accustomed milieu that we would not recognize a stranger until he behaved strangely, any more than we would feel frightened of the tiger at the zoo until we noticed that the cage door had been left open. But, of course, the cage doors are occasionally left open, our own and the other person's. It is in the relatively rare (or is it?) occurrence when we find ourselves looking into other eyes, without the accustomed bars of social privacy, that this 'first sight' impact makes itself felt.

But I raise the question of its infrequency because it is probably highly variable, being frequent, even a regular occurrence, at certain periods of life and almost unknown at others. One cannot observe the meetings of little children without being impressed by the immediacy of their attractions and aversions; adolescents on the whole go about with unbarred eyes; Hazlitt in middle life, separated from wife and children and contemplating divorce, feeling no one had ever loved him in his life, seems to have been particularly naked in the eyes.

But these times of nakedness, and in that sense vulnerability to the impact of strangers, do not preclude the possibility that the impact may always be there but pass unnoticed, as we might not notice that the tiger's cage door was open but might dream of it that night. It will not have passed unnoticed that my discourse has changed from considering the first impression as enveloping the entire person. I seem, rather, to be speaking of it as a primarily eye-to-eye phenomenon. This process of 'looking', though distinguishing between 'at' and 'into', need not place them in conflict or mutual exclusiveness. Rather, to look into another person it seems necessary to delve into his eyes within their setting in the landscape of his total person. This landscape includes not only the architecture of clothing but also the geology of the body beneath, structure and movement. Upon this graphic landscape is imposed the music of the speaking being, song and dance, much on show, some distant murmurs also.

We would, therefore, include the 'plausible professions and studied actions' by which Hazlitt is 'wheedled out' of his first impression, as part of the landscape of the person which need have no such wheedling power if we had been able to trust the emotion by which the unconscious mind informs us of the impact of the stranger. We do wheedle ourselves out of this impact by second thoughts.

Still, what are we to make of Flaubert's paradox about the impact of 'some peculiarity, some imperfection', odious in one person and enchanting in another? It seems to fall within the error of loss of context, and therefore to create a paradox where none exists. One might as well complain that a tree in the foreground of a Claude, half rotten or blasted by lightning, was a 'peculiarity or imperfection' in the composition.

This brings us back to what is perhaps the central and most emotive aspect of this enquiry: the origins of the power of the object which we love (or hate) at first sight. Or shall we phrase it more psycho-analytically: how does the unconscious make such immediate judgements? And if we understood its method of operation, would we still wish to place our reliance upon it rather than upon our conscious second thoughts?

Our answer, for what it is worth, must be this: the unconscious makes a dream involving the other person, the stranger. But what is the content of this dream, then? Why, it is our primal dream of love (or hate) in which we cast the stranger as protagonist and estimate his fitness to the part, as a stage director casts his play, and as the theatre critic views the opening night. Our minds are full of characters in search — not of an author, for we ourselves are the author — but of players to fit the parts. Thus does transference people the intimate area of our lives. If we go on learning from experience the drama changes and may require recasting. If we are neurotic, the drama remains fixed, and may require recasting as the actors grow jaded by the parts imposed upon them. With rare good luck the growing person finds like growth in his players and they write and play the new dramas together. With rare bad luck the neurotic finds his players never tire of their roles and they proceed through life in an interminable 'Mouse-trap'.

There is a widespread belief that hastening to bed forestalls the phenomenon of falling in love, and this is probably true. But the widespread belief that in-loveness thrives on sexual frustration is certainly a slander, an invention of the poverty of temperament which cannot distinguish between being in love and the Romantic Agony, with its delicious masochism. Freud made his own contribution to this pessimism by placing the phenomenon amongst the manifestations of obsessional neurosis. What is true, on the other hand, is that the dream of the perfection of the love object, of the man or woman who 'glows in the dark', is usually subject to disillusion. Meg Harris Williams's essay on *Hamlet* will greatly expand on this point, but the essence of the problem is fundamental to our understanding of the structure of the mind. To state that the phenomenon of falling in love is founded upon a primal dream of love entitles it to enlistment in the general phenomenology of the transference. But transference, seen as an externalization of an internal object or situation, falls into two great categories, infantile and adult. In analytic work we are concerned chiefly with the infantile transference. But there are no inconsiderable number of people who, in the course of childhood, have accepted the disillusionment in their omnipotent-omniscient expectations of parents without a significant loss of love for them. What has happened is that the infantile transference has been replaced by an adult one, whose maintenance the parents must continue to deserve by their actual qualities.

In like manner the infantile component of an experience of falling in love, being inevitably subject to disillusionment, may be allowed to lapse in favour of the adventure of getting to know one's love object more and more deeply. The consequence is unexpected, especially to the beloved person, for one of the terrors of one's love being reciprocated is the grim expectation that deeper knowledge of oneself will inevitably cool the passion of one's beloved. It seems far less likely to the lover that he will be cooled by discovery, only she. But what produces the (most pleasant) surprise (in the world) is that being in love has an astonishingly ennobling effect on one's character, that is, on one's view of the world and fellow human beings.

All of this is so marvellously described by Robert Louis Stevenson in his essay in *Virginisbus Puerisque* that I will not try to compete with his extraordinary bit of descriptive psychology. I presume it was written after the clever and brittle essays on marriage, that is, after he had met Mrs. Osbourne in France:

'Falling in love is the one illogical adventure, the one thing of which we are tempted to think as supernatural, in our trite and reasonable world. The effect is out of all proportion with the cause. Two persons, neither of them, it may be, very amiable or very beautiful, meet, speak a little, and look a little into each other's eyes. That has been done a dozen or so times in the experience of either with no great result. But on this occasion all is different. They fall at once into that state in which another person becomes to us the very gist and centre-point of God's creation, and demolishes our laborious theories with a smile; in which our ideas are so bound up with the master-thought that even the trivial cares of our own person become so many acts of devotion, and the love of life itself is translated into a wish to remain in the same world with so precious and desirable a fellow creature. And all the while their acquaintances look on in stupor and ask each other etc. —'

'Indeed the ideal story is that of two people who go into love step for step, with a fluttering consciousness, like a pair of children venturing together into a dark room. From the first moment when they see each other, with a pang of curiosity, through stage after stage of growing pleasure and embarrassment, they can read the expression of their own trouble in each other's eyes. There is here no declaration properly so called; the feeling is so plainly shared, that as soon as the man knows what is in his own heart, he is sure of what it is in the woman's.

'This simple accident of falling in love is as beneficial as it is astonishing. It arrests the petrifying influence of years, disproves cold-blooded and cynical conclusions, and awakens dormant sensibilities.'

'It seems as if he had never heard or felt or seen until that moment; and by the report of his memory, he must have lived his past life between sleep and waking, or with the pre-occupied attention of a brown study. He is practically incommoded by the generosity of his feelings, smiles much when he is alone, etc —'

'One thing that accompanies the passion in its first blush is certainly difficult to explain. It comes (I do not quite see how) that from having a very supreme pleasure in all parts of life — in lying down to sleep, in waking, in motion, in breathing, in continuing to be — the lover begins to regard his happiness as beneficial for the rest of the world and highly meritorious in himself.' — 'The presence of two lovers is so enchanting to each other that it seems as if it must be the best thing possible for everybody else.'

'Certainly, whatever it may be with regard to the world at large, this idea of beneficent pleasure is true as between the sweethearts. To do good and communicate is the lover's grand intention. It is the happiness of the other that makes his own most intense gratification. It is not possible to disentangle the different emotions, the pride, humility, pity and passion, which are excited by a look of happy love or an unexpected caress. To make one's self beautiful, to dress the hair, to excel in talk, to do anything and all things that puff out the character and attributes and make them imposing in the eyes of others, is not only to magnify one's self, but to offer the most delicate homage at the same time. And it is in this latter intention that they are done by lovers; for the

40

essence of love is kindness; and indeed it may best be defined as passionate kindness: kindness so to speak, run mad and become importunate and violent. Vanity in a mere personal sense no longer exists.'

'That he should have wasted some years in ignorance of what alone was really important, that he may have entertained the thought of other women with any show of complacency, is a burthen almost too heavy for his self-respect. But it is the thought of another past that rankles in his spirit like a poisoned wound.' — 'To be altogether right they should have had twin birth together, at the same moment with the feeling that unites them. Then indeed it would be simple and perfect and without reserve or afterthought. Then they would understand each other with a fulness impossible otherwise. There would be no barrier between them of association that cannot be imparted. They would be led into none of those comparisons that send the blood back to the heart. And they would know that there had been no time lost, and they had been together as much as was possible. For besides terror for the separation that must follow some time or other in the future, men feel anger, and something like remorse, when they think of that other separation which endured until they met.'

4   On Aesthetic Reciprocity

The little chapter on 'First Impressions' must serve as a guide-line to our exploration. We know from ethology the powerful effect of imprinting in establishing a bond at a primitive level, the level of adhesive types of identification, of conditioned reflexes and of automatic obedience (or disobedience?). We want to trace and explore the comparable phenomena at the level of mentality — of emotion, symbol formation, thought and judgement. There is indisputable evidence from the analytic therapy of psychotic children that the bonding at the imprinting level can be overridden by a failure of emotional bonding. Where this occurs we have been overly ready, as psychiatrists, to ascribe this deficit to extrinsic factors: foetal distress, immaturity, prolonged labour, etc. Almost always one can find some such extrinsic factor on which to hang a causal explanation. But the therapeutic process with such children — of which number James, described in the Introduction, is far from atypical — suggests a more intrinsic problem that requires our understanding. It has no explanatory power and must remain somewhat conjectural, but it is powerfully evocative. We want to suggest that these children, in one way or another, have been overwhelmed by the aesthetic impact of the outside world and the prime object that represents it both concretely and symbolically: the mother, her breasts and nipples, and her eyes and mind.

If we are to pursue this idea seriously, it is necessary likewise to confront the even more difficult question: why are not all babies so overwhelmed? Or are they bowled over but saved, in the nick of time, as it were, by something? I am going to describe a child who emerged crushed physically as well as mentally: Claudia, now eight years old. The consortium of extrinsic factors contributory to her crushing and the thera-peutic equipment, including analysis, that has contributed to her rejuvenation, are equally impressive. But the content of the analysis suggests a very surprising formulation of intrinsic factors, products of her own mentality. It suggests that Claudia was not saved from being crushed by the aesthetic impact of her beautiful mother because she experienced her mother seeing her as 'an ugly little clown'. Furthermore the material of the analysis suggest that she understood this to be a fact, that she was an ugly little clown, by virtue of the method by which she had been made, an ugly method. This latter explanation appears to have been the fruit of Claudia's later researches and thoughts about her parents and their relationship.

But before describing the clinical material, or, rather, before asking the therapist, Mrs. Giuliana Fortunato of Milano, to describe it so that I may comment, it would be useful to indulge in a bit of imaginative conjecture. I want to make up a little story about Claudia's experience of the latter months of intrauterine life, of the birth process, and the impact of her first experiences outside the womb. Emboldened by Bion's unselfconscious 'novel' (*The Dawn of Oblivion*, which is Book 3 of *A Memoir of the Future*), I will write it in the first person, but of course in a more sophisticated idiom than that of the eight year old Claudia, since we have no choice but to use language to express the inchoate emotional responses and proto-thought of the newborn:

> 'I have always found my world basically congenial ever since I began to find it interesting. When I was a fish I just swam about and had no thoughts, but once I found my friend Placenta we explored and shared our findings, I with humming and dancing, he with his reassuring souffle. It became clear that there were others on the other side who hummed a lot. One I could hear particularly well, a wonderful hummer. We thought of finding the Northwest Passage but it was too good a world to leave until it began to shrink. In fact it became quite unpleasantly restrictive, positively cramping, and when I pushed the walls they began to push back. I got cross and really kicked out, but this seemed to have an adverse effect, quite frightening squeezings. We decided to leave, though we both suspected we were being forced to emigrate to make room for some newcomer. I felt pretty angry at this usurpation, for I had lived there since the beginning of time, after all. So, foolishly, you might say, I kicked out with the full power of my immensely strong legs.

43

Well, I must have done some damage for a proper earth-quake ensued, a great chasm opened up revealing the Northwest Passage I'd dreamed about. I was rammed into it, head first, placenta following, but somehow in the chaos of the next few minutes or years, we became separated. I never saw him again. At the end of the passage everything was different, surprising, marvellous — and terrifying. My body became suddenly dense and heavy, immovable; some delicious smelling stuff ran into my chest and I heard myself, not humming but screaming. They must have thought I was screaming at them, those huge and beautiful creatures, so strong they could lift me with one hand while I couldn't even lift my own head. But it was the beauty of one that over-powered me, and I could see from the way she looked at me that I was tiny and ugly and comic. Then I realized I was to be thrown away, for kicking and screaming, I suppose, or for being little and ugly, perhaps. But I felt that these few moments before the end were somehow precious, just looking at her, though it hurt my eyes and I had to shut them. And her humming, pure music! By this time I was beginning to dry up, shrivel, shiver with cold and be tormented by a gnaw-ing inside I'd never had while Placenta was with me. Then she showed me the most beautiful thing in the world, to blind me, I supposed so that I should not see the abyss. Quite kind, really. My mouth stopped screaming and started sucking the anaesthetic stuff with which I was to be "put to sleep". Very humane. I could die laughing and crying and dreaming of being huge and beloved of her.'

It is a silly Kafka-esque tale, but evocative like a Woody Allen film. The grain of truth catches one. But the true story of Claudia is more affecting. In 1978, while on one of our teaching visits to Novara in Piemonte, Mrs. Harris and I were asked by Dr. Romana Negri to see a tiny brain-damaged child in order to advise about the paediatric and psychological management. The consultation, which took place in the hotel lobby, was attended by both parents with little Claudia in the mother's arms, drooping like a battered little rag doll. Her squinting, misshapen face hung loosely, drooling, eyes lifeless, a painful contrast to the delicate and elegant beauty of her mink-coated mother. Both parents spoke English well, the father being the active of the two in describing the history. He hovered about mother and babe, desperate to help, arousing compassion in the observer through his juxtaposition to the more resigned and dutiful but contained demeanor of the mother. I was reminded of Picasso's 'equestrienne' series of drawings, where the stateliness of rider and horse confront the little clown with his broken whip and burnt-out shoes. They were not very young to be having their first child.

We saw the parents and Claudia twice a year for the first four years of her life and were astonished to see how she came to life under the tender and dutiful care of father and mother, supervised at every step by Dr. Negri. The orthopaedic problems with her feet were corrected by splinting, the squint was operated on somewhat later, and the severe motor impediment was considerably helped by psychomotor therapy. By the age of four she was an odd little girl, in constant motion in what appeared to be a dangerously dyskinetic way, yet she never hurt herself. But any observer was kept in a constant state of anxiety for her safety as she lurched about. Her head was generally bent to one side and she seldom looked straight at one, only glancing glimpses. While seeming wild and wilful and isolated, she was nonetheless always listening to the adult conversation and would at times interpolate pertinent information.

By age five her parents were getting a bit desperate about her prospective schooling, had a brief excursion into some type of behaviour therapy against advice, but then requested analysis for Claudia. Mrs. Fortunato began seeing her three times per week. The following three sessions are from the third year of the analysis, approaching the Christmas holiday of 1986. I will present them one at a time and discuss each before continuing. It is a moving story of a child both acting in the transference and employing her therapist to research a developmental problem.

The clinical material that follows is in Mrs Fortunato's words, as translated from the Italian by Mrs. Mimma Nozziglia:

Monday, 1st of December, 1986: She came in carrying her usual toy horse, which she placed on the table and ignored for the rest of the session. She asked me to tie a belt around her waist, using the cloth that covers the pillow, and put a sort of belt that she made by rolling up a blanket around my waist as well. (About two months earlier the same blanket had for a few sessions been rolled to form a baby, 'the baby that came undone'.) Exactly the same belt game had been played some time before, when it had formed part of the preparation for a party. As it had then, the play on the word 'cinta' (belt) came to my mind because of its connection with 'incinta' (pregnant). When I mentioned this Claudia politely corrected me, saying, 'You should say 'cintura' (also meaning belt), but nonetheless immediately asked me to place a cushion over her stomach and tie it in place with the belt. She also placed a big cushion in position over my stomach to be tied by the blanket (the result being that the two pregnant bellies were very different in size). Next we had to go to the hospital for ecography to determine if our babies had been born (come to life?). As soon as it had been determined that they indeed had been born, we had to untie the belt to release them. They were both boys and both named Giuseppe. Claudia insisted that our babies were identical, despite the fact of the cushions being such different sizes, and differing in colour as well. Hers was about one quarter the size of mine, pink, with floral pattern and a label saying 'hand-painted'. Claudia noticed this and said that her baby's pyjàmas were hand-painted, but seemed worried that mine was not so designated. I said that she was pretending our babies were the same, meaning that we were the same as well, because she was afraid to admit that I knew things about babies that she did not know. For instance, did she wonder if babies were indeed hand-painted like the cushion or were they made in some other way.

Apparently unaffected by my comments, she went to fetch the trolley, putting her cushion-baby on the top shelf and mine on the bottom. She ordered me to give both babies the bottle, which I did. However, although she watched attentively when I was feeding her baby, as soon as I turned to feed mine, Claudia started to fidget about the room, putting her fingers up her nose and bouncing on the couch with her shoes on (which was usually discouraged). I said that it seemed difficult for her not to be jealous of my baby and envious of me, even though she claimed we and our babies were the same, for she was showing a great desire to dirty me, to get inside me with her fingers to snatch my baby away from inside me, and also to dirty and snatch away the nipple that was in my baby's mouth.

She listened to this. Then she came up to me slowly and asked in a whisper how a baby was really made. She said she wanted me to make a drawing, a drawing of her own Mummy and Daddy while they were making a baby, because she did not know how they did it. I told Claudia that such a drawing would be of no use, but her request became increasingly urgent and insistent. When she finally became plaintive and tearful, I told her that I thought she felt that my being grown up meant that I had had experiences which she had not yet had, and feared she might never have. The fear that she might never grow up made her unhappy and angry. She became calmer and, as it was the end of the session, she left silent and pensive, remembering to take the toy horse with her.

Discussion: Claudia has brought her toy horse, which she places in a commanding position but does not play with. The ensuing material suggests that this is an important symbol. One could say, 'What follows transpires under the Sign of the Horse', meaning that this symbol, so universal for beauty, strength, fertility and the capacity for useful work, denotes the area of life under exploration. Mrs. Fortunato's management of the setting and her interpretive comments move the material along very well, despite Claudia's attempts at domination and dismissal. Her first attempt to state the problem, and to solve it by magical means, is to fuse her identity with the therapist's (projective identification or possibly adhesive?). By this means she hopes to achieve parity with the therapist's skills and knowledge, even to the point of teaching her the correct word for belt, 'cintura'.

But the effort is feeble and unconvincing. It breaks down as soon as Mrs. Fortunato points out the disparity in size and quality of the pregnancy-cushions, having already been challenged by reference to the pun 'cinta:incinta'. As soon as the two Giuseppe-babies are yielded, masturbatory attacks break out, launched at the mother feeding the babies. But the finger-up-the-nose and the bouncing-on-the-couch-with-shoes betrays the intrusion inside the mother where the inside-baby is being fed by the daddy-penis which the mother holds and controls. As soon as this attack is interpreted, the mood of the session changes dramatically. Dependence of a clinging and pleading sort emerges, but it is wheedling and disingenuous, revealing inadvertenty the core of the problem. Claudia wants Mrs Fortunato to draw her a picture of the act by which her own parents, not adults in general, not Mr. and Mrs. Fortunato, make babies. The therapist correctly comments that such a picture would not help her, for it has been clear in earlier material that Claudia knows the mechanism of the act and its gross anatomy.

At this point, in tender response to the tearfulness and anxiety, the therapist correctly explains that the knowledge the child desires can only be achieved from the kinds of experience which only adults can have, but that Claudia is worried she may never grow up, for some reason. There is, after all, a limit to what can be taught that inheres in the limits of the possibility of verbal or graphic communication. Some things can only be 'shown' and can only be experienced, not merely seen or heard. Claudia would like Mrs. Fortunato to help her to peep into the nuptial chamber of her parents' relationship. We know from the history of art that this cannot be done except symbolically, for any attempt at direct representation either turns out to have a pornographic impact or is so innocently adolescent, like the Indian erotic sculptures, as to represent only fun-and-games.

By the end of the session we have no reason to think that Claudia is embarked on anything other than the ordinary 'sexual researches' of children, except, perhaps, for the degree of anxiety, tearful urgency and the already existing mechanical information which seems to satisfy most children of the latency period. Yet we have reason to be puzzled. Why 'under the Sign of the Horse'? Is it also 'under the Sign of the Cross'? The Christmas break is at hand, the celebration, after all, of the birth of the most-beautiful-baby-in-the-world! What is a child, or adult, for that matter, to make of the 'Annunciation'?

Wednesday, 3rd of December, 1986: This time Claudia brought nothing with her. She wanted, instead, to build things with the box of wooden blocks, the box of which had illustrations of the types of structures that could be made. But she was insistent that I must help her. She brought the little table and chair up close to where I was seated and decided to copy one of the pictures on the box, a rather complicated one with bridges and pillars and walls and arches surmounted by a clock. She worked away in silence, intent, but asking me for help at points when she felt in difficulty to interpret the picture or to balance pieces. The clock fell down several times and I commented how difficult this particular piece seemed to be, this monitor of time. Perhaps this was because the next session was to be missed because of a bank holiday, making a long interval, longer than usual. Claudia replied that she was not to go to school either and asked when the next session was to take place. Meanwhile she kept working away steadily, which rather struck me as it was the first time she had attempted to build anything. In the event the final product gave a distinctly triumphal-arch impression but very unstable.

Towards the end of the session she abandoned this constructive play and turned to the toys. She took a father, mother and son dolls, saying they were Gigi and his parents. The construction, which was on Claudia's side of the table, was to be their house. She placed the small dolls in sitting positions, the son between the parents, and asked if they could be left that way until the next session. She knew of course that this could not be allowed, and I said that she might be wondering if I would be able to keep something of hers inside me, this active Gigi-son who could build houses, during the interval. It might also be a question whether she could keep him inside herself for that period, for he seemed to be a child who separated his parents, as she perhaps would wish to keep me separate from my family, and keep my attention solely on herself. She offered no comment, as the session closed.

Discussion: We are not operating under the Sign of the Horse this time. Instead Claudia has come with a determined plan in her mind, intent on doing something she had not done before.

49

We would not know what to make of it were it not for the context of the previous session and the gap due to the Bank Holiday. Only at the end of the session, with the material about Gigi and his parents do we have evidence that there has been a shift from a feminine to a masculine point of view, both about babies and about parental sexuality. The theme seems to be that making babies is in fact a masculine activity which boys can do as well as men, for it consists of assembling the necessary pieces. By implication these necessary pieces are all available in the box of the mother's body, but they simply lie about unused until the masculine constructive urge makes itself felt. Accordingly, since little boys can do this assembling as well as daddy, it is reasonable to keep the parents apart until the child decides that a new baby is called for. We can only suspect that this shift to a masculine orientation has something to do with the approaching Christmas break, of which the Bank Holiday functions as a harbinger. Clearly little boys are treasured far beyond any estimate placed on little girls. We are seeing Claudia at this moment in her most latency configuration, a far cry from the anxiously pleading little girl of the previous session. She does ask Mrs. Fortunato for help, but as a mason's helper, not as the wise and knowledgeable analyst-mother.

> *Wednesday, 10th of December* (after the missed session). Claudia arrived once more with her toy horse and, as before, then ignored it. She announced enthusiastically that we were to leave for Turin, where her grandmother lives (in fact she has no grandmother in Turin), because I, who was now her daughter, needed an x-ray of my teeth. While we were getting ready for the journey she trod on my foot, as if by accident and I said that perhaps she was a bit cross about the session we had missed, adding something like 'feet can tread on feet, teeth can bite: danger looms.' Claudia turned toward me with a little smile and immediately put on me a white cloth that seemed something between a bib and a sheet. She said I was to drive. When I asked how old I was in this game and she replied that I was twelve years old, I pointed out that twelve year old girls are not allowed to drive cars. She replied rather irritably, 'Then you are eighteen. Come on, let's go.'
>
> While I was driving I also pointed out that, as I was play-

ing the part of her daughter, I must also represent herself, yet I was not her age. Perhaps she felt that her actual age was a very difficult one, with so many things to learn. But in order to be able to learn she had to admit that she knew very little, and this was very hard for her to do. There was no reply, but when we did arrive at the grandmother's house, it was I who had to play all the parts under her instruction, to say, 'Hello, Jessica, I am pleased to see you,' and then to reply as herself, 'Hello, mother, we've come because my daughter has to go to the dentist and so on. The dentist, whom I had to telephone, was unable, as it turned out, to give us an appointment until Thursday. I remarked that the teeth that can bite seemed to need some attention from the dentist-daddy, but that there seemed to be some difficulty, as shown by the fact that I had to play all the parts and that the appointment was delayed, in Claudia being able to accept the daddy's help.

She immediately said that now it was Thursday. The dentist arrived but I still had to be both dentist and his patient. The x-ray was taken, but suddenly the play was disrupted by Claudia's announcement that she was going to draw a clown. She went straight to the toy basket but immediately complained that her pencil was missing. I wondered aloud whether she wasn't afraid to find the pencil as it was right under her nose, and that her plea for help had really the meaning of needing me to share the responsibility for drawing the clown. She then picked up the pencil, and also a green felt-tip pen, but immediately began to moan that it did not write, and threw it back in the basket. I said that she seemed full of suspicion of me, that I didn't want to help her, wasn't giving her the right tools to be active. Claudia then picked up a large sheet of cardboard, of a type she usually used to cut strips from, brought her little table close to me and quickly sketched the clown, drawing also some diagonal stripes across its arms. But this was no sooner done than she began to whimper, 'It's ugly! Throw it away!', and seemed very upset. 'Throw it away! Throw it away!' she urgently repeated, but I told her I would never throw it away because I thought that her drawing contained something valuable, namely her attempt to understand something. I too wanted to understand. She looked at me with curiosity, paused a

51

moment and then said, very seriously, 'Why do they say, "You're a clown"?' When I asked who said this, there was no reply from Claudia. So I wondered whether she had, in fact, when she was very little, herself felt that she was just an ugly, unhappy little clown. Then I spoke at some length about the recent material and how it was related to the stripes on the clown's arms that made it look as if bound by ropes. I spoke of her jealousy of my feeding the babies, of teeth that could bite and feet that could tread on my feet, of the fingers up her nose that stood also for getting her fingers into her bottom in masturbation. They seemed to be connected with ideas of getting inside me to steal my good things, babies, the daddy's penis, my knowledge and understanding. The clown's hands were perhaps bound to prevent this, for fear that this getting inside could break everything there, making all that was beautiful become ugly, like the clown felt itself to be.

Claudia was listening intently through all this long interpretation, and while I was still talking, and she was still listening, she hurriedly and quite skilfully cut out the drawing of the clown with her scissors. She handed it to me and I placed it in the folder with her other drawings, but Claudia immediately picked up the remaining piece of cardboard from which the clown had been cut, handing it to me so that it might also be placed in the folder. This was the first time she had done anything of this kind. She also handed to me a strip which she had cut from the same sheet without my having noticed, saying that I was to keep it for the next session. Our time was up. Claudia picked up her toy horse and left the room, but asked me for a drink before leaving.

Discussion: we are once again operating under the Sign of the Horse and have returned to the world of femininity and matriarchy. In fact we now have three generations, grandmother, mother and daughter, all working together on the problem. But the problem itself has shifted from the generic question of how babies are made, after the brief detour through the realm of masculine omnipotent assembling. Under the sway of resentment about the missed session (treading on Mrs. Fortunato's foot) and presumably of the approaching Chirstmas break, the problem now finds a more definitive statement, 'Why are some babies ugly little clowns', implying that others are beautiful, perhaps like the baby Jesus.

Mrs. Fortunato is following, in her long pulling-together interpretation, the theme of the role of aggression, of jealousy and envy, in attacking the object through projective identification, spoiling its beauty, resulting in an identification with an ugly object. This Kleinian theme is undoubtedly there in the material. But there is something else in addition that is apposite to this child's history and takes into account certain other facets of the material. It has now, by the end of the third session, become apparent that the problem is an aesthetic one: not how babies are made, but what differential of baby-making methods results in some babies being good and beautiful while others are ugly and aggressive little clowns. Claudia is caught between a matriarchal and a patriarchal theory, neither of which seems to answer the question. In the matriarchal orientation females, old and young, are alike full of babies and only need the ancillary assistance of echographic and x-ray equipped daddies to make the babies be 'born'. But why is it that some are big and some are small, some are hand-painted with flowers and others are not? From the patriarchal vertex it is quite different: females are full of all sorts of baby-pieces, which males, boys and men alike, have the tools and skill to assemble. But why is it that some fall to pieces, and others grow big and strong and beautiful and can tell the time correctly?

No, neither of these theories are adequate. There is something that Mrs. Fortunato knows that Claudia does not know, that is designated by the Sign of the Horse. It has to do with what Claudia's mummy and daddy do in the privacy of their nuptial chamber, of which she knows the mechanics but cannot imagine as an experience. She cannot put the parents together in her mind in the mechanics of coition in a way that is in keeping with the beauty of the horse. What is more, she firmly believes that her mother is likewise limited in her conceptions, as evidenced by her not having more children. If the sheet of cardboard represents the body of the mother from which the 'ugly little clown' has been born, then what remains, this mother with a hole in her, is just as much in need of Mrs. Fortunato's help as the clown, whose bondage is no solution.

Accordingly Claudia gives the remainder of the cardboard to be preserved by the therapist as carefully as she has preserved and valued the clown which she refused to throw away. Even the secretly cut strip, perhaps representing the stolen penis-baby-bottle, is returned for preservation. Full of hope, Claudia asks for a drink before departing.

Clearly the crucial moment in these three sessions is at that point when Claudia begs Mrs. Fortunato to throw away the Ugly Little Clown and she refuses, giving as her reason that the drawing represents the child's striving for understanding. At that moment, I will contend, a new idea has been transmitted to the child, that the beauty of an individual, child or adult or even a baby, resides not merely in what is outside in its bodily being. There is something more, something that is inside which cannot be directly seen but can only be construed from evidences of its mind's qualities. In the present moment Claudia is exhibiting some of 'the daily beauty in her life' which inheres in her quest for knowledge and understanding, the qualities which make her a beautiful little patient for Mrs. Fortunato.

Knowledge of the history of the child's birth and observation of the parents during our consultations with them leaves very little doubt that the damage to the child at birth shocked both the parents, as one could only expect. The father's response, for clearly he was a man passionately attached to his beautiful and elegant wife, was one of deep sorrow, devotion and readiness for any sacrifice. But for him clearly the mother and baby were an indissoluble unit, an united object of his readiness for service. It is probably of little consequence for our purpose in this exposition that he was not a handsome man but conveyed some-how a tragi-comic impression, not unadmirable by any means. The mother, on the other hand, while commanding admiration for her beauty and upright character, disappointed one by her coolness and decisiveness. Seemingly without conflict she bore the pain of her disappointment, gave herself over to the necessary services to little Claudia, and ruled out the question of ever conceiving another child. Through the following years, as the baby came to life and commenced her idiosyncratic develop-ment, the mother followed it all with interest but without enthusiasm. She never gave the impression of seeing the spark of internal beauty in this child. Clearly something had been crushed, or, in Claudia's apparent imagery, she was a mother with a hole in her where a beautiful baby had been. Still, one would have to admit her willingly to the class of Ordinary Beautiful Devoted Mothers.

The point of presenting this thrilling material is two-fold, a major and a minor theme. I wish to discuss the minor theme first; the nature of what Freud called 'the sexual researches of children', to which he attached the significance of the fountain-head of the quest for knowledge. In his way of formulating the problem, no distinction is made between mystery and secret. The general impression is that children are driven by curiosity about the secrets of the parents' sexuality. It was perhaps for this reason that the concept lent itself so well to being coupled with that of sublimation, displacement and other types of self-deception by which essentially delinquent motives could be diverted into socially laudable avenues. In contrast Mrs. Klein's view of an epistemophilic instinct operative from the beginning of postnatal life, an instinct whose primary object of interest and inquiry was the inside of the mother's body, meaning also her mind, was a more imaginative approach. However, even she took many years to begin to make a clear distinction between a quest for knowledge and understanding on the one hand, and intrusive and salacious curiosity on the other. The alternation between dependent and intrusive (projective identificatory) modes of inquiry is clear in Claudia's material, for instance.

It has been quite in keeping with the materialist scientific spirit of the age that we should have been content to think that the quest for knowledge about parental sexuality in the minds of small children would be satisfied if one could give them lectures on embryology and genetics. Claudia's material, although rendered exceptional by the circumstances of her damaging birth, is in a wider sense in no way exceptional. It is a particular instance of a general class of questions inherent to cognitive development. In order to grasp their nature we have to make a shift in our adult way of viewing the world — a shift which is, after all, the burden of this book. It has a lot to do with our habits of speech; thus the descriptive term 'tail of the comet' inhibited astronomers from seeing that the so-called 'tail' was in fact in the lead, and not in the wake, of the comet's path of

55

motion. Similarly one might like to alter Wordsworth's description of the child 'trailing clouds of glory' who 'cometh from afar'. We would need to say, 'projecteth clouds of glory' as it 'journeyeth afar'.

The class of questions which preoccupy this child, as Claudia shows us, include such particularities as: 'Why do I feel ugly?', 'What kind of conjunction of my parents has produced this, either ugliness or feeling of ugliness?' This can be translated into terms applicable to any child in a manner forming a series of propositions: 'If I could see babies as beautiful, I would be able to feel myself, as a member of that class, to be beautiful; if I could imagine the conjunction of my parents to be a mysterious process possessing a degree of beauty that I cannot as yet imagine, I would be able to see their babies as beautiful, including myself; if my parents cannot convey to me that they experience me as beautiful, I cannot then imagine myself to be the product of a beautiful and mysterious conjunction but only of an ugly secret one.'

This is Claudia's dilemma to which Mrs Fortunato has so spontaneously responded by refusing to throw away either the ugly picture of a clown or the picture of an ugly clown. She has had a glimpse of Claudia's cloud of glory, her enquiring spirit, and with it, of course, her rich potentialities for development. This brings us to the second theme: the factors which encourage or inhibit the tendency of parents to see the newborn as an aesthetic object. The accumulating wealth of infant observation experience leaves little doubt that this is, in many cases, perhaps most, a delicately balanced situation existing in both parents faced with the newborn. Behind, in the background, and perhaps most important of all, is the quality of the parents' relation to one another, the degree of passion of their sexual union, the extent to which a child, and one of this sex, was yearned for. But then there are factors related to the baby itself. Of course the general formal qualities of a baby — its proportions, its helplessness and vulnerability, its delicacy of texture and colouring — have a universal impact; even baby snakes and alligators have a share of this charm. But specific to the individual situation, and crucial, are items related to family resemblance and the absence of blemish or damage. Claudia, of course, was both so blemished and damaged that family resemblance was quite obscured; even her viability was in great doubt.

But even in the most favourable circumstances it is not possible to equate this charm, of formal qualities and family resemblance, with the attributes we associate with the concept of aesthetic object. Despite the outraged cries of innumerable outraged mothers ringing in my ears, I dare assert that a newborn baby is not, in its formal qualities, beautiful. We must look more deeply to discover the essence of baby-ishness which makes of it such a powerfully evocative object. But is it not the same with regard to the aesthetic impact of the mother, her breast, her face, her embracing arms as they impinge on the baby? Is it not essentially her mother-liness, the manifestation of her interior qualities, that delivers the blow of awe and wonder? So it is, beyond all explanatory reference to instinct, racial inheritance or hormones, with the baby. Its interior qualities, in which it excels all other creatures, deliver a corresponding blow to the parents. What it possesses that is the essence of its baby-ishness is the potentiality to become a Darwin, a George Eliot, a Rembrandt, a Mme.Curie, a human being. Its baby-ishness impinges directly on the imagination and sets us peering into its future. This ravishment, the love-at-first-sight that it can evoke is, I contend, the sine qua non of the baby's tolerance to the aesthetic blow it receives from the mother. And which Claudia could not tolerate.

In the first blush of this love-at-first-sight on the part of baby and mother alike, the first feed, as love-making, is crucial to their continued hopefulness and toleration of the passion. Small wonder it is awaited with such anxiety and misgiving, such virginal anxiety, one might say. When this mysterious conjunction is consummated, a process of development ensues which is most beautifully described by Keats in a letter to his friend Reynolds (May, 1818). I insert it here to counterbalance the crudeness of the language of the imaginative conjecture about Claudia which opened this chapter:

'I compare human life to a large Mansion of Many Apartments, two of which I can only describe, the doors of the rest being as yet shut upon me — The first we step into we call the infant or thoughtless Chamber, in which we remain as long as we do not think — We remain there a

long while, and notwithstanding the doors of the second Chamber remain wide open, showing a bright appearance, we care not to hasten to it; but are at length imperceptibly impelled by the awakening of the thinking principle — within us — we no sooner get into the second Chamber, which I shall call the Chamber of Maiden Thought, than we become intoxicated with the light and the atmosphere, we see nothing but pleasant wonders, and think to delay there forever in delight: However, among the effects this breathing is father of, is that tremendous one of sharpening one's vision into the heart and nature of man — of convincing one's nerves that the World is full of Misery and Heartbreak, Pain, and Sickness and Oppression — whereby the Chamber of Maiden Thought becomes gradually darkened and at the same time on all sides of it many doors are set open — but all dark — all leading to dark passages — We see not the balance of good and evil. We are in a Mist — We are now in that state — We feel the "burden of the Mystery".'

5   The Role of the Father
in Early Development

The move from theorizing about mental states to building models of the mental apparatus enables us also to move from a linear phase-organized theory of development to a more imaginative field-description of the process. We evolve 'stories' about a mind that builds itself by 'learning from experience' and develops faults and distortions from the evasion of the truth about these experiences. The 'story' that we carry into our consulting rooms as the backdrop for understanding and describing the phenomena we encounter with each individual patient is something of a prototype. In no sense is it 'normal' statistically, yet it is far from idealized since it includes a description of the steps in cognitive development and structuring of the personality with many nodes of conflict. Each one of these nodes is a point for the origin of distortions and faults. A backdrop of cognitive development and structuring implies the operation of thinking to resolve conflicts of meaning and, while it undoubtedly contains an internal logic, it is in no sense linear in the manner of theories of ontogenetic biological development. Rather it tends to present a somewhat spiral configuration, like the analytical process itself, thus giving a new meaning to Freud's concept of working-through.

The prototypic story (model) of development tends, of course, to be weighted heavily on the side of the evolution of the mother-child relationship, to which the role of the father must be appended as an important modulating, and potentially modifying, force in the field. It is a source of some of the most important faults and distortions regarding both character and psychopathological constructs. It is no simple task to describe this prototypic story, mainly because it functions in the consulting room in a predominantly unconscious way, being dipped into by the countertransference, and furthermore changing all the time as new clinical (and personal) experiences generate new ideas and rearrange old configurations. Perhaps periodically there are also the 'catastrophic changes' which require the whole image to be set in flux and re-ordered. These (extended) moments, which seem in fact to last for several years, are apparently brought about by the impact of the genius of others. My own evolution as a psycho-analyst certainly has had two such periods induced by the assimilation of the work of Melanie Klein and, ten years later, of Bion.

If we repeat our prototypic story of intrauterine life and the emotional experience of birth in the language of psychoanalytic descriptive theory, it would go as follows:

In the latter months of intrauterine life (judging from the recent experience with ecography) the foetus begins to have a lively if limited mental life (defined in terms of the beginning operation of interest, attention, emotion and of symbolic processes for thinking). His interest and attention are drawn to three types of experience: those of his container (being largely auditory and kinaesthetic), the sound of his mother's voice, and the more muffled sounds of other external persons and things. His imaginative response to the emotions stirred by these impingements, coupled with the growing attention to his own body and its capacities, takes a symbolic form in the mode of song and dance, in which rhythm is overwhelmingly important. Of the three types of objects, the mother's voice is the most evocative and carries the first aesthetic impact, responded to passionately (used in the sense of an integration of love, hate and the thirst for knowledge: Bion's plus L, H, and K.) The impact of the birth process, both exciting and terrifying, prepares him for the immense sensual and aesthetic impact of the outside world, which greets his eager visual apparatus in particular. The intensification of his passion, now directed visually towards the mother, face and breast, is contrapuntally confronted with new types of physical distress, pulmonary at first, chilling, drying, and, above all, the gravitational experience of density and immobilization. The heaviness of head and limbs brings a new experience of helplessness from which the enclosing in the mother's arms and pulling-together aspect of nipple-in-the-mouth bring him almost instant relief. Although the breast-feed brings into his inner space an omnipotent and omniscient object to protect him, it also brings painful wind and bad objects which he expels with screams and defecation back into the mother. This enables him to retire into his inner world in sleep, but anxious about the mother who now contains his persecuting wind and feces; emptied also of the good things he took in from her. When he awakens again in need she is there, but the persecutors are around, threatening to get back into him, by mouth or anus, by eyes or ears. A protector is necessary and presents himself as the father with his powerful but mysterious penis, to guard the mother and to guard the baby's orifices, especially the anus, which is felt to lead directly inside where his precious objects have been lodged. A bad feces-penis might get in and either steal or destroy the breast mother. Uncertainty begins to intrude into this world of reliable satellite parent figures as longer hours of waking, more erotic contact with the mother at breast, bath and nappy change stir possessive feelings and controlling impulses. After all how does he know they are to be trusted? They leave him alone at night and he can hear the sounds of their talk and other more mysterious things. And he has noted the similarity between mother's nipples and father's penis. Perhaps it is *they* who are controlling *him*. And then there are those children, dubiously friendly. Perhaps others inside the mother, waiting their time to emerge as he had done. Not that he remembers others in there, but perhaps she is full of separate rooms, like the home. Surely the thing to do would be to keep the parents apart and to remove those penis-nipples which control his feeds. Sleep must be curtailed and vigilance instituted. Yet their combination seems all-important. Mother must be fed in order to feed the baby; the bad things he evacuates into her must be destroyed and removed; and what of the possible babies inside mother? What would happen should they die?

This pale language cannot, of course, begin to capture the richness of the dream and phantasy language of infantile thought as we are able to reconstruct it from analytic experience and infant observation. But it gives us sufficient background with which to describe the significance of the father in the life of the infant. The infantile image serves as the prototype, again, for the later more sophisticated conceptions. The father's functions have an import secondary to the role of the mother and any later movement into a role of primary importance sets in train a gross distortion of the world of human relationships. The conceptual basis for such reversals of primacy rest upon confusional states in which the series nipple-penis-feces-baby serves either as the source of poor differentiation or the matrix by which confusions are generated as a defence. Insofar as confusion of roles and functions exists in the minds of the parents as well they are likely to be reinforced in the child.

The father's functions are generally those of supply and protection to the mother-child relationship, and his genital is both the tool and the weapon of these functions. This genital symbolism for his mental functioning easily slides into concreteness when splitting processes reduce the whole objects to partial ones in the service of defence against the depressive position and the impact of aesthetic conflict. Splitting of the nipple-penis from the breast, which generates an eroticized penis and an envious breast-with-a-hole, seems to be the most serious impediment to development; while the paranoid distrust secondary to the confusion penis-feces-nipple which results in the malignant nipple undermines mental health. All of these confusional trends come into crisis at the time of weaning, which, however, also promotes the differentation between internal and external reality upon which foundation the move from a skin-container (exoskeletal) to an introjective (endo-skeletal) personality depends. This move carries with it a certain degree of disillusion about the omnipotent-omniscient qualities of the external parents. Such qualities thenceforth only appear in the form of transference love and paranoid hatred.

Childhood after weaning may be viewed as a continual working out and working through of this basic pattern of cognitive conflicts. And the mentality of the parents plays a major role in the field of forces upon which it is played out. But after infancy the parents no longer function as limiting factors to the child's development, for with the acquisition of mobility and later of language, the finding of other objects in the outside world to carry the transference significance of good objects becomes possible. In this way many qualities can accrue to internal objects which may be lacking in the parents.

In this model of the developmental process, the parents are

seen in the role mainly of providing a protected space where the child may have the kinds of experiences of intimate emotional relationships upon which the evolution of the personality depends. While the actual qualities of mind and behaviour of the parental couple appear in the social facade of the child's personality, mainly through the operation of narcissistic (projective and adhesive) modes of identification, the intro-jective core develops in a far more mysterious way. As Freud has described, the 'form' of internal parental figures may be derived from the outward form of external parents, but the functional qualities and the degree of aesthetic aspect have no such direct reference. Since internal objects at their best represent ideas, in the sense of forms, such as beauty, truth, goodness, justice, generosity, forgiveness, charity, wisdom; their essence is spiritual and bound in the innate preconceptions of the race and its millenial experience. For this reason the child's trust in parents is a transference phenomenon and subject inevitably to some considerable degree of disillusion. Within the prototype of development expounded here, it is the father and his genital that carries the greatest load of suspicion in the child's mind. But the child's trust in the mother also is subject to severe strain. This comes from two directions: the experience of separation (absent object) and the painful impact of her aesthetic in arousing his passions (present object). Of these two types of stress, the former tends generally to be displaced onto the father while the latter adheres to the mother. It is only very late in development that the aesthetic of the father and his genital appears as a force in development, through the emergence of introjective identification with the internal mother's view of him. This limited apprehension of its aesthetic quality greatly facilitates the conception of the import of the male genital as a weapon rather than a tool. Only with acceptance of the 'next baby' conflict does this weapon concept yield place to the tool-of-procreation and establish the role of the father in any degree of genuine glory comparable to that of the mother. Usually it is a very late acquisition indeed. Con-sequently ideas of male superiority can be firmly placed as paranoid-schizoid phenomena, based as they are on quantita-tive (size + power) rather than qualitative (goodness, creativity, utility, courage, etc.) criteria.

All of the foregoing relates to psychic reality, to the concept of father that arises when the adult self takes shape through the agency of introjective identification with the internal parents as Combined Object. In the realm of behaviour and emotion, we must speak, as with truth-fulness and mother-liness and baby-ishness, of father-liness. The first realization is that this must be a description of a set of feelings, attitudes and consequent behaviour which cannot have a necessary relation to the status of progenitor, nor even of masculine sex. The opinion has been given in the chapter on reciprocity between baby and mother that from a deeply animal, instinctual foundation, there arises as a product of imaginative thought a bonding at a symbolic level that has its richest manifestation as aesthetic impact, and consequent conflict. While it may seem likely that the aesthetic impact of the mother on the baby is largely founded on the sensual apprehension of her formal qualities, the mother's orientation to the baby has a far more imaginative base in her grasp of its teeming potentialities to become an evolved human being. This same configuration of mother-liness may arise in the putative (pater incertus est) father.

But the composition of his father-liness tolerates poorly such uncertainty, for it rests on a foundation of trust in the woman and the exclusiveness of their sexual union. Fortunately the miraculousness of nature usually comes to the rescue by repro-ducing unmistakeable likeness, at least to the father's family, if not at birth, soon thereafter. But this factor is complicated by the psychological aspect of being able to recognise the likeness when it exists (*A Winter's Tale*), or to see it where none exists. The burden of this is that, while the mother's mother-liness is directly related to the baby, the father's father-liness is contingent. And therefore, being more complex, more subject to disturbance, it is more unstable.

This contingent quality, this secondary response to the baby's existence as against a primary response to its baby-ishness, tends to favour some of the important distortions of fatherliness which have been so characteristic of cultural history as an accompaniment to the degradation of women. Pater-nalistic possession usually extends only to the son, the first or, later, the preferred son, and has implemented its tyranny characteristically through the laws of inheritance. On the other hand paternalism, and the patriarchal family, contributes to the continued degradation of women by unwillingness to make sacrifices for girls' education, opposition to the marriage of daughters — in the past, by controlling dowry, for instance — but most damaging of all, by lack of interest, paternal neglect.

Father-liness can often be simulated, or rather caricatured, by the competitiveness with the mother that interferes, controls, encourages maternal neglect. Similarly the tenderly supportive attitudes and attentiveness of fatherliness can be quietly replaced, as the children grow and their sexual attractiveness becomes more manifest, by erotic play and cuddling which easily escalates and also drives the children into secret sexual games and masturbatory habits. Certainly the patterns of paternal behaviour are in severe flux in our Western culture as the sharing of economic responsibility encourages domestic division of chores and favours househusbandliness. The difficulty this arouses can probably best be understood in terms of confusion between father-liness and mother-liness in the man. At the present moment, when redundancy for a man in his forties can so easily result in a prolonged period of unemployment, particularly in the middle classes, a permanent reversal of economic roles can take place, perhaps to the great gratification of the bisexuality of both partners. Its consequences for the children are unclear, for it cannot be compared with the consequences of derelict fathers or fathers living on unearned income.

On the other hand, the very contingent nature of fatherliness is also the source of its greatest strength and value. The concept of husband, as provident manager of the overall space of the family in the community, would seem to be in keeping with psychic reality. As provider and guardian of the space where the mother nurtures and rears the children, a differential of spheres of influence and responsibility is clearcut. One might say that it is his estate and her children, in the sense of responsibility rather than possession, as he faces outwards towards the community and she faces inwards towards the children. The Riddle of the Sphinx we could pose would run: 'Who stand back to back in the morning, side by side in the evening, and face to face in the night?'

6   The Problem of Violence

When Bion, in his pre-psycho-analytical work as a psychiatrist, first drew the distinction between the mental apparatus and what he called the 'protomental apparatus' (*Experiences in Groups*), he laid down the groundwork for the differentiation between those operations which involve meaning (and the formation of symbols for representing meaning), and those which merely involve signs and their manipulation by logical operations. *Signs* are indicators of *information*; but *meaning* must find its representation in *symbols* in order that the emotionality of human relationships may be thought about and evolved. States of mind may be communicated by primitive means such as projective or perhaps also adhesive identifications, but these transmissions have not of themselves the capacity for growth and evolution in complexity, sophistication, generalization or abstraction. Mathematics and logic are the sciences of signs and information; psychology and philosophy are the sciences of meaning and symbols. To seek to bridge them, worse still to confuse them, indicates a failure to grasp the central fact, that they relate to different worlds: the outside world, and the inner world of psychic reality.

This spatial view of mental life, so central to the Kleinian tradition, in its concreteness carries implications of different worlds, with differing premises, differing laws. For instance the world of projective identification, inside an internal or external object, is a world without the fourth dimension of time; past and future have only the meaning of 'out', in the sense of 'when I was out' or 'when I will be out'. You might say that the world of projective identification has tenses, but not time as a measurable dimension of reality. On the other hand, the difference between the emotional meaning of time in psychic reality and therefore with respect to the significance it has for intimate human relationships, and time's factual measurement in the physical world, is of the greatest importance, and a source of endless confusion in our culture. For while physical time as a dimension of the universe of physical phenomena is linear and relative, the time dimension of emotional relations may be either oscillating, circular or absolutely linear.

Given that the mental sphere proper, as distinct from the protomental (or what Bion later called the 'soma-psychotic'), must be apprehended in its geographic dimension of multiple worlds, it is necessary to make a distinction between the venues of the protomental and the mental with regard to the external world. Immediately we become aware of the differentiating gradient between public and private/secret areas. From the visual point of view, the public surface of a person's body is a variable area, depending on whether he is at a committee meeting, on the beach or in the hospital. From the tactile point of view the entire body surface is private, while from an olfactory vertex one might think a person's privacy extends several feet. If his odours penetrate further they become automatically public for a particular reason having to do with the conventions of social distance. In our culture if a stranger aproaches and stands closer than, say, eighteen inches, we feel threatened, slightly assaulted, even if the stranger asks an innocent question — the time or directions to Baker St. On the other hand at a cocktail party we would experience this proximity as a sexual invitation, whether we welcomed it or not.

Thus it may be said that each individual, in his planetary orbit, makes his daily round with an atmosphere whose boundaries threaten repellant action if trespassed, much as a meteor is burnt up on entry due to the friction of our surrounding gases. For this is the essential meaning of private/ secret: that entry must be invited. Consequently the spaces in which we are exposed owing to undress, lavatory or sexual functions, the requirements of quiet or undisturbed activity, tend to be enclosed, lockable. We may even resist telephone intrusion by leaving the receiver off. We may browse among a friend's books on the shelf but will not look inside his desk. We knock before entering the closed door of the bath even in our own homes. The establishment of this boundary of privacy/ secrecy is conventional and if we traverse it unawares we avert the eyes and hastily retreat with apologies.

But because the boundary is ambiguous in its import — privacy or secrecy — respect for it is a matter of judgment in our dealings with children. We do not accord this respect to the infant except when asleep — beyond, that is, the surface of his body. That privilege of trespass is reserved, generally, for the person in parental function. At all ages the orifices of the body are sacrosanct, even for the infant. This is clearly because we attribute to these entries the significance of portals to the internal world. Yet the senses, particularly the special senses, are also invested with this meaning; this raises a dimension of ambiguity that amplifies the privacy/secrecy equivocation.

In the public sphere of our lives in the external world we move about in conformity and adaptation to these conventions of trespass of the privacy/secrecy of other individuals. These conventions lubricate social movement and allow us to maintain casual/contractual relationships with a minimum of friction or tormenting uncertainty. But the activities necessary to this adaptation not only require skill and sensitivity to the responses of others, they are also vastly time-consuming. Maladaptation may be observed in two classes of individuals: those without the social skills and those who are unwilling to spare the time and effort involved. The former we associate with mental and emotional disturbances which estrange the individual from his culture, but it may also be seen in foreigners. The latter, which we are inclined to label as eccentricity, may be said to characterize artists, scientists, enthusiasts and fanatics whose special preoccupations make them intolerant of time-consuming convention.

Without any pejorative implication, it would seem reasonable to label this area of casual/contractual adaptation as mindless or protomental in the sense that we operate in this sphere with signs and not with the symbols formed autononomously from the operation of alpha-function and unconscious dream-thought upon our emotional experiences. That we operate with signs, is obscured by the fact that this involves the employment of received symbols functioning *as signs* in the particular basic assumption atmosphere active at the moment — dependence, pairing or fight-flight. The signs of rank and status are clearly displayed; but also are the evidences of the more private world of character, for, in time, each man comes to wear the face he deserves. These two displays, of rank and character, arouse in the casual observer curiosity and interest respectively, and thereby some degree of desire to penetrate the barriers of privacy/secrecy. We wish to understand more of the private person but also to ferret out his secrets. These two tendencies may be taken as driving forces towards intimacy on the one hand, and violence on the other.

Upon this conceptual background with its emphasis on spatial relationships, it is possible to construct a concept of violence which becomes synonymous with violation: violation of the boundaries of privacy/secrecy. It has many distinct advantages over the usual quantitative descriptive definition of violence in that it includes mental as well as physical violation of boundaries, allowing for a more minute investigation of the qualitative subtleties by which communication slides into social action. It should also allow us to explore with equal penetration the relations between individuals and between groups and organizations.

But before attempting such a preliminary exploration of the implications of this spatial viewpoint and the definition of violence as violation, it is necessary to say something about the 'binding' effect of thought, and the evacuatory significance of action in the evolution of the mental apparatus. It is a special virtue of the Bionic addendum to the Kleinian model of the mind that it makes it possible to see clearly the way in which the structuring of the mind in the course of personality development arranges, to use Freud's phrase, to 'interpose thought between impulse and action'. In Bion's model, the alpha-function which creates representations of emotional experience that can be used for thinking and stored as memory, binds the 'accretions of stimuli' of which the apparatus would otherwise have to 'unburden itself' through action or psychosomatic functions or hallucination. Actions of this sort have as their essential quality meaning-lessness. Bion cites as an example what he calls the 'beta-screen' type of meaningless talk; but strictly speaking the whole category of basic assumption group behaviour would have to be subsumed under this category. Although I described the central function of social conventions as lubricating the area of casual/contractual relationships, much time and vitality are squandered by people in activities and socializing which are essentially uninteresting — killing time, letting off steam, relaxing, restlessness, getting rid of tension.

Insofar as the personality structure has become able to

symbolize and think about its emotional experiences, impulse is bound; the steps of the horizontal axis of Bion's Grid are traversed through notation, attention and inquiry as the preludes to judgment, decision and action. The metaphor of atomic and molecular structure is helpful for envisaging this, but perhaps a clinical example would have more psychic reality. Many years ago Arthur Hyatt Williams told me a vignette from a patient which I have never forgotten, partly because it involved a dream which was almost identical to one I had just recently heard from the late Doreen Weddell. Dr. Williams at the time was doing analytic therapy with convicted murderers at Wormwood Scrubbs and told me of a patient whose analysis had commenced in prison, where he'd been confined for many years for murder in the course of rape. When parolled this man returned to his trade of bricklayer but found adaptation very difficult indeed. Some of these difficulties arose from his falling in love with a woman for the first time in his life, and during this turbulent period he had the following dream: *He seemed to be working inside a house, dismantling a partition wall. As he removed the courses of brick systematically, he suddenly came across a bolt of lightning lying bound in the mortar between two courses.* Within a few months of this dream a fulminating cancer was discovered and he died within half a year. In her section of *Explorations in Autism* Doreen Weddell had reported in the case of Barry the evidence that the structuring of the personality of this autistic boy under the influence of the therapy, had been secondary to the evolution of a functionally valid partitioning of the inside of his internal mother. One may speculate that for Dr. Williams' patient the stress of falling in love, with its turbulent conflict of jealousy and curiosity (aesthetic conflict?) was having a dismantling effect on his respect for the privacy/secrecy of his beloved and consequently of his internal mother at an infantile level. If his years of imprisonment had curbed his capacity for externally directed violence, as in the rape and murder, was he now left with only the psychosomatic avenue for unburdening himself?

To this reminder of the role of thought in structuring of the personality through the binding of impulse, it might be valuable at this point to add a note about the other great agency of control — the superegoideal. In Chapter VIII of the *Psycho-analytical Process*, I illustrated the thesis specified by Freud that the experience of other transference relationships beyond the original parent figures, assimilates additional equipment within the internal objects. In fact there is a good reason to think that Bion's differentiation of 'learning from experience' from 'learning about' the world, depends on just this type of introjection into the internal object of new ideas, as a primary step towards modification of the equipment of the self. This is a succinct reminder that 'thinking for oneself' is in fact an internal process of 'thinking with' an internal object, in many ways a pedagogic relationship between object and self. The more combined the object, the more creative become the thoughts — that is, the more poetic and idiosyncratic become the new and autonomous symbols, by contrast with the employment of received symbols. In the dreams of creative individuals the novelty of the symbols and the complexity of the interweaving of visual and verbal elements is often breathtaking, for example, our 'gold rush' poet.

We should now be able to go on to explore the implications of our spatial view of the distinctions public/private and private/secret, as the generalized descriptive concept 'violence' funnels into the more technical idea of 'violation'. In order to do this I want to keep in mind the family as prototype of the setting of all human relationships, using as the background the view of family life put forward in 'A model of the Child-in-the-Family-in-the-Community'. In that monograph by Martha Harris and the author (D.M.) a format for examining family life was put forward which emphasized the moment-to-moment variations in organization and functioning. The performance of certain emotional functions necessary for maintaining the family as a proper work group were detailed, and the forces operating to induce regression to various types of gang and basic assumption grouping were outlined. It is not necessary to repeat these special facets here, where we are concerned primarily with the relationships of individual to individual, carrying forward the assumption that the techniques of violation can be extrapolated to larger groupings.

The first consideration would seem to be an investigation of the social visibility of the boundary of privacy/secrecy. I have already indicated the dimension of physical distance as a sensitively variable convention. More difficult to describe is the quality of openess or closedness with which a person operates. This may be seen as a dimension on the one hand of the social armouring but also of the character as displayed in intimate relationships. It is subject also to more minute variations depending on the nature of the transaction at hand between individuals. A person is likely to be more open when expecting praise than criticism, for instance, more open when relaxing than when under the stress of work. This dimension of openess seems to have both an active and a passive aspect, both of openess to invitation to an increase in intimacy and also of issuing such an invitation. But it can be difficult to distinguish in action a certain aspect of secrecy when it is disguised by pseudo-openness. The social armour that presents as comradery and my-life-is-an-open-book is typical of the politician in our culture, just as the facade of typical-family-man is often the screen for dedicated perversity.

But the degree of social display of the boundary of privacy/secrecy is also a significant dimension. While privacy discretly displays its social boundaries of class and status so that they may be perceptible to interested persons, more flamboyant display of the evidences of rank is likely to be aimed at projecting intrusive curiosity, provocations to trespass. Similarly, clothing that attracts notice, induces sexual interest or flouts convention is likely to be projective in intent, regardless of rebellious motivation against the unreasoning restraints of custom. Cave canem on the gate and broken glass on the top of the wall may repel professional or delinquent invasion but they also provoke aggressive intent. Likewise the spikiness of irritability towards menials may keep the meek in their place but is also calculated to arouse spying and eavesdropping.

Now the balance in motivation between secrecy and privacy is in many individuals and under many circumstances a rather delicate matter. This instability may be understood as a function of the difference in the economics of mental pain and pleasure associated with privacy and secrecy. The theory of the work group throws considerable light on the self-containment of privacy and its overriding concern not to be interfered with by forces outside the task-group. Secrecy, on the other hand, probably derives most of its pleasure from the fact of being secret rather than from its specific content. What, after all, could be the pleasure in having a secret if no one knows you have a secret? Although children display this most flamboyantly, chanting, 'You don't know what I did', the adult is hardly more subtle in his cat-that-got-the-cream demeanour.

This brief exposition is far from exhaustive, but it seems necessary to conceptualize the scintillating qualities of the privacy/secrecy boundary in order to grasp the relevance of the theory of aesthetic conflict to this problem of violence, when construed as violation of the space of privacy/secrecy.

This would seem to be the appropriate place to introduce a concept without which we are rather helpless to understand the means that a person uses for guarding the boundaries of his privacy, as well as to distinguish the motives which may leave these bounds unprotected from violation or transform them into the confines of secrecy. The process of degradation involves the quality of relationship between self and love-objects, both internal and external, and therefore a coarsening of ethical values. In analysis it is possible to obtain a very detailed representation of these processes of degradation. Melanie Klein's delineation of paranoid-schizoid and depressive positions, as both a structural formulation regarding integration-disintegration, and one describing oscillations in ethical values (egocentricity versus object-love), has been richly filled out with clinical detail over the past half century. Bion's work on groups, the evolution of the structural view of narcissism (narcissistic organization of infantile parts of the self), and the concept of the gang have widened the field of investigation.

Through the concept of aesthetic conflict, we are in a position, to add yet another theoretical dimension, albeit one which is in fact familiar to every analyst who examines dream material closely. The concept of splitting processes, which gave such clinical point to Abraham's theory of whole- and part-objects, finds its clearest representation in dreams. For not only do they make explicit the planes of cleavage (good-bad, male-female, top-bottom, front-back) by which the self and objects are cleft from whole to partial states, but dreams also show clearly the process of degradation. This follows a clear path of internal logic, moving from identifiable person to unidentified person, to animal to vegetable to inanimate machines and matter like faeces. When on the other hand non-human

73

objects are utilized as symbols (of the beauty of nature or of man's ingenuity, for instance), it is necessary to distinguish such representations from the concreteness of degradation of the self or objects in psychic reality. But alertness to the manifestations of aesthetic conflict soon makes one recognize that the most important aspects of the degradation occur in this very dimension: degraded beauty of the objects and degraded capacity to experience the aesthetic impact in the self.

Before proceeding to clinical material to illustrate these processes, it might be appropriate to insert here a brief note, related to the chapter on aesthetic reciprocity, concerning the aesthetic of the image of the self and the capacity to accept other people's aesthetic response to oneself. To consider oneself an aesthetic object is not the same as to aspire to be one (Milton's aspiration to "become a true poem", being already a true poet). To hold an image of oneself as an aesthetic object must surely be called vanity, and be the result of a narcissistic mode of identification with the object. Hamlet's acid comment about 'the much beautified Ophelia' seems unkind in view of the evidence of her passion for him. Certainly one of the chief items in men's distrust of the aesthetic impact of women relates to the motivation behind their 'beautifying'. Is it a manifestation of vanity? Is it predatory? Or can it be trusted as a function of their generosity? It seems to be not in the nature of the aesthetic problem to experience the self as such an object, but it is possible to allow the "eye of the beholder" to do so, without begrudging the pleasure and without accepting it as objective fact. After all, we move about the world as representatives, envoys, accepting with pleasure the tribute paid — not to ourselves — but to 'them', our household gods.

A young Scotsman, good-looking and vain of both his appearance and his steady climb towards success, had come to a London teaching hospital with an academic career in psychiatry in mind. While working on the psychotherapy service, finding it all surprisingly interesting, he bethought himself to have 'some analysis' to fill out his CV. He had married recently, after a very successful career as a bachelor-among-the-nurses, and presented a very respectable and erudite demeanour. His parents had separated and both remarried when he was in his early teens, but, being the eldest and a very self-reliant child, he found the changed way of life quite congenial, even something of a relief. For in the last years of the marriage the father had been quite alcholic and, when coming home drunk, had been in the habit of entering the patient's bedroom to abuse him with criticism of his character.

The early months of the analysis came as something of a shock to him, partly because he found himself able to remember and report dreams, which was out of keeping with his previous experience; but more because these dreams revealed unsavoury aspects of his character that had a rather striking congruence with his father's drunken accusations. Opportunism, exploitation of women, greed for money and status, cowardliness and deviousness all found a rich dream-documentation. But he took it all in good heart until he was shaken by a nightmare, that a *small, aboriginal man in a loincloth and armed with a 'longbow' and arrows was creeping into his house to shoot him.* It clearly had a reference to the transference and the interpretation of primitive and infantile phantasy, but also referred to his father's intrusions, perhaps drunk on cider 'Strongbow'.

As the first summer holiday of the analysis approached and the material seemed to centre around the opportunism of his educational history and approach to psychiatry, there seemed evidence that the process was seizing his interest, but also threatening his life's plans for achieving status, security and privilege. In this context, and on the eve of having to make a case presentation before the professor, he had a second near-nightmare. In it *he was gathering his papers and slides, but could not find the latter. Although they were in no way essential to the material he intended to present, they were part of the customary paraphernalia of the professorial unit, to which he aspired to be promoted. And to make matters worse, once he had found the slides, he discovered, on reaching the auditorium, that the video machine was not working properly. He got into a panic, frantically tried to contact the technician of the video equipment. Once he realized that the time for the presentation had already arrived, he wondered in desperation if he could send in a message to the professor that he was ill.*

On enquiry it turned out that the presentation concerned an elderly woman with florid hypochondria and the video was of an interview with her in which she described the moment-to-moment processes of migration of her hypochondriac delusions.

My patient was intending to show that her florid disturbance was in fact a symptom of an underlying depression. His dream lent itself to the same formulation: when faced with a public exposure of his capabilities, he suddenly discovers that his techniques for projecting an image of himself as perfectly adapted to the established community, are no longer available, because his internal mother (the video equipment) who does his thinking for him is not functioning (is ill) and needs to be repaired by the technician-daddy (who has gone on the long summer holiday break). The only way to evade the pain of the situation (the depressive pain of having damaged the mother by his opportunism and exploitation; and the persecutory pain of public exposure of his limitations) is to identify with the damaged object, to become ill himself.

The burden of the dream is the patient's growing realization that he is ill and needs analysis, that he has hidden this from himself and from others for years (at least from the time of the disintegration of his family) by using the 'equipment' of the culture, submission to those above and exploitation of those below in the social hierarchy. If he is going to begin to think for himself (as, for instance, to put forward the idea that hypochondriacal symptoms are a form of depressive illness) he will discover his dependence on his internal parents, and on his analyst who is at present carrying the transference of these objects. It can be seen that the panic in the face of criticism from his professor in this dream (in reality he would not be so frightened) has a link to the terror of the wiry aboriginal man in his loincloth with his 'longbow' and arrows, an image of his tipsy father.

This discovery, that thinking for oneself is dependent on the services of internal objects, comes often as a shock to the well-adjusted people who come to analysis for professional reasons. But it usually takes a long time before they realize that to think for oneself, to form one's own opinions and judgments and to act upon them, carries a serious threat of becoming maladjusted. A man in his mid-thirties, well-educated and charmingly boyish in his enthusiasms and high-mindedness, came to analysis as part of long-standing plan to become a psychoanalyst. Having grown up in a well-to-do family of strong Anglo-European culture, it had been long accepted that he would be a doctor and perhaps a psycho-analyst, but at university he had decided to change course. He changed from medical studies to PPE for his degree and entered accountancy en route to being groomed for a place in his father's group of industries. His private (or secret) plan was to work for a number of years until he was wealthy enough to sustain a period of low income, and during this initial period to marry and establish his family with the young woman with whom he had fallen deeply in love at university. Perhaps his father was somewhat disappointed that his eldest son should not fulfil his own frustrated longings towards medicine and psycho-analysis, but he welcomed him into the industrial scene where he treated him with a deference that quite obscured any 'boss's son' aspect of his rise to wealth and responsibility.

After two years of analysis he felt ready to enter upon his new career and began to investigate the various trainings within reach of Oxford while also looking for employment that would contribute to his development in this field. His first job was more administrative than clinical, as locum for a woman director of an organization of post-mental hospital hostels and day centres. But he threw himself into the work with such enthusiasm and managerial skill that by the time the directress returned from her study leave, the hospital board was loath to have her back and to lose my patient. Despite ample warnings from the analytical material he had pursued his 'boss's son' behaviour, and was eventually astonished at the implied treachery to the directress in so exceeding his brief as locum. It made more real for him the formulation of having abandoned his dependence on his mother to become 'daddy's heir apparent'.

So he decided he had best take a more humble and purely clinical post as nursing assistant at a hostel for adolescents in care. His first weeks there quite overwhelmed him with confusion, for the differential roles of staff and patients (or were they clients — or inmates — or guests?) seemed quite nebulous at the auxiliary level while the medical level seemed to function like a mental hospital. His managerial soul entered on a period of torment of uncertainty between adaptation and the need to think for himself — and face the consequences. It was not the aggression, the suicidal gesturing, the absconding and uncooperativeness of the patients, but the absence of clear guidelines for staff that impinged on him so disturbingly. One night, after having decided to watch and wait rather than call the consultant when a young woman alleged to have swallowed some razor blades, he dreamed the following:*the family was at a country fete on a lovely day and part of the entertainment was a military display. There were in fact two lines of soldiers, a front row in modern battle dress with automatic weapons, and behind, a row of redcoats with muskets, all firing at random. The patient was standing with the vicar* (who is chairman of the village school board of which he is a parent member.*) He felt slightly alarmed at the random shooting but assumed that blanks were in use, until he noticed that a soldier had stepped forward from the front rank and was in fact being wounded by the bullets. He turned appalled to the Vicar, who merely gave him a kind of boys-will-be-boys sort of reply and he burst into tears and awoke sobbing.*

The dream threw up immediately two lines of association: the first was his having taken upon himself the responsibility of not calling the consultant, who would have ordered the girl to be taken to emergency for x-rays to determine if she had really swallowed razor blades (she was known to have swallowed pins in the past). The second line of association surprised him, for it related to his children. He had found a dead baby bird while walking in the garden with two of the children after breakfast and his daughter, aged seven, in her competent way, had run into the house to fetch a little box in which to take the bird to school for their nature study exhibit. But the boy, aged nine, looked on sadly, his eyes rimmed with moisture. 'Fallen out of the nest' seemed to mean, then, 'out of step', 'out of line'. Was this the inevitable consequence of thinking for oneself, of relying on one's own judgment? My patient recalled that it was only as late as the Boer War that the red uniform had been abandoned in favour of a more camouflaged battle dress. But then again this had hardly been more humane under the conditions of trench warfare in the First World War. Were the ethics that dominated the relations of medical to auxiliary staff at the hostel any different from those of the General Staff to the troops in the field? Did a person who got 'out of line' become indistinguishable from the 'enemy'? One is reminded of Ibsen's great play, *An Enemy of the People*.

I have chosen these two pieces of clinical material to illustrate the problem of degradation by the demands for conformity to the group ethos, because the first seems to illustrate well what happens to the internal objects when degradation is yielded to, and the second shows what happens to the self at the hands of the group when it is resisted. My first patient, fairly young in analysis, has been experiencing a process of de-idealization of the good adjustment he had relied on as a defence against the confusion and despair consequent to his parents' separation and divorce in his pubertal years, preceded as it was by experiences of disillusionment in his father for his weakness, drinking and hostile abuse. In the context of this loss of self-idealization he found himself excessively anxious to please the professor, for whom, in fact, he has rather little admiration because of his narrowly biological viewpoint and his bullying tactics with younger staff. In the dream he becomes panicky because his equipment for thinking, his internal parents, have been reduced to the video-machine mother and the maintenance technician father, who cannot be found — presumably because (like the analyst soon), he has gone on holiday. What looks on the surface like a banal realistic dream can be seen on deeper scrutiny to reveal the degraded state of his internal parents owing to his yielding to the opportunism of the group, thus compromising his capacity for independent and creative thought in the face of the professor's prospective bullying. It is of special interest that in this way, in his dream, he has revealed an understanding of the unconscious processes underlying hypochondriasis which is completely at variance with the mundane medical modes of presentation in the paper he had prepared.

In this chapter thus far, we have pleaded the move from the usual descriptive concept of violence, with its explosive, physical-and-external world overtones, to a more abstract one of 'violation'. We have been busy demonstrating the advantages deriving instead from a geographic or spatial vertex. By differentiating the public and private spaces of the individual, we find ourselves in a position to make a clearer distinction between 'private' and 'secret', from the intentional point of view: namely that secrecy is directed toward an external audience, while privacy indicates inner world functions. All of this finds its prototype and meaningful core in the distinction between internal and external worlds in our model of the mind.

Bion and Bick, in their different ways, have pointed to the evolution of the personality structure from an earlier skin-container (exoskeletal, two-dimensional) to a later internally oriented (endoskeletal, three-and four-dimensional) state in which the internal objects perform mental functions (superego-ideal) which the self cannot undertake and without which it cannot grow. This schema places adaptation and growth in a certain degree of conflict with one another, partly by virtue of the economics of time and vitality, but, more important, because of the constant danger of both objects and values sliding into degradation.

This essentially Chekhovian slippery slope, this Strindbergian trap, this Shakespearean impasse looms every day in our consulting rooms, and requires of the analyst a capacity to carry the transference of objects which can contain and modulate this conflict so as to allow time for its clarification and working through. The difficulty of the task is lessened if it can be contained in the transference relationship itself, but, as so often happens, the conflict envelops other areas of the patient's life as well, as illustrated by the previous two examples of disturbance in the professional area. When it also involves the intimate love relationships, the problem is delicate in the extreme. To tease out the narcissistic acting-out from the evolving adult intimacy can hardly be managed without the help of the patient's dreams, so intense is the parental counter-transference. Also, with highly verbal patients, the subtlety of their cynical misuse of language, the skill and speed with which they argue their point so overpoweringly, all combine to reduce the analyst not merely to waiting but almost to praying for a dream.

Some years ago a talented writer of forty came to analysis in a state of suicidal desperation. The highly organized way of life that depended for its stability on regular periods of paedophilic excursions to the East had gradually burnt out. This reduced him once more to the state of despair and loneliness which had brought on a breakdown at university, had taken him into a Trappist monastery for some years, and from which he had only gained release by capitulating to his sexual inclinations. Despite his demeanour of contempt for analysis and high-handed patronization of the analyst, he brought rich material which made it possible in the first half year of therapy to demonstrate to him that his paedophilia was based on a fetishistic attraction to the bare knees of little boys in short trousers, that his phantasies were essentially heterosexual, that he was smitten by the beauty of young women to a degree he could not bear and that his masturbatory phantasies were essentially masochistic. The consequence was somewhat daunting: he fell madly in love with a seventeen year old Malay girl student in a creative writing course he was giving at a polytechnic.

What ensued during the next eighteen months had a distinctly Romeo and Juliet quality, for he felt in danger of being thrown out of his job (although this seemed unrealistic and had its history in the days when he'd been a schoolmaster with paedophile inclinations), while she felt that any news of the relationship reaching her parents in Malaysia would result in her immediate recall. Virginal timidity, combined with caution and distrust on both sides, conspired to move the relationship very slowly from out-of-doors walking and talking to indoors kissing and petting. During the summer holiday she returned home and drew from her educated and reasonable parents permission to continue to explore the relationship, with severe restrictions on the sexuality. He waited on tenterhooks in a state of constant upper respiratory illness, constantly threatened by returning paedophile memories, although not desires. In fact he found himself unable to acknowledge that the activities with boy prostitutes had been perverse, despite much evidence of dreams that sadistic and degrading intentions towards prospective boy siblings contributed a significant element. He'd been an only child of parents who divorced and remarried, leading a boarding school and divided life from age seven, with the exception of one halcyon year between his mother's second and third marriage when he had lived with her at the seaside. In fact in that year he had been in love with a girl cousin four years his junior, whom he seldom saw later and never forgave for marrying 'a rich man'.

Juliet's return in the autumn brought them both great joy and the sexual restriction of her parents accorded well with their mutual anxieties about the sexual act. However the escalation of their intimacy and desire for one another gradually began to weigh heavily in the balance with these strictures. With no

Nurse to arrange for her defloration and no Friar Lawrence to organize their elopement, the complexity and tension between them began to take on a sado-masochistic colouring. He found himself badgering and bullying her to defy her parents, while at the same time being visited during their petting by flashes from his paedophile days. Early in October an interesting event, followed by a revealing dream, took place. During one of their prolonged sessions of petting and kissing, Romeo suddenly, to his own astonishment, pushed his finger deep into his partner's anus, so deep that it became soiled with faeces. Nothing was made of it by either of them, at the time; but the next day he noticed two things: first, that his bullying tendency was increased; and, second, that she seemed to like it, in fact said so. This troubled my patient, for he could see that, in her youth and inexperience, it would be so easy for a masochistic enslavement to him to ensue.

A few nights later he had a very revealing dream: *he seemed to be a soldier in the First World War, in the trenches and the mud, being ordered to fire on a German strong-point, a pill-box with machine guns firing. He was told to aim at a small slit, which he did, and kept shooting until the enemy fire ceased. He then cautiously approached, climbed on top and opened what looked like a lid to peer in. The sight that greeted him was extraordinary: there were two WW I type tanks, each lying on its side facing one another, their treads slowly moving and seeming to interlock like the bits on a slide fastener. They moved more and more slowly and then ceased, like dying animals.* The principal association to the dream was surprising, for it related to his mother's, not his girlfriend's, background. It seemed that his mother had been wealthy when his parents married, having inherited the proceeds of what had been a flourishing business in the nineteenth century — virtually a monopoly in the production of little boxes for pharmaceuticals, pillboxes. The implications seemed undeniable: in putting his finger into Juliet's anus he had enacted a phantasy of assault on the inside of his mother's body to destroy her internal objects (she would have been born during World War I), represented as armoured and aggressive monsters of Victorian morality. This was the link to his girl's Malaysian parents with their Moslem morality which forbade him to penetrate her. Thus his bullying and badgering had the same meaning as inserting his finger deep in her anus, with its link to memories of his paedophilic past.

I found this dream image very evocative, for it seems to move on various levels and draw on various formal sources for its imagery. I was very struck by the image of the two dying tanks, partly I suppose because it recalled to mind Bion's descriptions of his experiences during that war as a tank commander (*The Long Weekend*, Fleetwood Press). Remembering the shape of those early tanks, I was also struck by the image, as if looking through a microscope watching two paramaecia 'conjugating'. This is the process by which these 'slipper animalcules' revitalize themselves periodically by exchanging nuclear material, thus achieving potential immortality. To place that image in a pillbox would also link it with capsules of medication as health-giving agents. But here the image is degraded by the armouring of morals hostile to youthful love, as he himself has been hostile to his mother's love relationships or to his little beloved cousin growing up to marry 'a rich man', becoming in his mind 'the painted whore of Babylon'.

Out of this evocative imagery, as from an archaeological site, there arises in the mind the image of the Nuptial Chamber, whose privacy and mystery need to be guarded only by the love and respect of those outside. But when this love is lacking and the mystery and privacy are seen as secrets of power, the chamber becomes a fortress, the site of catastrophe, its historic remains ranging from Ur to Dachau. This inner world structure, which has always been imaged in the architecture of religion, and which lies behind the 'arras' (how ironic that this should also have been the name of the battlefield where Bion met his catastrophic change) — this is the 'heart of mystery' where meaning is generated. The place of this creative intercourse, so prosaically called the parental bedroom, is the locus of awe and wonder in the internal world. Or more correctly, here is where the alpha-function takes place, where the creative act of symbol formation quietly proceeds through the night. By its operation we can go to sleep fatigued and confused and awaken vitalized and once more amazed at the beauty of the world and the wonder of being live, feeling and thinking creatures.

7   The Undiscovered Country: the Shape of the Aesthetic Conflict in *Hamlet*

i) *The Mould Of Form*

Hamlet is probably Shakespeare's most enigmatic play. Founded on the metaphor of internal 'eruption', it explores the endeavour to find a container for the new and monstrous mystery which rears its beautiful and ugly head. Both the world of the play and the constitution of the hero are shaken by turmoil when it appears that the phenomenon of psychic growth is not a naturally-unfolding process but 'shakes our disposition' with 'thoughts beyond the reaches of our souls'; and the structure of the play correspondingly expands or rather cracks and undermines the classical self-contained model of the revenge tragedy which is its anti-type.

The quality of 'mystery' which everyone recognises in *Hamlet*, is of its essence: not just in relation to the theme of not 'plucking out the heart of the mystery' as Hamlet describes it, but also in relation to the complex and ambivalent way in which the play takes hold of our imagination, as observers and in a sense participants in its emotional struggle: we who, like the puzzled crowd at the end, are 'but mutes and audience to this act'. The play makes it clear that the experience of mystery is not a facile or passive one of wondering acceptance, but one which involves violent antagonism and ambivalence; its latent drama seems to exist in images beyond the reach of our thoughts — as in the oedipal conflict which lies, suggestively, always between the lines, and often grating against the overt drift of the revenge plot. As mutes and audience we follow the hero, with a peculiar mixture of adulation and irritation, as he attempts to disentangle the riddle of his 'uncle-father's' incestuous marriage and murder, from the mystery of the 'undiscovered country' from which no traveller returns. This is ultimately his own inner self, whose image hovers always out of reach, sometimes glimpsed beyond the images of his mother or of Ophelia — yet, as with Orpheus and Eurydice, always frustrated or falsified by the unreal responses of others, whenever any potential point of recognition or mutual understanding appears within reach. Time and again, attempts to pursue the developmental mode of 'exploring the mystery' are converted, through an instantaneous switch of energies, into the essentially destructive and violent mental mode of 'solving the riddle': not just by the visionless characters but also by the hero. And this contrast between two distinct mental modes which are operating in parallel — exploring the mystery and solving the riddle — is what constitutes the texture of the aesthetic conflict throughout the play. It accounts for the ambivalence of its fascination; and for the fact that the latent imagery of the play never reaches a conclusion or a solution. This is why it is a 'problem play' rather than a proper tragedy; why the end of the 'sweet prince' who receives a soldier's burial is on one level satisfying (certainly not ironic), yet on another level deeply disturbing, since it is made clear that the real 'story of Hamlet' is in no way contained by the comprehension of those who remain on the stage. Instead, this onus of understanding is transferred back to us as readers with the implicit message that now we have to begin the play all over again, and without much guidance save that of Horatio, whose function throughout — as Hamlet's close friend and observer — is to direct our attention to our faculty of observation, with the additional instruction that this need not, in fact cannot and should not, be dispassionate. The point about one who 'in suffering all, suffers nothing' is that somewhere, amidst the *dramatis personae* of the mind, service is required of a faculty which, though it is not immune from pain, can see what is going on without disintegrating.

The name Hamlet means 'the Idiot'. As has often been noted, his social function in the court of Denmark is as a version of the king's Fool, who under the guise of jest can tell the truth, the child who sees the emperor's new clothes. Hamlet is a more sophisticated version of the Socratean gadfly, the 'hectic in the blood' destined to lead a live wire to the electrically charged store of emotional and spiritual values which are liable to become damped by social and political formalities. In the midst of the oily and superfluous rhetoric of the court (Claudius' first word, we remember, is 'Though'), he is the only one concerned with the difference between 'is' and 'seems'. His main departure from the role of Fool, of course, is that his quest is for the truth about himself and the landscape of his soul, by comparison with which the truth about Claudius's crime is a side-issue or rather a red herring. On his first appearance he complains that no 'forms, moods, shapes of grief' can 'denote me truly':

> These indeed seem,
> For they are actions that a man might play;
> But I have that within which passes show . . .

He indicates that the problem of self-knowledge is simultaneous with that of self-expression. But self-expression requires some form of external resonance; and much of the drama of *Hamlet* is based on the hero's failure to find any such resonance, any intimate relationship whose answering reverberations will 'denote him truly'. The 'antic disposition' is not only a guard but also the external indication of a search which never finds a containing form. Before the death of the previous king and the subsequent appearance of 'rottenness' in the state of Denmark, Hamelt is the ideal Renaissance prince, with the 'courtier's, soldier's, scholar's, eye, tongue, sword', as Ophelia describes him: 'the glass of fashion and the mould of form/ Th' observed of all observers'. His shape seems ready-made, to others and perhaps also to himself, until he is faced with the necessity for *becoming* a prince, as opposed to merely *acting* the prince through any of the various 'actions that a man might play' — any form of acceptable role-playing. Society's pressure on Hamlet to conform, is proportional to its unspoken need for him to do something different and provide a new model of princeship; throughout it is acknowledged by all that though the authority is Claudius's, the hope is Hamlet's, for the fruitful continuance of Denmark — he is the 'expectancy and rose of the fair state'. Like Horatio his fellow-student, Hamlet is 'a scholar': one who knows in principle how to speak to ghosts, but not how to contain the emotional turmoil which arises when he is called upon to transmute this scholarship into action. He is called back from comfortable monastic seclusion at Wittenberg to witness a change in the state of Denmark, when his cardboard idealised image of a father is, like his own reflection in the glass of fashion, replace by an alternative, apparently antithetical yet closely related, 'uncle-father'. Old Hamlet and Claudius pair together like two sides of the same coin, 'Hyperion to a satyr', the god and the beast in man. The Ghost himself is an ambiguous creature, veering between the majestic and the clownish, the sorrowful and the spiteful. Hamlet's new awareness of the beast in his uncle-father is simultaneous with the dawn of love for Ophelia. Suddenly a different complexion is put on the qualities of a royal marriage: 'lust' and a 'radiant angel' are seen to be 'linked' together in a 'celestial bed' and 'preying on garbage'. Together these form part of a single mental development, focussed on the symbolic pageant of marriage, funeral and coronation, breaking out of quiescent uninvolved scholarship and into turbulent emotional experience which poses problems both deeply philosophical and 'beyond philosophy'.

For outside the haven of Wittenberg, the idea of 'knowledge' takes on forceful and even violent implications of feeling upon the pulses, as opposed to mere academic omniscience. When Hamlet returns to his home, it appears that a corollary to this marriage-funeral-coronation is that Denmark is in a state of approaching invasion, with soldiers on guard and a sense of undiagnosable 'sickness' all the more sinister because it seems excluded from the language and consciousness of the court. Even on the plane of feeling, it is only recognised by the occasional insignificant soldier shivering on the dark, cold battlements. The ostensible reason for the watch is young Fortinbras with his 'shark'd up list of lawless resolutes'; yet other associations stemming from Denmark's troubled internal state rise to the surface; 'something is rotten in the state of Denmark'. It is suggested later that Denmark's sickness could be 'th'imposthume of too much wealth and peace' rather than of war; meanwhile Old Hamlet himself, erstwhile guardian of the realm, is described as 'the King that was and is the question of these wars'. The imagery which overwhelms the first act, of deep ulceration coming to the surface, indicates the internal eruption now manifest in the stalking of the ghost, making the state vulnerable to invasion. Hamlet's initial function, as an element in the Mind of Denmark as a whole, is to bring this indefinable sickness on to a plane where it is at least seen and acknowledged; and after this, to attempt to carry the process of thought further into 'undiscovered country', the sphere of the unknown. Hamlet is the only one to whom the Ghost, representative of the shadowy spiritual world ignored by the court, will speak; and Hamlet's impassioned plea, from the claustrophobic condition of present knowledge, is: 'let me not burst in ignorance!' His 'prophetic soul' is receptive to two kinds of information which the Ghost conveys, and to the ambiguity of the Ghost himself as a vehicle of either truth or lies, or perhaps both together. On the one hand the Ghost tells him of his foul and unnatural murder and extorts a promise of revenge; he incites, intimidates, infuriates and tantalises his son with bombastic talk about the 'secrets of his prison-house' and his wealth of experience and powers of story-telling — which, however, he is not going to unfold:

> I could a tale unfold whose lightest word
> Would harrow up thy soul, freeze thy young blood,
> Make thy two eyes like stars start from their spheres . . .
> But this eternal blazon must not be
> To ears of flesh and blood.

This 'devilish' aspect of the Ghost drives mad the son who cannot denote himself truly, and invites the detective or riddling mentality in Hamlet; it encourages him to use the melodramatic 'blazonry' of the players in the Mousetrap to try and 'catch the conscience' of both kings — laying a trap to test the Ghost's veracity at the same time as Claudius's guilt. On the other hand, however, the Ghost implicitly and poetically conveys to Hamlet a different kind of knowledge, about the emotional experience of 'marriage' and the whole aura of birth and death behind it — an area where policy-making and discursive reasoning fall short, and whose mystery rather than secrecy Hamlet in his turn states to Horatio, once has has glimpsed its existence: 'There are more things in heaven and earth, Horatio,/ Than are dreamt of in your philosophy'. These are the 'things' which cannot be trapped for inspection, but only known through processes of identification, as when the prince recognises himself as an 'arrant knave', 'crawling between heaven and earth' and exploring the mystery after the pattern of the infant climbing on its mother's lap.

Thus in a seminal, poetic speech, the Ghost recounts to Hamlet what is in effect his version of a fall from Eden — an encounter with knowledge, and the accompanying sense of sickness or death which this brings:

O Hamlet, what a falling off was there, . . .

. . .

Sleeping within my orchard,
My custom always of the afternoon,
Upon my secure hour thy uncle stole
With juice of cursed hebenon in a vial,
And in the porches of my ears did pour
The leperous distilment, whose effect
Holds such an enmity with blood of man
That swift as quicksilver it courses through
The natural gates and alleys of the body,
And with a sudden vigour it doth posset
And curd, like eager droppings into milk,
The thin and wholesome blood. So did it mine,
And a most instant tetter bark'd about,
Most lazar-like, with vile and loathsome crust
All my smooth body.
Thus was I, sleeping, by a brother's hand
Of life, of crown, of queen at once dispatch'd,
Cut off even in the blossoms of my sin,
Unhousel'd, disappointed, unanel'd, . . .

The Ghost's description of his poisoning, the infiltration of his innocent smooth body by that alter-ego his brother, justifies its existence not so much on the plot level (where its detail is superfluous) as on the level of dream-imagery. His speech provides the fountainhead for Hamlet's soliloquies and attack on his mother; their language is based — in muted and modulated form — on the expression, more than the message, of the Ghost. The poisoning is described in such a way that the external infiltration through the 'porches of the ears' (thoughout the play seen as the body's most sensitive organ, representative of all exits and entrances and points of contact with alien forces) appears to be the consummation of an internal eruption, bringing out weals upon the skin and cutting him off in 'the blossoms of his sin'. The leprous, reptilian quality of the

89

scales then becomes figured in the chain-mail armour he wears as Ghost. Through one form of alien entry he is deprived of his umbilical link to life, crown and queen at once; his blood curdles as the milk turns sour which had hitherto kept him like an infant 'secure' in his afternoon sleep in the garden. The infant king who ruled his mother like a Jove, Hyperion or Hercules (as Hamlet describes his father), finds that even in his secure hour he is 'unhousel'd' by some serpent or satyr-self from his original smooth womb-like skin or shell: 'what a falling off was there!' In his new nakedness, no longer king of infinite space, he accuses the Queen of 'falling' in virtue when he feels himself falling and has not yet gained any new sense of beneficence in space. This is the dream-sequence which lies behind Hamlet's poignant exclamation: 'O God, I could be bounded in a nutshell and count myself a king of infinite space — were it not that I have bad dreams'. This is the emotional world, full of the psychic dangers of bursting out of claustrophobic ignorance, which provides the dark irony behind Hamlet's satirical complaint to Rosencrantz and Guildenstern that 'I lack advancement' — a complaint which they can only interpret in terms of worldly ambition.

The eruption over the smooth body of the kingship, therefore, expresses a matter deeper than a merely circumstantial killing. It is connected with the sin within the father and by implication within Hamlet himself, being as prince 'subject to his birth' and obliged to work not only on his own behalf but on behalf of the entire Mind of Denmark. He inherits not only the idealised heroic father who overcame Old Fortinbras in a primitive Beowulf-style combat in some mythical chivalric age, but also the greedy scavenging father whose pattern of manhood consists in 'stealing the precious diadem from the shelf and putting it in his pocket'. This is Hamlet's description of Claudius, but in fact the play's imagery associates the 'vicious mole of nature' which has erupted in Denmark, as much with the dead king as with the lustful and ambitious live one. It is Old Hamlet who is described by his son as an 'old mole', a 'worthy pioner' (a military miner, in the sense of *under* miner; just as the devil was known as an 'old collier'): 'Canst work i' th' earth so fast?' His father's memory materialises round the misty ramparts and watch-towers of Elsinore (like the 'heaven-kissing hill' Hamlet sees as an appropriate association), but by the end of the ghost-scene is seen as quite at home in the lower regions of the castle. Hence the macabre dance in which Hamlet leads his companions round the stage following by ear the Ghost's movements below the trapdoor with 'Come on, you hear this fellow in the cellarage?' This dance echoes the poison coursing through the gates and alleys of the body, and anticipates how a king may make a royal 'progress through the guts of a beggar'. The structure of the stage itself, with the trapdoor the traditional location of hell, symbolises both mother earth and man's body with its channels and apertures, its points of catastrophic change, where death or understanding occur. Its confines range beyond the vertical dimension to the 'removed ground' where the Ghost first speaks, where cliffs overhang the sea and 'draw you into madness'. Its dusty timbers both represent and undermine 'this most goodly frame the earth . . . this majestical roof fretted with golden fire', which appears — when the stagey illusion is penetrated — 'a sterile promontory', with man 'a quintessence of dust'. All of this dream- or night-time landscape contrasts with the bright artificial glamour of the court with its tapestry-covered recesses and spyholes: a world which has no language for spiritual realities and no consciousness of the revolution fermenting under its floorboards. So in the court, the 'wild and whirling words' of Hamlet's 'antic disposition' echo the process of mining and undermining set by the Ghost as he patrols his night-time kingdom after his hearsed bones have 'burst from their cerements'. And Hamlet obstinately hangs on to his dark mourning clothes and then his antic dress, not merely to show the Court they don't understand him, but to remind himself that he cannot yet denote himself truly without some reference to this shadow world which he feels holds the key to his prophetic soul.

Unlike Prince Hal, who is destined to become an ideal earthly king, a model for patriotism, and who only appears to be a misfit whilst he is in fact opportunistically strengthening the social grounds for his eventual rule, Hamlet is a genuine misfit or 'idiot', with a concept of princeship as yet unborn and unknown to himself. His initial university-inspired efforts to assume a liberal role (as when he insists on 'your loves, as mine to you' when his friends offer him their 'duty' in the ghost-scene) peter out as he comes to realise love is not a freely available commodity, and only Horatio follows him without self-interest. As the play progresses, all hints of a *Julius Caesar*-type conspiratorial mentality are shed; and the value of being 'beloved by the people' (as Hamlet is said to be) becomes debased during Laertes'rush into the palace at the head of the rabble. Hamlet's embryonic princeship is as distinct from these younger-generation models as it is from the heroic mode of Old Hamlet or the *real-politik* of Claudius (whose efficacy is also overturned during the play). The Queen, Claudius tells us, 'lives by his looks'; and with the Ghost's command to 'remember' him, Hamlet is hauled out of a sort of prolonged babyhood, like 'a fat weed rooting itself in ease on Lethe wharf', to review the genesis of his feelings and source of his spiritual nourishment. The new prince is out of his nutshell but unfledged, in a condition akin to madness; and his quest in shuffling off his old redundant 'mould of form' and seeking a new shape, is figured in the play's underlying metaphor of the infant soul struggling to achieve accommodation in an unknown, 'undiscovered country'.

It is clear, then, that Shakespeare's task in evolving *The Tragical History of Hamlet, Prince of Denmark* is likewise not one which can be contained in any of the lyrical or classical moulds which have up to this point in his career comfortably encompassed his search for a hero. The drama of *Hamlet* will, like the Ghost, 'burst its cerements' and take on a genre of its own: one which, in its five hours of playing time, does in one sense negate the very concept of a stage-play (despite its rich 'variety' as Johnson called it, and high entertainment value). It corresponds to Polonius' caricatural description of 'pastoral-comical, historical-pastoral, tragical-historical, tragical-comical-historical-pastoral' etc., being indeed a 'poem unlimited'. The play, like its hero, is in search of a new mould of form. It contains Shakespeare's most savage attacks on acting and theatre, both implicit and explicit; and could be described as evolving a type of dream-play — not as a genre in its own right as with the later romances — but through a process of violently cannibalising the revenge-tragedy structure which is its ostensible vehicle. Before plunging further into the thick forests of the play's poetic delineation of emotional territory, therefore, let us digress for a moment to consider what kind of play we are trying to grope our way through. *Hamlet* is not a classical play — to use 'classical' in a general formal sense, as when Aristotle defined plot as 'the soul of tragedy'. Aristotle referred to the encapsulation of meaning through the rigours of form. Not only is plot *not* the soul of *Hamlet* — but we continually have the uneasy feeling that attention to plot diverts us from some other level on which the play is functioning, some obscure emotional experience which it is evoking in us. Shakespeare seems to use formal expectations in a negative way, as if he chose the genre of revenge tragedy with its well-known demands and expectations as a deliberate foil, to set off a series of evocative dream-images which seem to evolve as it were through friction against the plot. Thus the ultimate message of the Mousetrap (if there is any) is not, for us, that 'Claudius is guilty' nor that 'Hamlet knows Claudius is guilty', nor even 'Claudius knows that Hamlet knows . . .' etc.; the message which gets across to us is better summarised by something like 'truth is not a mouse'. Shakespeare uses the conventions of plot-denouement to force our attention in a different direction. In a similar way, the Queen delivers a long account of Ophelia's drowning in a way which corresponds, formally, to a classical 'messenger speech' — which is always an eye-witness account of the events related. Yet clearly, in terms of plot, the Queen cannot have been an eye-witness; and this sort of formal dislocation serves to strengthen our poignant impression of the speech's dreamlike quality and of the Queen's farewell to her younger maiden self; her image of the drowning serves to fill out the exclamation about her own 'sick soul' which she gives as an aside; not an analytic character, she only achieves self-expression through the fate of Ophelia. Again, there are such riddling plot-matters as, did the Queen commit adultery before her husband's murder; did she suspect the murder and if not why not; does Ophelia know her father and the king are behind the arras — and does Hamlet; or, how can Horatio be a contemporary of Hamlet's and yet describe from memory the duel between Old Hamlet and Old Fortinbras which occurred on the day of Hamlet's birth? Again, is Fortinbras really just passing through, when in Act IV his entire army marches across the stage, apparently unnoticed by anyone except Hamlet; and how can we be expected to take seriously Hamlet's account to Horatio of his rescue by means of the pirate ship — when Hamlet reappears on Danish soil, we are tempted to believe with Claudius that he never really left, but 'checked at his voyage'. His absence seems a matter of hours on the one hand, while Ophelia distributes some flowers and Claudius has a few words with Laertes; yet on the other hand there is a sense of years passing, while Hamlet (according to the universal feeling of readers and play-goers) seems to pass from about age eighteen to age thirty. In other words, the play is full of riddles, should we choose to focus our attention upon solving them on the superficial level of plot-significance. And even if we do — with the full exercise of ingenuity — find answers in terms of the plot's necessity, these are invariably strangely empty and unsatisfactory. We find we have been 'hunting the trail of policy', like Polonius when he sets out to 'find where truth is hid/ Though it were hid indeed within the centre'. Yet we are no closer to the 'heart of the mystery' until we realise that the dream-imagery of the play is working on us on a level which actually clashes with the plot. Time and again the unsatis-factoriness of a plot-explanation is precisely what illuminates the dream-like quality of the latent imagery.

Hamlet is the figure on whom the world of the play is totally dependent for awareness of the mind's predicament. If he were not there, doing what Coleridge would call 'delving in the metaphysic depths', the state would appear on the surface to be running smoothly, under competent leadership. (This is not entirely our impression; thus Claudius's reliance on 'impotent and bedrid' old Norway to curb young Fortinbras's irrepres-sible empire-building, shows real-politik in a more satirical light than with Bolingbroke for example.) Claudius, despite having murdered his brother, is portrayed however as no blacker than any everyday politician who has unintentionally lost the capacity for contact with his spiritual life; the play has no 'villains' in the sense of an Iago or an Edmund. Renewal of this lost contact is associated throughout the latent imagery of the play with the feeling of sickness: the 'sick soul', 'thought-sickness', 'sicklied o'er by the pale cast of thought'. And the sense of sickness, together with the foreboding of prophecy as in

Hamlet's exclamation 'O my prophetic soul!', is the first sign that a thinking process is attempting some imminent eruption in the primitive mind of Denmark. Yet instead of helping thought to emerge, the other characters block channels of meaningful communication with the hero in a Kafkaesque manner, so that all the mental action is concentrated on Hamlet alone. This means that the reader or play-goer is brought into uncomfortably close proximity with the figure of the hero, in a way which has been likened to the first-person novel; though while that tends to rest on a comfortable feeling that somebody knows everything, however subjectively, *Hamlet* gives the sense of unfathomable mystery behind every opened door. As Hazlitt said: 'Its reality is in the reader's mind. It is *we* who are Hamlet . . . we are more than spectators, faced with the original text.' This makes it difficult to maintain the kind of stance which Brecht advises in tragedy, of 'sympathising' but not 'empathising' with any one character. The Romantics revelled in the almost adhesive identification which *Hamlet* impels through its powerful 'incantation' (in the Stokesian sense); twentieth-century liberalism on the whole has recoiled from it, fearful of being accused of sexual hang-ups. Shakespeare abandons the containing function of the classical play (which can cathartically absorb the most gruesome horrors), in order that everything should be shapeless except the hero's inner conflict, resulting in what Eliot called an 'artistic failure' (*Selected Essays*, 1932).

We are told that Shakespeare did not know Sophocles; however, a glance at *Oedipus* will help us to define our problem in experiencing Shakespeare's enigmatic play. *Oedipus* is the archetype of the play in which plot is the soul. In both *Oedipus* and *Hamlet* the search for self-knowledge, the making of a true king, is founded on the hero's obsessively and in a way unnaturally honest determination not to avoid the disturbing implications of the emotional knot which is in effect the foundation for the mind's entire development. But in *Oedipus*, the city-state — the mind as a whole — already knows that it is sick; in *Hamlet*, the murder of the king is unknown (here Shakespeare differs from his source-stories), so that even this limited recognition of mental disease finds no expression in society until Hamlet returns to provide a focus for the state's madness. In *Oedipus*, the situation of a general awareness of

95

sickness makes the time ripe for an investigation in which plot is the soul. The subsequent unravelling of Oedipus' history *is* the emotional meaning of the play. Like the Chorus we sympathise but not empathise as the hero's fatal mistake is revealed in a way which makes it clear that the accident was no accident but the will of the gods — an inevitable expression of the human condition, which the hero takes on his shoulders on behalf of us all, thus cleansing the state of pollution and arousing cathartic satisfaction in the audience. Oedipus' first act of knowledge, solving the riddle of the sphinx, brought him worldy status and cured one kind of sickness in the state. In his second act of knowledge he is punished for previously thinking he knew the answers, for omnipotence, and has to painfully identify with Tiresias' blind insight. The search for knowledge is then directed inwards, to the mystery which was not solved by the riddle. And in *Oedipus*, unlike in *Hamlet*, logic leads to the second answer as well as the first. Plot or external circumstance unravels according to the requirements of the mind's internal condition; retracing history leads to the ultimate act of self-knowledge; the second or true riddle — that of Oedipus' parentage — becomes fused with the Mystery. This is true tragedy, as in *Lear*, with 'we that are young/ Shall never see so much, nor live so long'.

In *Hamlet*, however, Shakespeare seems deliberately to reject the classical equivalence of direction between plot and self-knowledge. There is a world of difference between Lear's 'ripeness is all' and Hamlet's 'the readiness is all'. This is epitomised by the supreme anticlimax of the announcement in the last scene that 'Rosencrantz and Guildenstern are dead', which pulls the carpet from underneath tragedy's dignified roll of meaningful deaths. Shakespeare uses tragedy's conventions only to undermine them. The play has what Kitto called a 'spreading' rather than a 'linear' structure (*Form and Meaning in Drama*, 1956); or, in Wilson Knight's terms, the 'temporal' element (of plot) is dominated by the 'spatial — the omnipresent and mysterious reality, brooding motionless over and within the play's movement' (*The Wheel of Fire*, 1949). Reading or watching *Hamlet* with Shakespeare's recent classically-constructed plays *Julius Caesar, Henry V* or *Richard II* at the back of one's mind, it is impossible not to be struck by how much more complicated has become the attempt to define the thinking hero, the poet-prince; how much messier the structural background; how much more ambivalent our entire response to the viability of a search for self-knowledge which strikes at the depths of the oedipal conflict to uncover the mind's fertile morass of thriving ulcers and rotting vegetation (the play's basic fount of imagery). 'The time is out of joint'; the mind, like the body-politic, is in a state of dislocation and hidden eruption. The embryonic prince, 'born to set it right', is faced with the Ghost's impossible and ambiguous command:

> But howsomever thou pursuest this act,
> Taint not thy mind, nor let thy soul contrive
> Against thy mother aught.

The 'act' which Hamlet has to pursue is not necessarily the simplistic one of revenge, demanded by the 'devilish' aspect of the Ghost, but the complicated one of self-development. In his relations with his mother, Hamlet is already both innocent (the state's 'rose') and tainted, by virtue of his psychic inheritance, and of his fateful inborn propensity to the pale cast of thought, which brings out weals on the skin. The mould of form is broken, revealing ulceration, bursting from ignorance, under the pressure of new emotional facts which neither the Renaissance prince nor the Wittenberg scholar have been trained to assimilate.

(ii) The Lobby Of Dreams

Hamlet's immediate reaction to the Ghost's revelations is, following his university training, to write something down — not only in the 'table of his memory' ('the book and volume of my brain'), but literally in his 'tables'. But he seizes them in vain, since the real problem is impossible to formulate, and he can only arrive at the platitudinous precept that 'one may smile, and smile, and be a villain'. He finds that telling a story requires aesthetic correlatives, not merely the instinctive urge to spill it out. Throughout the play, he is then plagued by the sense that everyone else wants to write his story, play upon his stops, pluck out his mystery, before he can even envisage himself: 'Ere I could make a prologue to my brains, /They had begun the play'. His antic disposition protects him in one way but exposes him in another, as an object of curiosity whose 'very cause of lunacy' may by some process of detective riddle-solving be ferreted out and explained: 'by indirections find directions out'. The idea of 'playing' therefore becomes a byword for manipulation, rather than for discovery-through-art; in *Hamlet*, all types of acting and action tend to be false moves rather than fictions about revelation; they are all 'actions that a man might play'. Instead, playing is contrasted with the idea of 'holding', the capacity to observe without interpreting, which comes to focus substantially on Hamlet's relationship with Horatio: as in, 'If thou didst ever hold me in thy heart ...' or in Hamlet's declaration of love immediately before the play-within-a-play begins, standing out in contrast to its anti-revelatory nature:

> blest are those
> Whose blood and judgment are so well commeddled
> That they are not a pipe for Fortune's finger
> To sound what stop she please. Give me that man
> That is not passion's slave, and I will wear him
> In my heart's core, ay, in my heart of heart,
> As I do thee.

And although Hamlet speaks here as if Horatio had always held this significance for him, our impression is on the contrary, that the context of events and of Horatio's reaction to them, make the idea of Horatio more meaningful and eventually indispensable to Hamlet; thus on his first appearance, Hamlet appeared barely to recognise Horatio, did not travel from Wittenberg with him, and was unaware that he had been present at Elsinore throughout the funeral, marriage and coronation. Horatio's integrity as an observer is also stressed by the small detail that even Claudius employs him at one point to keep an eye on Ophelia (a post in which, since he can never affect the active course of events, he might seem to fail dismally — except that by some obscure means, the drowning of Ophelia shortly comes to the Queen's notice). He complements Hamlet's function as misfit or Fool through also being an outsider, always on the fringes of the court yet never receiving nor requiring 'advancement', so remaining 'poor'; and 'why should the poor be flattered?' Despite or rather because of his passivity, Horatio comes to provide a vital aesthetic dimension to the story of the Mind of Denmark. Where everyone else is engaged in action, he is one who 'in suffering all, suffers nothing' — that is, though seeing and feeling all that is done, he does not disintegrate or allow his self to become denatured. Without Hamlet's depths of exploration, he is not of princely or heroic calibre, but neither does he slip into defensive omnipotence (like Claudius and Polonius) in the face of phenomena he does not understand. And although he has few words to speak, his presence in the play is strongly felt. At the end, when Fortinbras the simple soldier-prince (an outsider in the sense of being uncontaminated by ideas) receives the election of the state, bequeathed with Hamlet's 'dying voice', Horatio receives the legacy of Hamlet's 'story'. He is still there to hold together the facts of the story, just as he was there at the beginning to introduce Hamlet and us to the Ghost, though he is no more a protagonist than are we ourselves. So in terms of the spatial quality of *Hamlet* as a whole, the Horatio dimension, which is defined gradually and almost imperceptibly, is essential to the reader's grasp of Hamlet's 'act' — the drama of dreams which is taking place between the lines, and which, unlike the linear plot, does not end definitively in a dying voice.

Horatio's un-prominent significance begins to take shape only after Hamlet's heroic effort to explore alone the 'undiscovered country' of his mind in the 'To be or not to be' soliloquy. This is an exploration which terminates abortively in the nunnery scene with Ophelia, and is never resumed so hopefully. The soliloquy stands at the centre of the play, in spatial as well as temporal terms; it is the eye at the centre of the whirlwind; its implications radiate outwards from this key point in the Hamlet consciousness. In terms of linear plot progression, this speech appears to have no business here — embedded as it is in the midst of the Mousetrap sequence, between Hamlet's first meeting with the players and the fruition of his scheming to 'catch the conscience of the king'. The plot is thickening and gathering speed, and this introspective and abstract soliloquy seems to stand in the way of the main action of the play, which has finally got going — so much so that sometimes in productions it has been lifted out of context and placed nearer the beginning, where Hamlet is more depressed and less manic. Yet, as we shall see, this detachment from the main action of the revenge tragedy (the play's superficial form) is essential to the play's *latent* drama, with its conflict between an omnipotent detective mentality and an exploratory, symbolic mentality. The soliloquy is given in the Lobby, where Hamlet is known to walk for hours on end, pacing his chosen cage and masticating 'words, words, words', thereby reinforcing his sense that 'Denmark's a prison' (as he tells Rosencrantz and Guildenstern). The Lobby is partly open to the sky, making a sort of artificial outside within the claustrophobic heart of the court; it is the place where Polonius and Hamlet discuss the shapes of the clouds, and Hamlet implies that the shape of the prince he is looking for is not that of a camel or a weasel or a whale; a place which Hamlet regards as but one step from the grave, as when Polonius asks him: 'Will you walk out of the air, my lord?' and he answers 'Into my grave?' The Lobby as a space, also echoes the Ghost's 'prison-house' of purgatory, whose 'secrets' he is 'forbid to tell'. All in all, it is ambiguous as to whether the Lobby is a chamber of dreams or a prison for nightmares. In it the prince is bounded in a nutshell, rehearsing the interaction between infinite space and bad dreams.

In 'To be or not to be', the latent spatial tensions of the underlying dream-play in *Hamlet* take on an almost microscopic character, barely visible to the naked eye. Here Hamlet makes an approach to the cloud of unknowing which contains the shape of the undiscovered country at the heart of his mystery:

> To be, or not to be, that is the question:
> Whether 'tis nobler in the mind to suffer
> The slings and arrows of outrageous fortune,
> Or to take arms against a sea of troubles,
> And by opposing end them. To die — to sleep,
> No more; and by a sleep to say we end
> The heart-ache and the thousand natural shocks
> That flesh is heir to: 'Tis a consummation
> Devoutly to be wish'd. To die, to sleep;
> To sleep, perchance to dream — ay, there's the rub;
> For in that sleep of death what dreams may come,
> When we have shuffled off that mortal coil,
> Must give us pause ...

As Dr Johnson saw, the speech 'shows connections rather in the speaker's mind, than on his tongue'; if one reads only the argument, it appears to be the refined expression of a string of Renaissance commonplaces; but if one reads the images beyond the 'tongue', it evokes in a semi-abstract way the tentative journey of a soul tasting a new world in a way which transcends the sterility of 'words, words, words'. The 'sea of troubles' echoes the sea of madness figured by Horatio in the ghost-scene, towards which Hamlet was led by the armed Ghost, who was himself invulnerable to the soldiers' sword-stabs; and the beating of the waves on rocks lies faintly behind the 'shocks' on 'flesh', the soul's armour and sounding-board, just as the 'mortal coil' suggests both tightly-wound rope and a snake shedding its skin. The mind's body no longer seems a 'sterile promontory', but quivers in anticipation. Hamlet's evocation of 'the heartache, and the thousand natural shocks/ That flesh is heir to' opens a new perspective on the observation of everyday suffering, as if through a microscope: expressing the drama which escapes the stage, the shock of feeling which normally goes unnoticed. Hence it stands in stark contrast to the play-within-a-play which is being engineered in the background, and the bombastic rhetoric of the players, which one part of Hamlet regards as a travesty of genuine feeling: 'What's Hecuba to him, or he to Hecuba, that he should weep for her?' Hamlet's picture of the newly-transmuted soul which has 'shuffled off this mortal coil' and 'pauses', disoriented in its new nakedness, for unknown 'dreams to come', is a startlingly poignant revision of the standard image of release from the body's prison. We remember the tranquil, secure sleep in which the Ghost was painfully assaulted by a kind of dream of being poisoned — the fundamental dream-sequence to which Hamlet is 'heir', both fulfilling and undermining the 'consummation' of life. This underlies the emotional upheaval which is the genesis of the poetic exploration in 'To be or not to be', and which leads out of the smooth nutshell to 'the pale cast of thought'. Now the embryonic prince pauses, at the threshold of the land of dreams, the undiscovered country, then crosses back to the world to capture aspects of worldly injustice ('Th' oppressor's wrong, the proud man's contumely, /The pangs of dispriz'd love'); then again makes another approach to the caesura of death, the moment of change, at which

> the dread of something after death,
> The undiscover'd country, from whose bourn
> No traveller returns, puzzles the will . . .

At the very threshold again, 'dread' is strangely transmuted into disorientation, as 'must give us pause' becomes 'puzzles the will'; and the word 'puzzles', emphatically placed, gives the idea of confusion an almost physical impact as in 'amazed'. Yet it is still delicately contained on a spiritual plane; the idea of 'something after death' is no longer that of the hell-fire torments threatened in the Ghost's 'eternal blazon' speech; these have melted away, like 'too too solid flesh', leaving — not a filled-in picture — but a pause and a space for the 'undiscovered country' at the heart of the mystery, a glimpse of a landscape whose features are unknown. The rhythm of the verse carries the voyaging soul into death and back again.

The values hinted at by this pause in the overt argument (whose logic has lost its impetus) deprive worldly enterprises, including those of 'great pitch and moment', of even 'the name of action':

> Thus conscience does make cowards of us all,
> And thus the native hue of resolution
> Is sicklied o'er with the pale cast of thought,
> And enterprises of great pitch and moment
> With this regard their currents turn awry
> And lose the name of action.

The new prince is no longer sure, not only of what action to take and when, but of what constitutes 'action' — what kind of action has reality. The Ghost's injunction was to 'pursue the act' without 'tainting his mind'; now the question arises, what 'act' is Hamlet really pursuing? For in this soliloquy the revenge-action and the superficial question about Claudius's guilt have been far transcended. Hamlet puts in the background the melodramatic blazonry which surrounds the idea of the revenge-act and other pseudo-actions usually considered heroic or important, and concentrates instead on the poetic and genuine aspects of the Ghost's suffering, the 'unhousel'd' infant soul on its lonely journey. He retraces the Ghost's travels through a refinement of imagery, by 'suffering in the mind', until the traveller who returns from the undiscovered country is no longer the same as the one who went. The Ghost who was 'unhearsed' and 'cast up' from the grave, is given a place in 'conscience'; the literal disfigurement of his body ('bark'd about most lazar-like') is transmuted into 'sicklied o'er with the pale cast of thought'; the blood coursing through the 'gates and alleys of the body, curdled 'like eager droppings into milk', becomes the 'currents [which] turn awry' as action metamorphoses into thought. The pure milk which fed the infant soul becomes contaminated at the moment of simultaneous sin and thought, when the boundaries of the mind extend beyond the womblike nutshell which it believed was infinity, and a glimpse of the undiscovered country hoves in view. The very process of 'suffering in the mind' expands the horizons of thought, in a way antithetical to the process which Hamlet in the previous scene had described as 'unpacking my heart with words'. The latent imagery of 'To be or not to be' occupies a space between the lines which is as far beyond 'words, words, words' as 'action' is beyond its 'name'. It exemplifies Hamlet's struggle to get beyond philosophy into poetry, to exchange riddling for the heart of the mystery, to achieve 'beneficence in space' (to use Stokes's phrase).

Immediately at the end of the soliloquy, without even half a line's pause, Ophelia appears:

> Soft you now,
> The fair Ophelia! Nymph, in thy orisons
> Be all my sins remember'd.

Her presence at this point seems to derive from two opposing lines of force, the real 'mighty opposites' which govern the drama of the Mind of Denmark: on the one hand, she appears the answer to Hamlet's dream of an 'undiscovered country', and his spiritual voyage seems to conjure up her presence (though it seems she has in fact been present in the background all the time); on the other hand, she has been planted as bait by Claudius and Polonius, who have arranged themselves as 'lawful espials' behind a pillar in the Lobby while 'To be or not to be' is being spoken and Ophelia is 'loosed' to Hamlet. The clash between these two forces meeting in the person of the innocent Ophelia, arouses an explosive violence in Hamlet which is matched only by his verbal attack on the other woman he loves, his mother, for being soiled by experience. The name 'Ophelia' (according to the Arden edition notes) seems to have two derivations: in a word meaning 'succour', and in 'Apheleia' meaning 'Simplicity', described by Jonson as 'a nymph pure and simple as the soul or as an abrase table'. As the partner to Hamlet's soul, or the earthly image of his own soul, Ophelia both offers succour to the 'puzzled' embryonic prince within him, and stresses its vulnerability. As Laertes later tells the priest, 'A ministering angel shall my sister be/ While thou liest howling'. Hamlet fresh from 'crawling between earth and heaven', immediately addresses her as if she might somehow provide a container for his 'sins', for the puzzled, howling, crawling child within him which she may 'remember' through innate knowledge. Yet her tabula-rasa quality reacts two-dimensionally, appearing simply to reflect back his sins in the form of returning his gifts: 'My lord, I have remembrances of yours/ That I have longed to redeliver. I pray you now receive them'. She acts in automatic obedience to her father who told her to 'lock up' her 'chaste treasure'. Hamlet intuits the fact that, as tabula-rasa, she is merely acting as a vehicle for another force, but far from excusing her, this inflames him because it is the very force which he regards as his enemy — the enemy of the true aesthetic action which, he implies, can somewhere 'shape' offences into thoughts:

> Get thee to a nunnery. Why, wouldst thou be a breeder of sinners? I am myself indifferent honest, but yet I could accuse me of such things that it were better my mother had not borne me. I am very proud, revengeful, ambitious, with more offences at my beck than I have thoughts to put them in, imagination to give them shape, or time to act them in. What should such fellows as I do crawling between earth and heaven?

The very act of birth makes a sinner; the infant exploring the territory of his world-mother between its upper and lower regions, is sinning and simultaneously seeking for a mould of mental form, a shaping spirit of imagination. Hamlet implies that if Ophelia merely redelivers offences, instead of shaping them, her proper place is in a 'nunnery' — a type of chastity which has, in his view, associations with bawdery; he feels Ophelia is displaying herself towards him in a way that is not herself but a species of 'painting' or false art: 'I have heard of your paintings . . . God hath given you one face and you make yourselves another'. The nunnery and the brothel are both places where the real body or self is hidden, a tantalising but immune secret. In these passages Hamlet is really speaking to the Polonius-behind-Ophelia, whom he calls a 'fishmonger' (bawd) and warns not to let his daughter 'walk i' the sun' (with a pun on 'son' — namely himself), 'lest she may conceive'. For it is Ophelia's stance, rather than any literal suspicion of the eavesdroppers on their conversation, which prompts him to see the ghost of her father in her, and to make the sudden accusation: 'Where's your father? . . . Let the doors be shut upon him, that he may play the fool nowhere but in's own house'. Hamlet feels Polonius too belongs in a nunnery or asylum, in return for engineering the false non-meeting of minds which occurs in the nunnery scene and which converts the Lobby of Dreams into a cage, as if Hamlet and Ophelia were animals in a zoo marked out for insemination in captivity, 'breeding maggots'. (Hence after the forthcoming murder, Hamlet against all rationality insists on 'stowing' Polonius in a cupboard on the stairs, on the way up to the Lobby — not to disguise his crime, but because it seems to him an appropriate confinement.) Polonius regards the mystery of whatever may be 'brewing between' the young lovers much as he regards the mystery of the madness inside Hamlet — as something which can be trapped for inspection, a phenomenon which may be encompassed by the politic language of bargaining, manoeuvring, hunting, playing and selling.

Yet Hamlet's rage against Ophelia derives not only from his antipathy to Polonius, but from his own failure to communicate with her — the conventional absurdity of his love-letters, which belong just as much to the realms of courtly artifice as do Polonius' manoeuvres, rather than to the true expression of feeling; and in particular, his unspoken guilt at his behaviour during his last meeting with her, when he intruded half-dressed into her closet while she was sewing in order to project onto her his anxiety after the meeting with the Ghost. In Ophelia's account (for this offstage encounter constitutes yet another dream-image, expressing Ophelia's intuition of Hamlet's state of mind), he came 'As if he had been loosed out of hell/ To speak of horrors', and echoing the Ghost's torments, with a sigh that seemed 'to shatter all his bulk/ And end his being'. Hamlet's attempt to convey his experience of the Ghost is beset by the devils of aggressive artifice and 'blazonry', echoing his diffi-culty in receiving the real experience from the ambiguous Ghost in the first place. Hence his intrusion into the closet is less a communication than a species of attack, a type of play-acting or false art in the same mode as the Mousetrap. The vision of the teasing, frightening Ghost is directed at Ophelia without any digestion or modification of the image, and it is inevitable that it should simply reflect back again without understanding. In a sense Hamlet gets his just deserts in the nunnery scene, since the anti-aesthetic element in his relations with Ophelia is initiated by himself not Polonius; he has never presented his sins or 'remembrances' in a form which gives her a proper chance to receive or remember them. Ultimately Ophelia, in her effort to understand him and receive his image truly, takes the weight of his madness upon herself (she is the only character with a literal belief in it, and it affects her literally), and sinks with all his sins remembered, drowning. The 'rose of the fair state' and the 'rose of May' are at the same time idiot-fool and innocent-fool, suggesting a fundamental bond of sympathy which never finds any language of interaction, any aesthetic correlation. After the nunnery scene, therefore, Hamlet's mania redoubles in energy, and he includes Ophelia, too, amongst the participants in a poisoned marriage whom he tries to trap in the play-within-a-play.

(iii) The Queen's Arras

The wider dramatic context of the 'To be or not to be' soliloquy, then, against which it stands out in sharp contrast, is one in which relationships of mutual manipulation, framed by the rhetoric of artifice and bombast, vie with each other in their process of subverting truthful poetic expression and substituting the political power of stage-management. The full force of the aesthetic conflict initiated by the Ghost is felt in the movement towards anti-revelation which is fulfilled by the Mousetrap. We remember how man, 'the beauty of the world, the paragon of animals', appeared to Hamlet a mere 'quintessence of dust' against the background of an earth like a stage:

> This goodly frame the earth seems to me a sterile promontory, this most excellent canopy the air, look you, this brave o'erhanging firmament, this majestical roof fretted with golden fire, why, it appeareth nothing to me but a foul and pestilent congregation of vapours.

This goodly frame contains a spirit of disease-ridden vapour, still ambiguous in its quality like all the imagery of fertile eruption, but sterile in so far as it is stage-like, a mould of form which is an empty vehicle. The stage-set behind 'To be or not to be' is of Claudius' and Polonius' making, 'lawful espials' behind a pillar. Their false stage is erected with the notion of hunting down the cause of Hamlet's pregnant madness, the 'something . . . o'er which his melancholy sits on brood'. To Polonius in particular, Hamlet appears a figure full of spiritual mystery: 'How pregnant his replies are!' — a mystery which he treats as a secrecy and attempts to penetrate through stage-management, inevitably unearthing only a foul and pestilent congregation of vapours. Meanwhile, correspondingly, the Players are rehearsing Hamlet's version of *The Murder of Gonzago*, another 'monstrous . . . fiction, a dream of passion', whose stilted display of fake emotion is intended to catch the conscience of the king. The elements of the oedipal drama are stiffly caricatured in the extracts from the *Dido* play, enacted by Hamlet and the Player King, just as they are afterwards in *Gonzago*: we have old baby-like Priam with his 'milky head', helpless before young Pyrrhus the 'painted tyrant' 'Roasted in wrath and fire' and 'o'ersized with coagulate gore, / With eyes like carbuncles'; we have Queen Hecuba, shorn of her royal robes and wrapped in a blanket, 'a clout upon that head/ Where late the diadem stood'; and the moment of drama known as 'Pyrrhus' pause' when Pyrrhus is taken 'prisoner' by the 'ear' before he recovers his sense of purpose and starts to make mincemeat of Priam. Hamlet is both fascinated and disgusted by the performance, which on one level appears to model his

107

role as revenger in the context of dilapidated, humiliated parents (in *Gonzago* the king is even more clearly past it — 'his operant powers their functions leave to do'); yet on another level, is clearly empty and meaningless: 'And all for nothing! For Hecuba!'

Hamlet is therefore as deeply committed to the anti-aesthetic mentality as are his enemies, Claudius and Polonius; and although he is most deeply critical of it, they are not completely happy either about 'pious actions' which 'sugar o'er the devil himself', or how

> The harlot's cheek, beautied with plast'ring art,
> Is not more ugly to the thing that helps it,
> Than is my deed to my most painted word.

(these are Claudius' last words as they hide themselves in the lobby to watch Hamlet and Ophelia). Although all the struggle focusses on Hamlet, the problem of achieving integrity and sincerity is common to the entire Mind of Denmark, and everyone is swept up in a monstrous fiction against their will. The incipient violence brewing in the centre of the play has Hamlet and Polonius as the foreground protagonists, as they are most actively involved in the riddling, trapping, detective mentality. Hamlet warns him obliquely, through comparison to Jephthah, that his omnipotent behaviour may result in the sacrifice of his daughter; but Polonius is masochistically prepared for sacrifice, as when he offers to remove his head from his shoulders ('take this from this') in the service of exposing the 'very cause of Hamlet's lunacy'. During these scenes, Hamlet is both at his most easily infuriated by Polonius, and at his most Polonioid himself. He tries to catch, not only both kings, but this third internal father-figure, who comes into prominence through Ophelia. Hamlet and Polonius are hand in glove over the Play business — their disagreements about acting and rhetoric being very much the sort that occur between those who speak the same language and have the same interests and values. They are both amateur actors; Polonius praises Hamlet's Pyrrhus, and Hamlet sneers at Polonius's Caesar, 'so capital a calf'. Earlier Polonius criticised the quality of Hamlet's versifying to Ophelia ('beautified' is 'a vile phrase') in a way which Hamlet, dissatisfied with his ability to get his meaning across in his lovemaking, would seem to endorse. Polonius' instructions to his children about deportment (in Act I) are echoed by Hamlet in his instructions to the Players:

> Be not too tame neither, but let your own discretion be your tutor. Suit the action to the word, the word to the action . . . For anything so o'erdone is from the purpose of playing, whose end, both at the first and now, was and is to hold as 'twere the mirror up to nature . . .

Excitable and verbose, swept away by misplaced reforming zeal, Hamlet harangues the players until (like Polonius with his advice) he loses his usual intuitive awareness and cannot recognise that they have had enough of him. He overrides their polite objection 'I hope we have reformed that indifferently with us' and carries on for another lengthy paragraph: 'O reform it altogether. And let those that play your clowns speak no more than is set down for them . . .' Doubtless the content of his lecture is sound and well-informed (as is that of Polonius), but its dramatic function is to portray Hamlet wildly removed from the reality of his spiritual quest. Coleridge distinguishes between Polonius and Hamlet in terms of the man of maxims versus the man of ideas; but they are more intimately related than that; in both there is a conflict between maxims and ideas, but Polonius the older man has ossified on the side of maxims, whereas Hamlet is striving on the side of ideas but whenever he is confronted with Polonius, cannot resist playing against him with the same weapons — maxims, riddling and verbal trickery. Polonius still has ideas to the extent that he can recognise the spiritual world in Hamlet, and is the only one to find his condition interesting as opposed to merely aggravating; he clearly regards him as a kind of son — one for whom he has much greater admiration than for Laertes. While Hamlet's attitude of barely suppressed rage towards his Polonius-father is like that of Caliban towards Prospero: 'You taught me language, and my profit on't is, I know how to curse' — his form of 'cursing' being word-juggling and play-acting. At the same time, Hamlet regards the Polonius who is on the verge of his second childhood as a sort of younger sibling or overgrown baby, who is playing a dangerous game by continuously swaddling himself behind arrases and women's skirts, 'in the

109

ear of their conference', with the mistaken notion of thereby gaining some omniscient knowledge, some position of privilege, from which the truth can be riddled out. He calls Polonius 'that great baby, still in his swaddling clothes', and (in the sinister wordplay before the Mousetrap) a 'capital calf', implying that he is a sort of deluded Little Claudius, a mere acting-Caesar whose imperial ambitions will bring disaster on his head. This feeling of Polonius as a diminutive Claudius, a baby king, lies very much behind Hamlet's response to the murder in the closet: 'Thou wretched rash intruding fool, farewell./ I took thee for thy better.' The same feeling, transposed into a key where the note of pity is more dominant, is caught up by Ophelia later, in her mad songs which express a correlation between the death of the nascent love between her and Hamlet, and the death of the babylike father whom her obedience had failed to protect: 'I cannot choose but weep to think they would lay him i' the cold ground'.

During the Mousetrap sequence, then, Hamlet abandons himself to being his most Polonius-like and omnipotent, acting as puppet-master and riddle-solver, and misusing potentially artistic equipment for expression, for avoiding emotional dilemmas rather than exploring them. He forces the actors to become agents in acting out a plot of his own concoction, just as Polonius uses Ophelia or his servant Reynaldo or Hamlet himself; and inevitably, the action is far from revelatory. The Mousetrap is Hamlet's bid at proof-theory: 'if a' do blench, I know my course'; in the event, Claudius does blench, but Hamlet's course is no clearer than before; the mysterious quality of 'pursuing the act' is not elucidated. And the court appear to be confused and upset less by any specific message conveyed by the play (about how Claudius-Lucianus murdered a king who seems anyway to have been on the verge of passing away, or about how Hamlet-Lucianus may be threatening to kill a king himself), than by Hamlet's omnipotent behaviour. As the (otherwise superfluous) dumbshow emphasizes, the meaning of the play is by no means self-evident; by way of conversation Ophelia asks Hamlet what it 'means', but it is clear that she and the whole court do not expect to find meaning in any real, intimate sense, in what they regard as merely a social entertainment, and would have sat quite happily through

Gonzago with or without Hamlet's additional lines, and remained totally unaffected. The only real actor in the Mousetrap is Hamlet himself; he directs the whole show and injects the only meaning there is, through his aggressive asides, mainly to Ophelia: 'Be not you ashamed to show, he'll not shame to tell you what it means'. He arranges a tableau such that he is both on the outskirts of the event, and at the centre of things — symbolised by reclining his head in Ophelia's lap (wrapped in the woman's skirts, as Polonius will be shortly in the arras); his eyes are 'rivetted' on Claudius and, one stage beyond that, on the actors who are to present his own doctored version of the original Scene in the Garden. He is the ultimate interpreter; as he says to Ophelia, 'I could interpret between you and your love, if I could see the puppets dallying' (puppets being genitals and actors). The framework of obscene 'interpretations' highlights the composite fantasy of poisoning and marriage, a mutal consummation, which Hamlet is moved to present: figuring a kind of false marriage service into which he has trapped Ophelia, following (he feels) the example set by his various parent-figures. 'Is this a prologue, or the posy of a ring?' he teases her, insinuatingly: 'So you mis-take your husbands'. The fantasy is underlined by Horatio's joke, an attempt to defuse Hamlet's mania, before the play begins: in promising to observe Claudius for signs of guilt, he says 'If he steal aught the whilst this play is playing/ And scape detecting, I will pay the theft' (stealing the crown, or diadem, being one of Hamlet's metaphors for the act of murder sex and coronation). So not only is the play-within-a-play 'life at a second remove' (as Hazlitt objected), but its whole texture of layers of illusion wrapped inside each other is one which expresses false art or pornography, with the titillating unreality condemned by Plato — the mystery of art's inner world, like that symbolised by the inside of woman's body, being converted into a secrecy which holds no secrets for an omnipotent interpreter.

Yet the other side of Hamlet, the explorer of the mystery in 'To be or not to be', is aware at an intuitive level of the anti-revelatory nature of this type of manipulative mentality, since it is precisely what constitutes the 'hectic' in his own blood, as well as Claudius's. For this reason he makes sure that he has a different type of observer on the scene, in the person of Horatio, to counteract the delusorily objective observation carried out by himself from his position as possessor of Ophelia's lap. Ostensibly Horatio is to keep an eye on Claudius, but his real function is to observe Hamlet himself, and provide an alternative dimension to the manic action. Hamlet's long and significant differentiation of Horatio's character from his own (as 'passion's slave') is placed immediately before the play begins, contrasting lyrically with the surrounding context of plotting and trickery, to which (like 'To be or not to be') it seems irrelevant. Horatio is not 'played on like a pipe', as Rosencrantz and Guildenstern try to play on Hamlet, or as Hamlet plays on Claudius and Polonius — and Ophelia. From this point onwards, Hamlet makes sure he has Horatio at his elbow to get his facts straight. When at the end of the Mousetrap, Polonius screeches 'Lights! Lights! Lights!' and the entire cast of court and players whirl about and rush off the stage in different directions, Hamlet and Horatio are left alone. Hamlet is in a state of manic self-satisfaction (as he suspected he would be); but he has enough of a dialogue with Horatio to establish the alternative perception that this kind of acting is not good enough. To Hamlet's announcement that he should 'get a fellowship in a cry of players', Horatio replies ironically: 'Half a share'. When Hamlet tries to elicit a more dramatic reaction, Horatio makes it clear that he has observed everything, and that he is not impressed:

> *Ham:* Didst perceive?
> *Hor:* Very well, my lord.
> *Ham:* Upon the talk of poisoning?
> *Hor:* I did very well note him.

Hamlet makes up a vulgar rhyme about the turn in the realm's fortunes:

> For thou dost know, O Damon dear,
> This realm dismantled was
> Of Jove himself, and now reigns here
> A very, very — pajock.

The conversion from Jove-ruler to a pajock-ruler (suggesting both peacock, and tramp) represents the two kings, the two-sided image of a father; but Hamlet, despite his recent freedom with pornographic innuendo, coyly refrains from completing the rhyme with the word 'ass', to which Horatio objects: 'You might have rhymed'. The integrity of Horatio's mode of observation can have no effect on the action, but it is essential to the alternative drama of non-action, to the latent evolution of thought, the search for sincerity, which is struggling throughout to find a voice despite the overwhelming progression of the revenge tragedy, whose action is unstoppable once it has started. The riddle of the Mousetrap represents a kind of caricature or anti-type of the classical, devastatingly logical sequence of self-revelation found in *Oedipus:* it is a vehicle for lies, not truth. Once its impetus has gained the ascendance, Hamlet succumbs to the role of the revenger which he mocks at the same time as enunciating it: 'Come, the croaking raven doth bellow for revenge . . . Now could I drink hot blood'. And although this would appear to lead him straight to Claudius (whom he immediately stumbles across, praying), that encounter merely serves to stress that Claudius is not really part of the motivating pageant of false art in Hamlet's phantasy — at least, not in that position of prayer. Hamlet cannot find the stimulation to kill him, despite the whole rationale of the Mousetrap and despite his state of murderous excitement. He carries on to the false heart of the mystery, the Queen's chamber or arras, where he finds a stage-set that answers more appropriately to his instinctive desire to plunder the inner world which has proved so elusive.

Finally, therefore, Hamlet gains a private interview with his mother. As if answering to his phantasy, she is not alone, but the Polonius father-baby is ensconced there in secret to be 'in the ear of their conference', behind the arras — in the private parts of the Queen's closet or body. Still acting as the stage-manager of the Mousetrap, Hamlet starts by giving her a lecture on aesthetics which is at the same time an attack on her inmost contents, made by 'words as daggers' which only narrowly escape being 'sealed' (as Hamlet puts it) by actual physical violence:

> *Ham:* You go not till I set you up a glass
> Where you may see the inmost part of you.
> *Queen:* What wilt thou do? Thou wilt not murder me?

The veiled threat is almost immediately realised in action with the spearing of the 'intruding fool' who thought himself securely wrapped in the Queen's arras. And though Polonius appears to be forgotten after Hamlet's first few words of regret, yet the implications of having the baby-like intruder now a heaped and formless mass of 'guts' beneath their feet, seep into the imagery of the entire dialogue between Hamlet and his mother, becoming its underlying subject. Indeed owing to its poetic inevitability, the murder seems less an accident and more an integral feature of the quarrel between them. Hamlet continues to rend the Queen's flesh verbally — to 'rend her flesh', 'if it be made of penetrable stuff', with his 'wagging tongue'. The mystery of the inside of his mother is as it were ripped open to expose a riddle — first the Polonius-baby and then the riddle of his uncle-father. The idea of the Queen's 'heavenly' face, glowing and sorrowing over the wound in her earthly body and the 'solid mass' which seems to have been dragged out of her, seems to be present in Hamlet's odd image:

> Heaven's face does glow
> O'er this solidity and compound mass
> With tristful visage, as against the doom,
> Is thought-sick at the act.

This ostensibly accuses her of immorality, yet in fact reads more like a description of her spirituality, larger than life and majestic like the Ghost, against the background of 'the doom'. It is she rather than some abstract Heaven who is 'thought-sick at the act' in which the 'soul' is 'plucked from the body of contraction', as the symbolic baby is plucked from her. At the same time, the imagery of violence and disease is part of the complexity of experience and of fertile 'stewing in corruption', the 'blister' which replaces the 'rose of an innocent love'; the internal 'mutiny in a matron's bones' links the Queen with the Ghost's underground travels (the 'worthy pioneer'); 'rank corruption mining all within' is the first step in becoming sick with thought. Hamlet is in a sense accusing the Queen of experience *per se,* of having given birth to him, rather than of immorality. In having 'Eyes without feeling, feeling without sight, Ears without hands or eyes, smelling sans all', she has the capacity for identification with the foetoid state which was (and is) himself, as well as the dead Polonius deprived of his senses.

The second — and related — aspect of the Queen's mystery, which Hamlet also treats as a riddle under his stage-management, concerns the two kings. When Hamlet produces his two portraits, 'the counterfeit presentment of two brothers', saying: 'Look here upon this picture, and on this', he appears to be asking not only, 'how could you allow two such contra-dictory figures inside you', but also, 'how could this be the same man?' The two brothers form a neatly emblematic contrast, like the two masks of comedy and tragedy: one an idealised god-like figure compared to Hyperion, Jove and 'the herald Mercury/ New-lighted on a heaven-kissing hill' and in liaison with the Queen's upper regions; the other a bestial satyr, source of contagion, 'like a mildew'd ear/ Blasting his wholesome brother'. (Hamlet, as heir to both, is simultaneously asking how they can both be part of himself.) The mystery reaches a climax with the appearance of the Ghost in the room — this time not in armour but 'in his habit as he liv'd', in soft clothes (tradition-ally, in his dressing-gown.) Hamlet with his cutting words is busy dismembering the Queen, and having depatched the 'milky head' of Priam-Polonius, proceeds to describe Claudius as 'a vice of kings,/ A cutpurse of the empire', who 'from a shelf the precious diadem stole/ And put it in his pocket' — words which in effect apply to the underlying phantasy of his own procedure in relation to the 'empire' of his mother, whom he treats as if like Hecuba she were wrapped in an old blanket with a cloth round her head instead of a diadem. The desecration is accomplished by himself as the 'glass' which he holds out to her 'inmost part', reflecting his innerworld, adopting the omni-potent stance of God at the day of judgment. But Hamlet's description of Claudius as 'vice of kings' and 'king of shreds and patches' is interrupted in midstream by the entry of his other father, Old Hamlet; and it is less an interruption than a conjuration in response to the cue of his words, the image which is on his mind: 'A king of shreds and patches — Save me and hover o'er me with your wings,/ You heavenly guards! What would your gracious figure?' Thus one aspect of the kingship enters when the other is announced; clarifying the fusion of split aspects of the father's identity. The gracious figure is at the same time a 'vice' or buffoon, a 'pajock', who is as much at

115

home softly clothed in the Queen's chamber as stalking about the battlements in armour. His shreds/folds of clothes/skin are ridiculous yet also even more awe-inspiring than the leprous chainmail from which they have metamorphosed. The ambivalent appearance of the original Ghost, who was not only heroic and majestic but clownish (an 'old mole' digging in the cellarage, the lower vaults of the castle), is fulfilled.

The immediate result of this apparition is that Hamlet's stage-management (with the glass, the portraits, etc.) is totally upset; and as in 'To be or not to be', his will is 'puzzled' and loses direction. He comes too close to a moment of truth; the Ghost tells him that 'amazement on thy mother sits', and that he must 'speak to her' (rather than haranguing her). The possibility of communication seems to unexpectedly emerge; the riddle threatens to become a mystery. Instead of holding a glass to the Queen, Hamlet finds that his own gaze is seized, his eye 'bends on vacancy', and his mother finally looks at her son. She does not see the Ghost directly, but she sees the ghost in Hamlet, as if for the first time noticing that there is something within him which 'passes show'; her recognition of his spirits 'wildly peeping' forth at his eyes, and his hair standing on end like 'the sleeping soldiers in th'alarm', echoes the original ghost-scene when the soldiers on guard first alerted us to trouble within the Mind of Denmark. Meanwhile, for a long, significant moment, Hamlet's dagger-campaign is aborted in midair (as when Pyrrhus stood 'like a neutral to his will and matter' and 'Did nothing'), as he begs the Queen:

> Do not look on me,
> Lest with this piteous action you convert
> My stern effects. Then what I have to do
> Will want true colour — tears perchance for blood.

There emerges the frightening, and 'piteous' possibility, that action might become sicklied o'er with the pale cast of thought, blood be converted into tears, melodramatic blazonry modulate into the artistic imagery of the undiscovered country of an emotional relationship, the meeting of minds. But we remember that Gertrude does not, any more than anyone else in the court, possess any language for the facts of feeling; in the first act she could only urge Hamlet to consider death as 'common' — that is, not to think about it. And here, she cannot pursue her glimpse of Hamlet's inner world any further than to diagnose it as 'madness' or 'ecstasy' — that is, she explains it as something outside her ken, distancing herself from Hamlet. Instantaneously, their potential intimacy dissolves away, and Hamlet is enabled to recover his original omnipotent control of the situation. He delivers his final precepts on virtue and vice, echoing his instructions to the players to 'reform altogether' the old bad acting habits: ' O throw away the worser part ... And live the purer with the other half'; the split in the heart is re-established. The 'devil' must be 'lodged' or thrown out, and to set an example in this, Hamlet proceeds to 'bestow' Polonius in a cupboard next door — or rather 'the guts', the spirit having departed, leaving the Queen drained of life like Polonius himself. Her words, 'I have no life to breathe/ What thou hast said to me', apply not only to her promise on the plot-level not to expose Hamlet's 'madness in craft', but also to her emotional state after the interview.

Thus Hamlet concludes his invasion of the Queen's Arras by 'safely stowing' the body of Polonius (which he has prized out) whence it came, in a compartment of mother earth where it is left 'at dinner' with 'a convocation of politic worms'; this is Hamlet's false version of aesthetic appropriateness, and he recognises that it seals his own fate, placing him too with the undermining worms like the Ghost in his tortured travels: 'I will delve one yard below their mines/And blow them at the moon', he says of Rosencrantz and Guildenstern and the projected voyage to England; and of Polonius, 'This man shall set me packing'. In packing him, Hamlet himself is packed:

> For this same lord,
> I do repent; but heaven hath pleas'd it so,
> To punish me with this and this with me,
> That I must be their scourge and minister.
> I will bestow him, and will answer well
> The death I gave him.

He finally recognises the kinship between himself and Polonius, in terms of their packing and their punishment, in the slow and deliberate 'me with this and this with me'. The 'answer' to all their acting, rehearsing and debate of 'words, words, words', is

117

silence — 'most still, most secret, and most grave'. Hamlet and Polonius leave the Queen's closet, 'drawing towards an end' together.

(iv) The Yet Unknowing World

The short chaotic scenes immediately following the murder of Polonius constitute the only period in the play during which Hamlet genuinely appears to be mad; other than here, he does noting which — as Johnson said — he might not have done with the more appropriate reputation of sanity. Once Polonius is 'safely stowed', Hamlet's madness is contained by his parallel confinement within the ship bound for England (land of madmen); the King and plot choose one method of purgation but Hamlet finds another within its boundaries, metabolising a bad dream. But the aesthetic conflict is over; Hamlet is no longer in the position of 'pursuing the act' — rather, the act pursues him. His role as omnipotent manipulator passes in cruder unambiguous form to Claudius and his henchman Laertes. Hamlet says 'let it work', and it works — the mindless revenge action takes over and the play swiftly runs towards its end on oiled wheels. But meanwhile the dream sequences — Ophelia's madness and drowning; the drama of the pirate ship; the graveyard meditations — brood over and above the primitive, automatic career of the plot, in an attempt to define the emotional quality of Hamlet's remaining quest, which is no longer how to become a new prince, but how to leave a truthful image of his struggle to the 'yet unknowing world'. After Ophelia's death, the earthly dimension of the spiritual quest becomes hollow, as does the role of action in any form; Hamlet's philosophising also ceases; meaningfulness passes entirely to the dream-sphere with its focus on Hamlet's 'story', wrapped in its cloud of unknowing.

We remember that the prologue to the closet scene involved Hamlet's protection of the 'heart of his mystery' from Rosencrantz and Guildenstern, the pipe-players; followed immediately by Polonius announcing that 'the Queen would speak with you', to which Hamlet replied by directing his attention to the clouds: 'Do you see yonder cloud that's almost in shape of a camel?' After making Polonius echo his subjective vision of the cloud's changing shape, he concludes: 'Then I will come to my mother by and by'; the implication of the context being that Hamlet's mystery is in his mother in the clouds, and that the pipe-players (followers of the 'strumpet Fortune') cannot help him to comprehend it. Now, in his fourth and final soliloquy, after the play's central catastrophe, Hamlet disengages himself from the self-idealising species of cloud-following ambitious prince, in the shape of Fortinbras, whose airy spirit derives not from awareness of a spiritual world but from its absence, and whose forward career is founded on the relentless march of an army takeover, oblivious to the thousands of mute souls crushed beneath its heel:

> Examples gross as earth exhort me,
> Witness this army of such mass and charge,
> Led by a delicate and tender prince,
> Whose spirit, with divine ambition puff'd,
> Makes mouths at the invisible event,
> Exposing what is mortal and unsure
> To all that fortune, death, and danger dare,
> Even for an eggshell.

This delicate prince is a caricature of the new prince heralded in 'To be or not to be', who is puzzled by the undiscovered country. This one, puffed with ambition and self-importance, pours scorn on 'the invisible event' — the mysterious potential birth to come, the embryonic soul and the thousand natural shocks that flesh is heir to. The eggshell becomes the newly-hatched soul's grave: a plot of earth 'hardly tomb enough and continent to hide the slain'. Through the apparition of Fortinbras' massy army marching across the stage, led by their invisible prince, Hamlet in effect reflects on his own false position inside his mother's arras, where Heaven's face sorrowed over 'this solidity and compound mass' — the 'example gross as earth' of Polonius' dead body. Fortinbras represents a false identification with the 'divine' embodied in the mother, with the invisible event of the ghost, and with the mortal and unsure,which ends in the eggshell-grave-cupboard where Hamlet stowed Polonius: a piece of land which a sensible common soldier would not farm for 'five ducats', 'a little patch of ground/ That hath in in no profit but the name'. The false

119

divinity of fame is no more a container for the mystery than is the strumpet Fortune. Yet, as in the earlier soliloquy with 'all for nothing! For Hecuba!', the intense insight accruing to the poetic imagery of Hamlet's expression, finds no correlation in the argument about his course of action. The poetic implications of Fortinbras' murderous emptiness seem untranslatable and even unrecognisable when Hamlet tries to derive from his meditations a model for action. Unable to digest them he therefore continues, through a characteristic twist of wordplay, to draw the opposite moral from that clearly demonstrated by the aesthetic sense:

> How stand I then,
> That have a father kill'd, a mother stain'd,
> Excitements of my reason and my blood,
> And let all sleep, while to my shame I see
> The imminent death of twenty thousand men
> That, for a fantasy and trick of fame,
> Go to their graves like beds, . . .
>   O, from this time forth
> My thoughts be bloody or be nothing worth.

Hamlet finds the process of 'suffering in the mind' as attempted in the 'To be' soliloquy — intolerable to maintain without external resonance, and converts his struggle into a simpler one of actuality: as if, after the murder of Polonius, he had (as the ambiguous syntax suggests) actually killed a father and stained a mother. Before the Mousetrap he believed that confirmation of Claudius' crime would make his course clear; now he speaks as if it would become clear (and the only clear course is a 'bloody' one) if he could regard himself as having committed the specific Oedipal crime. Nevertheless in this soliloquy, the emphasis of the emotional force is different from earlier passages using an equivalent logical twist for self-deception. The concluding couplet does not have the manic incitement of 'drink hot blood' or 'catch the conscience of the King'; on the contrary, its triteness stresses the hollowness of the overt argument; just as the real 'shame' expressed by poetic emphasis, applies not to Hamlet's inertia (the ostensible subject) but to the fact that he is about to lead the entire court to their graves like beds, helplessly acquiescing in the identification with Fortinbras which is now inevitable. So this soliloquy marks the beginning of the play's final phase. Hamlet philosophizes no more, since it is now clear that no depth of insight thereby initiated, can find proper reception in an overall model of integrity; and insight alone, without any containing dimension in the mind, just 'puzzles the will' even to the extent of madness. After the shipboard action, Hamlet submits his body passively to the various roles which society requires him to play, no longer in need of madness to cover an evolving identity; he 'follows the King's pleasure'; while at the same time, he tries to prepare less perishable aspects of himself — his soul, his name — for a different kind of 'shaping' reception.

The backdrop for the soliloquy is an army takeover, clearly imaging the forthcoming fate of Denmark, with state and stage strewn with corpses: a sight which according to Fortinbras 'well becomes the field, but here shows much amiss'; the field is his, as presaged in the first act. The operation is masterminded by Claudius, who sees that sorrows come 'in battalions', and that his person — as head of state — is being arraigned 'in ear and ear' as if by a 'murdering piece', in many places giving him 'superfluous death'. His subsequent plotting (a mixture of ruthless bullying and 'a little shuffling'), ensures that this premonition is fulfilled in actuality. The first bringer of infection is Laertes, who like Fortinbras is wrapped in a vain cloud of mindlessness,

> Feeds on this wonder, keeps himself in clouds,
> And wants not buzzers to infect his ear
> With pestilent speeches of his father's death.

Claudius and Laertes between them enact a sort of tedious, absurd, petty-minded caricature of the relationship between the Ghost and Hamlet, using the same basic rhetorical figures but drained of their emotionality. Thus instead of the sea of madness which lies beyond Elsinore's battlements and cliffs in the ghost scene, and toward which Hamlet tentatively ventures, we have Laertes rushing in to the palace at the head of the rabble, like the ocean who 'overpeering of his list/ Eats ... the flats with impetuous haste'. The Ghost's imagery of hell-fire becomes Laertes' conventional 'vows to the blackest devil' and 'daring damnation' as he immediately slips into the standard revenger's role which Hamlet found too meaningless; the imagery of poison becomes Claudius's coarse political slang: 'But to the quick of th'ulcer:/ Hamlet comes back', while the rose and blister of innocence and experience revert to their unambiguous conventional derivation as Laertes screams that, if he were to remain calm, his blood would cry cuckold to his father and brand the harlot on the unsmirched brow of his mother. Meanwhile Claudius, in order to channel Laertes' instinctive outbreak into the required direction, expatiates in a tediously rhetorical description on the heroic model of a centaur-swordsman, a Frenchman who rode 'incorps'd and demi-natur'd/ With the brave beast' and who, he says, was effusive in his praise of young Laertes as a swordplayer: 'he cried out 'twould be a sight indeed/ If one could match you'. In other words, he echoes the account in Act I of the larger than life heroic combat of Old Hamlet as he 'smote the sledded Polack on the ice'; producing the age-old card of a god-like father for emulation — which Hamlet (saying he was 'no Hercules') tried to resist and see in more complex terms. To cap the conventional picture he adds that Hamlet is 'envenomed with envy' of Laertes' reputation, and sets the notion of good brother/son against that of bad brother/son. Laertes responds to Claudius' bullying manipulation and becomes his pawn as does England — which, being still 'raw and red/ After the Danish sword', obsequiously accepts Denmark's dirty work. The way Laertes falls into all the traps Hamlet has avoided, shows him to be stupid rather than bad-natured; thus his immediate emotional reaction to Ophelia's death is one of empathy ('Too much of water hast thou, poor Ophelia'), yet he cannot do anything with his 'tears' — the womanly part of himself — other than momentarily indulge them, and then get rid of them: 'When these are gone, /The woman will be out'. He is not capable of a struggle towards integration and therefore can be played on like a pipe, even when it is 'against his conscience', as he feels during the duel.

Meanwhile it is Ophelia, in her pregnant madness, who carries the implications of the cloud of unknowing on behalf of the Mind of Denmark, during Hamlet's temporary absence in the lunatic asylum — the deathbound bark which he 'checks' in midstream. She also takes to the water, as a species of sacrifice, gathering to her all the spiritual values which have found no place in the court, but unable to sustain them other than through the death of innocence. In contrast with the emptiness of Fortinbras and Laertes, her cloudiness is full of meaning, like her 'unshaped' speech which suggests 'there might be thought' within it, but of a kind which is not expressible in the words, words, words, of social discourse:

> Her speech is nothing,
> Yet the unshaped use of it doth move
> The hearers to collection. They aim at it,
> And botch the words up fit to their own thoughts,
> Which, as her winks and nods and gestures yield them,
> Indeed would make one think there might be thought,
> Though nothing sure, yet much unhappily.

She is thought-sick, and evokes in the Queen the helpless recognition of her own 'sick soul', as she evokes in everyone the sense of a whole world of potential emotional communication between 'thought' and 'thought' rather than word and word, in this play which annihilates the values of all mere *forms* of expression and places all its emotional weight on an unknown, undiscovered country whose features and languages remain always out of reach. So far has the court become divorced from the world of feeling that even the ritual forms sanctifying spiritual life are deformed and cannot be kept up — Polonius and Ophelia are both interred 'hugger-mugger', with 'maimed rites'. The pageant of flowers surrounding Ophelia's madness and death fulfils these grave-rites as well as suggesting the 'blossoms' of the court's sinfulness which, as Rose of May, accrue to her, being her response to the smooth body of the ghost-within-Hamlet becoming encrusted with weals representing the 'blossoms of sin'; for as Hamlet said, his father was taken with 'all his crimes broad blown as flush as May'. The grave and the marriage-bed are again linked as the Queen, scattering flowers, says 'I thought thy bride-bed to have deck'd, sweet maid, /And not have strew'd thy grave'. And Ophelia's madness is a type of expression of marriage with Hamlet, in which she remembers his sins instead of handing them straight back to him; but it is a complete empathy and acceptance, rather than a battle and compromise leading to continued earthly existence. Her Valentine song suggests she felt raped by his madness: he 'dupped the chamber door,/ Let in the maid that out a maid /Never departed more'. Hamlet and her father are fused in the image of the pilgrim with 'cockle hat and staff' and 'sandal shoon' who is embarked on a journey out of this world,

> Larded with sweet flowers
> Which bewept to the grave did not go
> With true-love showers.

It is as if she intuits Hamlet's strange return from the sea with his sea-gown scarfed about him like a shroud, and their final meeting at the grave, and the sarcastic undertones of Resurrection and Day of Judgment with which Hamlet challenges the pseudo-Godlike King, in his missive beginning:

> High and mighty, you shall know I am set naked on your kingdom.

'Naked' and 'alone', the soul returns to its native soil for rehabilitation. All this forms part of the 'unshaped' thought of Ophelia, who says 'Lord we know what we are, but know not what we may be'. Her ultimate achievement of self-expression is to drown 'in her own defence' — an image which, as Eric Rhode shows in *On Birth and Madness* (1987), is often associated with the process of childbirth, and which is caught and intimately understood by the Queen. Here Ophelia appears both native and foreign to her watery element as, making herself into a flower-boat, she beautifies the 'ingrained spot' in Denmark's soul:

> Her clothes spread wide,
> And mermaid-like awhile they bore her up,
> Which time she chanted snatches of old lauds,
> As one incapable of her own distress,
> Or like a creature native and indued
> Unto that element. But long it could not be
> Till that her garments, heavy with their drink,
> Pull'd the poor wretch from her melodious lay
> To muddy death.

Denmark's tears (the water) and the flowering of the fair state, are concentrated on and in her, her clothes like rose-petals drinking like the symbolic infants associated with her metaphoric pregnancy, until they enter the 'heavy' sleep of muddy forgetfulness, thereby echoing and reforming the fat weed rooting itself in ease on Lethe wharf, which was Hamlet.

The ultimate container for offences, the grave, is dug on the stage in between the accounts of Ophelia sinking, and Hamlet rising from the sea. As the Grave-digger implies, she drowned herself 'in her own defence' when the water 'came to her'. The ships are coming in to land, as the Grave-digger sings while he throws up skulls:

> But age with his stealing steps
> Hath claw'd me in his clutch,
> And hath shipp'd me intil the land,
> As if I had never been such.

Goodman Delver's house will 'last till doomsday', and Hamlet's commentary on it suggests that it is capacious enough to contain the whole court if not mankind itself, from 'Cain that did the first murder' onwards. The comic and casual disturbance of the court's bones suggests that even in this apparently final resting-place, boundaries must still be crossed back and forth. Their bodies may have reached the land, but only to be 'cast up' once again on the shore, like the unhearsed Ghost, in a 'fine revolution': 'Did these bones cost no more the breeding but to play at loggets with them? Mine ache to think on't.' Here in the ultimate private parts of Fortune, Hamlet comes across metaphorical associations about breeding maggots, skin-deep paintings, soul-houses and singing or wagging tongues, which he has been in the habit of taking in vain and using as ammunition for aggression; now he finds the same ammunition, mixed with clods of earth, flying back in his own direction, thrown by a 'mad knave' who has 'no feeling of his business' and 'sings in grave-making'; and he acknowledges that his own bones 'ache to think'. And here, amongst the bones being used for playing at loggets, Hamlet confronts his father once again, in yet another form. When he asks the Grave-digger who this universal grave belongs to, the reply is 'Mine, sir'. The Grave-digger is a sort of Polonius now on the winning wicket and able to answer Hamlet back, giving better than he gets, and outdoing Hamlet in defensive-aggressive wordplay: thus ''Tis a quick lie sir, 'twill away again from me to you' echoes 'These words are not mine' — 'Nor mine now' (between Claudius and Hamlet) or 'What man . . . what woman then?' echoes 'Man delights not me . . . nor woman neither'. Now, Hamlet recognises that 'equivocation will undo us'. At the same time, as the name Goodman Delver suggests, the Grave-digger represents a down-to-earth transfiguration of the Ghost, that 'worthy pioner' who has been digging in the cellarage throughout the whole play. He started his job, digging the court's grave, on the day of young Hamlet's birth, the same day as the remotely chivalric duel between Old Hamlet and Old Fortinbras, which now appears a kind of celebration of the 'cost of breeding' the new prince. We remember that Horatio also was present in journalistic capacity at this duel-birth; and taken together, these coincidences image a composite emotional event at the root of Denmark's present sickness and vulnerability.

It is often regarded as curious that the Ghost, who sets the whole drama rolling and takes up a large part of the first act, should disappear completely from the play and even from Hamlet's reflections, after the closet scene (as Ophelia also disappears). But he reappears in a different form in the graveyard: partly in the verbose gravedigger who teases Hamlet with his superior wit, and partly in the mute skull of Yorick. Hamlet's 'Alas, poor Yorick' echoes 'Alas, poor Ghost!' —

Alas, poor Yorick. I knew him, Horatio, a fellow of infinite jest, of most excellent fancy. He hath bore me on his back a thousand times, and now — how abhorred in my imagination it is. My gorge rises at it. Here hung those lips that I have kissed I know not how oft.

When Hamlet follows the 'noble dust of Alexander' to 'a bung-hole', pursuing for the last time a train of association which Horatio calls 'considering too curiously', he is in effect relinquishing the old image of his father in heroic mould, together with the awe and irritation and latent competitiveness, and contempt, which went with it:

Imperious Caesar, dead and turn'd to clay,
Might stop a hole to keep the wind away.

O that that earth which kept the world in awe
Should patch a wall t'expel the winter's flaw.

In a sense he wonders at his own fury at Polonius-Caesar and his
own fear of Jove-like man, the empire-builder holding sway over
the world of Denmark and his mother. It seems as unreal as a
stage-set by comparison with the world momentarily bounded
by Yorick's stinking skull — the 'rag and bone shop of the heart',
as Yeats would say. Hamlet's own 'equivocations' are matched,
undone, purged by the Grave-digger, as they reach the end of the
road — fit only to stop a bunghole. Instead, from the grave of old
associations, emerges the single evocative picture in the whole
play of a father-son relationship: the seven-year-old child on the
jester's back. The jester is the lost player-king whom the acting
Player King could not revive or impersonate; he is another
version of the buffoon-like 'king of shreds and patches', the 'vice
of kings' who could cast off his majestic armour for the absurdity
of a dressing-gown, along with 'gibes, gambols, songs, and
flashes of merriment'; he is Gilbert and Sullivan's 'wandering
minstrel, a thing of shreds and patches'. Hamlet has finally made
his way to the unofficial presentation of king and prince: somewhere between or beyond Hyperion and the satyr, stands the
kind of father who made Hamlet, not only the glass of fashion
and the mould of form, but the court's Fool.

Dusty Alexander is a fiction, a superficial mask of kingship;
but the skull with the lips hanging on it, superimposed by
imaginative remembrance, and evoking a complex reaction of
wonder and revulsion, is reality: the reality of an inner world.
Here, as well as the boy hanging on the jester's spine, is Ophelia
with the petal-clothes hanging on her and drinking; here in the
quality of 'infinite jest' in constricted confines, is infinity in a
nutshell, not an empty eggshell of hot air. Yet Hamlet himself
finds this image of the Mystery too painful to contemplate for
long, and in his subsequent vulgarisation of it, paves the way for
the trap in which he will shortly be caught when the revelation
of Ophelia's death comes upon him; the funeral procession is
already making its way as Hamlet announces, with a sort of
premonition:

Now get you to my lady's chamber and tell her, let her paint
an inch thick, to this favour she must come.

Ophelia, in the chamber of the coffin, is already coming: her own innermost chamber envisaged through Yorick's fleshless chops, but — like the Queen's 'inmost part' seen reflected in Hamlet's 'glass', only revealing in the negative. For the second part of this peculiar and perplexing recognition scene consists in confirmation that the undiscovered country is a lost cause. The features of this scene recall those surrounding the 'To be or not to be' soliloquy — the false painting; the ultimate nunnery of the grave; the metaphysical speculations which culminate in the presence of Ophelia as the earthly partner in their fulfilment. Hamlet's 'What, the fair Ophelia!' echoes 'Soft you now, the fair Ophelia!', and again Ophelia is presented by father-figures whose jealous and curious guard Hamlet feels antagonistic and debasing of his own aspirations. The mystery of Ophelia's chamber or inner world, suddenly becomes fused — by an omnipotent father — with the secrecy about the ownership of the grave, which the Grave-digger has succeeded in withholding throughout the long scene despite Hamlet's efforts to worm the information out of him. The teasing word-player finally reveals his trump card, hoisting Hamlet with his own petard. Hamlet realises he has been ultimately out-tricked and out-played, not by his external enemy Claudius but by an enemy within, part of his paternal inheritance. His sense of outrage at this lies behind the scuffle and ranting match with Laertes over the grave:

> Woo't weep, woo't fight, woo't fast, woo't tear thyself,
> Woo't drink up eisel, eat a crocodile?
> I'll do it. Dost come here to whine,
> To outface me with leaping in her grave?
>   . . . Nay and thou'lt mouth,
> I'll rant as well as thou.

In this play in which 'words, words, words' are synonymous with self-deceit, Hamlet's single phrase 'I lov'd Ophelia' is (like the undramatic expression of regret at Polonius' death) drowned by the 'bravery of grief'; Hamlet makes his contribution to the display, artificial and mocking as it is, out of despairing acceptance of the conditions of instinctive mindlessness to which he too is subject against his will: 'The cat will mew, and dog will have his day'. After this, wordiness and rhetorical flourishes pass to the ludicrous and harmless figure of Osric, where they are relieved of their sinister connotations and become merely empty and absurd, a barrier to conveying the simplest items of information; Osric with his 'yeasty' concoctions, 'fanned and winnowed', gathers to himself the airiness of Fortinbras 'puff'd with ambition', and like Fortinbras with his eggshell, Osric becomes a 'lapwing running away with the shell on his head'.

In the midst of the verbal flourishes which act as prologue to the 'shuffling' of rapiers during the duel, Hamlet indicates how such trickiness suffocates the hidden problem of 'knowing oneself':

> *Osr:* I know you are not ignorant —
> *Ham:* I would you did, sir. Yet in faith if you did, it would not much approve me. Well, sir?
> *Osr:* You are not ignorant of what excellence Laertes is —
> *Ham:* I dare not confess that, lest I should compare with him in excellence; but to know a man well were to know himself.

Hamlet comes to define his tragedy not in terms of knowing about the activities of his father, but of knowing himself, the key to absolute knowledge-as-mystery. Between the two fights with Laertes, in which Hamlet accepts his appearance as 'umbrage' to one who has a sort of brotherhood with him (just as he agrees to 'follow the King's pleasure' in all matters of form), Hamlet recounts to Horatio a different kind of 'fighting in his heart' during the sea-voyage which took him away from and back to Denmark:

> Sir, in my heart there was a kind of fighting
> That would not let me sleep. Methought I lay
> Worse than the mutines in the bilboes.

His account of his dream and ensuing dream-action recalls the rebellious hell 'mutinying in a matron's bones' which was his image of his mother's internal state on marriage, and suggests a dream-world bounded by the mother's body, a kind of ship, founded on the original secure sleep in the orchard whose confines were cracked by the infiltration of bad dreams. This time, the bad dream is accepted as a vehicle of knowledge, a type of inspiration contrasting with the tricky omnipotent 'deep plots' of the Claudius or Polonius within him: 'When our deep

129

plots do pall ... /There's a divinity that shapes our ends, / Rough-hew them how we will'. Hamlet escapes from the 'play' which was benetting him, and leaves the deathbound bark with the authentication of his father's 'seal'. Horatio makes his moral objection to the fate of Rosencrantz and Guildenstern, but this time Hamlet overrides him, since for once he is motivated by a different kind of identification with his father, in line with a sense of 'heaven ordinant', a sense of being guided and preserved rather than manipulated. It is the first time he really recognises his royal descent, and accounts for his announcing himself as 'This is I, Hamlet the Dane' in the burial scene, as if he had in some way come to terms with the fact that he was destined to be a prince not a liberal politician. Yet this in itself sets a trap for the soul, expressed in the rationalisation: 'Is't not perfect conscience/ To quit him with this arm?' Events are closing in, and the space and time which remain to Hamlet for being himself, may be bounded in a nutshell: 'It will be short. The interim is mine./ And a man's life's no more than to say "one".' After this, Horatio makes no further moral rebukes, as if for the first time realising the depth of Hamlet's predicament — beside which the correctness of his attitude to the despatching of the two ambassadors seems superficial. After the dream on ship-board, it is clear that Hamlet's ship, also, is coming in to land:

> There is special providence in the fall of a sparrow. If it be now, 'tis not to come; if it be not to come, it will be now; if it be not now, yet it will come. The readiness is all. Since no man, of aught he leaves, knows aught, what is't to leave betimes? Let be.

Echoing Ophelia's words in her madness, 'we know what we are, but know not what we may be', Hamlet's final achievement in the face of the mystery appears to be the knowledge that he knows nothing: neither what he leaves nor what leaves him. Yet at the same time, there is a new quality in the equation of Hamlet the Dane with 'a sparrow', which suggests the incorporation in his image of himself, of the foetoid Polonius who fell so easily, and of the femininity which his brother Laertes rejected with 'the woman will be out': thus Hamlet describes his sense of 'how ill all's here about my heart' as 'the kind of gaingiving that would trouble a woman'; and in saying 'let be', he is neither throwing this out, nor attempting the Herculean feat of opposing this internal thought-sickness to the mindless onrush of political events which is about to conclude the play. His recognition of the lack of knowledge is therefore less an expression of nihilism than a Socratean first step in confronting the mystery.

As always, Hamlet's intimate colloquy with Horatio, providing the emotional touchstone for the internal drama of dreams, contrasts with the dénouement of the revenge-plot which is taking place around it. Witholding his inner self entirely from the forms of action, courtesy and rhetoric which society and his mother demand from him (asking him to use 'some gentle entertainment' to Laertes), Hamlet's final formal speech — in which he dissociates himself from his 'madness' — has a hollow and artificial ring, quite the opposite from the declaration of self-revelation which one expects at the end of a classical tragedy. It is precisely owing to this disengagement of his soul, that once the action has started, Hamlet is keen to make an end — refusing to examine the foils despite his suspicion of treachery, and finally having to taunt Laertes to give him his 'best violence' and let the play finish, since it is clear that otherwise Hamlet would have won the duel, given Laertes' qualms of conscience. Within a minute or two the stage is strewn with corpses, and Fortinbras enters from where he has been waiting in the wings, to receive Hamlet's 'dying voice' and take over the kingdom to which he always felt he had some 'rights of memory', and on which his march was always set: focussed on the court's 'little patch of ground'. Through the casual, clumsy and meaningless chapter of deaths which concludes this tale of 'accidental judgments, casual slaughters', Shakespeare stresses the antagonism of the plot to the emotional drama. But in the midst of the unrevelatory action, Hamlet and Horatio once again and for the last time, emerge to take the centre of the stage: seizing prominence amongst the pile of corpses and the irrelevant surge of extraneous characters. Hamlet has already said 'I am dead' twice, when — on seeing Horatio with the poisoned cup — he completely sheds his attitude of fatalistic acceptance of events. Suddenly filled with energy he rises up to snatch it away:

131

> As th'art a man
> Give me the cup. Let go, by Heaven I'll ha't.
> O God, Horatio, what a wounded name
> Things standing thus unknown, shall I leave behind me.
> If thou didst ever hold me in thy heart,
> Absent thee from felicity awhile,
> And in this harsh world draw thy breath in pain
> To tell my story.

Hamlet's fatalism refers only to the fulfilment of the revenge plot which he saw, after the closet scene, would 'work' to its close automatically and mechanically, overrunning the Mind of Denmark as inevitably as the army battalions. Throughout, Hamlet has been struggling to write his story, to find an aesthetic correlative to image the idea of a new prince. At each potential point of revelation he has, through lack of resonance from the other protagonists, fallen impulsively into collusion with an anti-aesthetic mode — such as play-acting, pursuing directions through indirections, or trying to riddle out the heart of the mystery as if it were a secrecy. But though the struggle may not have availed, he has no intention of allowing it to sink into oblivion. He is content to hand the 'election of the state' to a simplistic figure like Fortinbras; but the inner 'story' which has been taking place in the latent structure of the play, has yet another revolution to undergo, another species of labour before it may be born into a form which speaks to a further generation. Horatio is chosen to translate 'things thus unknown', drawing breath in pain and holding in his heart, to 'th'yet unknowing world': 'let me speak to th'yet unknowing world/ How these things came about'. Horatio may not yet understand Hamlet, but he has been trained to observe him, and the quality of his observation is steady (unlike the Queen's, who could not stand it for more than a moment — owing to her position as a protagonist, with everything to lose); and Hamlet may not know aught he leaves, but he has come to trust Horatio's ability to see and contain the facts. For Hamlet, beneficence in space — 'felicity' — is dependent on a further mental transformation which must take place outside the Mind of Denmark, perhaps in conjunction with those who are 'mutes and audience to the act'. 'It is *we* who are Hamlet . . . we are more than spectators, faced with the original text'. The Horatio dimension can do no more nor less than to deliver the text, open-ended as it is. The play ends on a half-line, 'Go, bid the soldiers shoot'; with the discharge of the cannon, Hamlet's soul dematerialises to the characteristically discordant accompaniment of angelic singing united with gunfire:

Now cracks a noble heart. Goodnight, sweet prince,
And flights of angels sing thee to thy rest.

Particles embodying the thousand natural shocks that flesh is heir to, disperse from the infinitesimally small explosion of a heart cracking — the fall of a sparrow. The resultant cloud of unknowing gathers to hang over our heads like the 'omnipresent and mysterious reality, brooding motionless over and within the play's movement'.

So *Hamlet* dramatises the conflict between intrusive, voyeuristic types of identification which aim to penetrate and control the aesthetic object from within, and the kind of projective identification which has a matching-oneself quality: exploration in a symbolic mode. Its dream-language is founded on the different kinds of resonance between inside and outside the aesthetic object. While anti-knowledge follows a clear and old-established pattern (the mould of the revenge form), the traditional path towards knowledge — through cathartic revelation — is not only cold-shouldered but undermined. The play wrenches us back and forth between knowledge and delusion, truth and lies, inviting or rather insisting on our participating in the aesthetic conflict in a way too close for comfort; at the same time maintaining its inviolate mystery. Hamlet's investigation of symbolic representation and its false theatrical umbrages/shadows, models an exploration of mental space which is also our own. But because tragedy's usual catharsis is rejected, unusual confusion and anxiety are aroused in the audience as we feel that the pattern of true knowledge will never be made clear. The play continues to envelop us beyond its own boundaries (which are in any case fluid and elusive), maintaining 'a process that seems to be happening on our looking' (Stokes); and neither Horatio nor Shakespeare will confirm whether our close identification with the hero is ordained to be our doom or our salvation.

8   The Place of Aesthetic Conflict in the Analytic Process

In considering the conflict of emotion aroused by the aesthetic impact of the object, it is necessary to relate this struggle to our existing model of the mind in its various dimensions, in the sense of extended metapsychology. Earlier chapters have dealt mainly with the dynamic, economic, genetic and geographical aspects, but aesthetic conflict has an important relation to mental structuring also. Insofar as the conflict over the manifest exterior and the ambiguous interior of the object stirs the epistemophilic instinct, it clearly makes an important — perhaps the major — contribution to the shaping of the place of K in the balance of L, H and K in the knowledge-seeking life of the individual. Melanie Klein and Bion, in particular, have traced the importance of the qualities of the object with regard to the evolution of the super-ego functions of internal and external objects. The vigilance, intelligence and uncorruptibility of these objects are surely the infantile basis of honesty; for long before an ethical preference can be embraced, despair of being able to deceive one's objects enforces integrity. The policeman at one's elbow is an essential bar to self-deception; love of the truth comes much later.

But the contribution of aesthetic conflict to the development of the ego-ideal functions of objects is less apparent. When objects are fully formed and loved their force in promoting aspiration towards excellence seems unnecessary of explanation. But aspiration, even in the sense of Milton's aspiration 'to become a true poem', is not the same as inspiration. And, unless we propose to deal with inspiration as mere allegory, we must take account of the 'Muse' in our consideration of ego-ideal functions. The psycho-analytical literature is unclear about the modus operandi of the inspirational role of the ego-ideal in promoting development, although it seems clear to many workers that the efficiency of introjective identifications derives from its aspirational stimulus, thus accounting for the gradual emergence of *identified qualities* in contrast to the

134

immediacy of the effect on the *sense* of identity induced by narcissistic forms of identification. This absence of a clear psycho-analytical view of inspiration can be seen to have the same roots as the failure to take account of the aesthetic impact of objects on personality development. Probably the tacit assumption has been that children have emotions but not passions, while on the other hand passions have never been given status among the emotions except on a quantitative basis as intense or excessive emotions. Certainly one of the aims of this book is to establish the term 'passion' as a specific response to aesthetic objects: as a *qualitatively* distinct consortium of L, H and K, which is therefore subject to very specific forms of attack by negative links. One need hardly document the virulence with which the anti-aesthetic forces in the mind, as in the culture, mount their attacks on aesthetic objects and aesthetic experience.

Much of this thesis on the attacks against the breast as an object of trusted dependence, was outlined in the chapter on the 'Threshold of the Depressive Position' in *The Psycho-analytical Process*. But at that time my attention was mainly focussed on the breast as part object, valued and even loved for its functions. These functions were mainly seen in Kleinian terms related to introjective processes, for the work of Bion had not as yet really found its place in my consulting room. The thinking breast, the assimilation of the mother's eyes to her nipples, the function of her reverie in making available to the baby the food for thought, the alpha-elements and dream-thoughts (rows B and C of the Grid) that enable the baby to deal with emotional experiences rather than to evacuate them — none of this had worked its way into my theoretical framework or model of the mind. Consequently the conflicts over the feeding breast, while recognized as structured in terms of the outside versus the inside of the object, were viewed mainly from the point of view of greed, envy, and possessive jealousy (of the inside-babies).

At present I would think all of that as substantially tenable, but from the viewpoint of recovery, rather than the achievement, of the depressive position. The super-ego aspect of this primal part-object was attributed to the nipple as the paternal element of the combined object of breast and nipple, endowed with qualities of strength and authority, presiding over the

135

feeding process. I would now see the nipples as associated primarily with the mother's eyes whereas their secondary link to the father's penis opens the way to erotization and zonal confusion. On the other hand the ego-ideal function of the combined object of breast and nipple was felt then to reside in the depressive problem of the shift in values, from ego-centric to object-related concern, consequent to and intrinsic to the shift to a depressive economic principle.

I think still that this is a useful way of looking at the ego-ideal functions of internal objects. The depressive orientation is essentially aspirational in its ethos; worthiness as a goal is at the heart of the experience of love and gratitude. But, it seems to me, it cannot cogently describe the inspirational aspect, which must be at the root of the transition from useful productivity — using received equipment of ideas, knowledge and skills — to true creativity. I do not wish to use this term loosely, bandied and battered as it is by promiscuous employment. Studying letters, essays and diaries of great artists suggests that even among such persons inspiration is a rare and fleeting phenomenon. How momentary or non-existent must it be amongst lesser figures? But it is a phenomenon and our model of the mind must be able to describe it, though we bow before its essential mysteriousness.

Psycho-analytical contributions to any theory of inspiration and creativity must, of course, be derived from experience of the analytical process. In my opinion, although reference to aesthetic experiences past and current must necessarily make up some part of the patient's material, the entry into the transference of an aesthetic apprehension of the analyst's modes of thought, of the analytical method and of the process of development that it generates, makes a late appearance in the therapy. It is by no means coincidental that its appearance tends to be simultaneous with another phenomenon: the tendency to impasse at the threshold of the depressive position, as described in *The Psycho-analytical Process* in 1967. At the time of writing the paper 'The Apprehension of Beauty' (1973), I read a paper on impasse to my colleagues which was fiercely resisted. I ascribed this characteristic tendency to inertia and impasse in the therapeutic process to the economics of mental pain in a general way. That is, I reported my observations on the waning of persecutory anxieties and the incipiency of depressive pain, as primarily related to 'the writing on the wall' or the 'whiff of grapeshot' of inevitable weaning and termination of the dependence.

I still think this is a legitimate generalization, but more point and descriptive power can be added to the concept by correlating the tendency to impasse with the emergence of aesthetic experience in the transference and its attendant problem of the love of truth. Two recent clinical experiences have helped me to clarify the inter-relation of these two ideas — namely, of the ego-ideal functions of the aesthetic impact of the primal objects, and the relation between the appearance of aesthetic conflict in the transference with the crisis of the Threshold of the Depressive Position, and its attendant tendency to impasse.

The first experience illustrates the emergence of the aesthetic conflict in the transference as a new experience for the patient and the crucial role it plays in the evolution of love for the truth. A young woman, slim and attractive, coming from abroad but speaking perfect, if somewhat inaudible English, had been seconded by the charitable organization for which she had worked for some fifteen years, to study personnel management in this country for a period of three years. During this time she undertook an analysis as part of her training and had been in therapy four times per week for some five years at the time of the present material. These five years had seen very extensive changes in her character, which had been chaste, withdrawn and colourless, deeply religious and asexual. A moderate degree of coming to life was reflected in changes in her interests, mode of dress, attraction to men, improved liveliness and lessening of her piety. When her personnel training was completed she asked to stay on to do a further training in counselling, to which her parent organization agreed in view of her long service at a very low stipend. Eventually she asked to be released from her contract, to which the officers of the charity not only acquiesced, but gave her a bonus of some seven thousand pounds as a severance gift. At that time, one year before the current material, we had agreed that she should continue the analysis at the greatly reduced fee that her organization had been paying, on the assumption that she would barely survive economically even with the help of her bonus until she returned to her country at the end of the analysis.

Within the next six months she completed her counselling course, found some rather menial employment and made preparations to leave when her student's visa would expire. Her analytic progress was slow and there seemed reason to doubt that time would be adequate for a satisfactory resolution of the difficulties that prevented her forming relationships of any depth of intimacy, especially with men. The same problems appeared in the analysis as very stilted communication, colourlessness of voice and vocabulary, a marked tendency to rehearse inwardly before speaking, and an adamant insistence that the relationship was necessarily impersonal because of her lying on the couch and because the analyst gave no information about himself. However she was a fine reporter of dreams and grudgingly developed some understanding of the spitefulness and princessly pride which held her back from acknowledging or showing feelings.

During the next months her social life seemed to pick up, her style of dress became markedly more youthful and attractive and the material began to revolve more around the men she met, mostly at her work. She talked of moving closer to the area of the analysis, now that she was no longer having to go to her course on the other side of town, and this seemed also to imply that she could now rely on public transport and save the expense of running a car. However she did not move, did not give up the car. Then one day she brought a simple little dream that *she was carrying a typewriter from one room to another and dropped it, but it was not damaged.* Inquiry elicited the information that it was not her typewriter, but an electric one which she does in fact borrow from a fellow lodger, who does not actually own it either. It seems to belong to a woman who had gone back to her native land, leaving the machine to be shipped to her. How long ago was this? Several months. Why had it not been shipped? Oh, the girl didn't seem to be in any hurry to have it!

The cat was out of the bag. I began to review her financial situation with her and discovered that she was now working full time, also had some private clients (illegally), had never touched the seven thousand pounds nor even the interest on it, since she was planning to buy a flat for her sole occupancy in

138

order to have more privacy and to see her clients. Had she considered raising her fee to me to approximate my regular charge? Yes, she had thought about it but decided that the analyst had been satisfied with the low fee during the previous years. The brazen ingratitude rather took my breath away.

Having clarified the problem, I rather left her to struggle with it, which her sullen demeanour reflected and her dreams documented. She grudgingly offered a compromise, to pay three quarters rather than half my regular fee, but seemed quite unable to grasp the issue of the cheating and the money that represented it. She was just like a monkey who gets his fist in the bowl of nuts and cannot get it out because he cannot let go of the nuts. She argued, she sulked, she flattered, she wept, but fortunately she also dreamt. *She was on a train going through exquisitely beautiful country in the vicinity of a city called Queenstown, but she was standing in the driver's cab rather than sitting in a passenger carriage. There was also present an attractive man and a young boy. She was looking at the man, wondering was he married, was he perhaps homosexual.* When I inquired about the driver the patient replied that she didn't know, she didn't notice him. I suggested that this train journey was meant to represent the analysis and her training which had finally brought her into a state of mind where she could notice the beauty of the world and this life, not relegating it all to Heaven; that Queenstown was London and the driver whom she didn't notice — being too busy finding a husband — was myself.

This dream had some effect and led to some movement towards understanding the enormity of her ingratitude and dishonesty with me as the parents who help her to develop towards womanhood in a world of beauty and sexuality. Two weeks later she had a dream clearly a sequel to the Queenstown one, that *she was sitting in the back seat of a car behind a couple; they might have been her parents or the analyst and his wife. The car came over the brow of a hill and revealed a magnificient vista of valleys and hills with the sea in the distance. But coming towards them was an articulated lorry, a juggernaut, and she felt frightened it would crash into them. Then she noticed by the side of the road a splendid horse, unsaddled and riderless, but with a bridle on its head.* I felt that the juggernaut represented that part of herself which attacks the parents as a combined object and which threatened to destroy the progress she was making towards acknowledging her dependence. The man of the Queenstown dream seemed to be replaced by the splendid horse, which I suggested implied that she was now more able to see the possibility of beauty in a man and his genital instead of simply husband-hunting in a predatory way. There was perhaps a pun, bridle-bridal.

The charming thing about this material is that the acting-in-the-transference is so transparently childish, and in a sense innocent, prior to thought. We need not be amazed (since Bion), that people can go far in their contractual adaptation to the 'world' without being encumbered by this troublesome faculty — imaginative thought. But intimacy cannot far proceed without it, for its evolution depends upon getting to know one another. These imaginative incursions into the ambiguous interior of the other's mind, which my patient attempts in her dream regarding the man in the train-cab, are little facilitated by simply looking. There must be interaction and communication to supply the unconscious with that wealth of data which can comprise an emotional experience. The mere aesthetic impact of the other person's exterior, even when it delivers a hammer-blow to the heart, as in love-at-first-sight, cannot generate the alpha-elements from which thoughts spring forth. This lady's habit of rehearsing her communications so impoverishes her vocabulary and the music of her voice that she fails to make an 'impression' on another person's mind. It is clear that without her excellent recall of dreams — which, however, must always be supplemented with interrogation for detail — little comprehension would ever have germinated in my mind. The analysis would have remained as drought-stricken as her other relationships.

Clearly this young woman is not an unethical person. She is an un-thinking one, and therefore insensitive to the position, feelings, needs and attitudes of others. All little children pilfer. To some degree it has the meaning of scavenging, but this can hardly be the case when a child systematically steals from her mother's handbag, buys sweets or is hoarding her loot to buy a dolly. The innocence is shown in the naiveté of their self-revealing crimes. Had I been more alert I would have noticed the parade of new clothes long before the typewriter dream gave the game away. The role of projective identification and attendant confusion of identity in this naiveté is shown in a dream the patient had a few weeks after the juggernaut one: *she was in her parents' bedroom and her mother came in, saying that there was dirty water left in the bath, implying that the patient should clean it up. But she was annoyed because she felt sure that it was mother who had taken the bath.* It is as if to say that she comes to analysis to afford me the opportunity of correcting my misconceptions about her. In such an instance, thinking in terms of mechanisms of defence, one cannot say with certainty whether the patient is confused or is employing confusion *as* a defence. In the latter case, in more epistemological terms, the truth is being bowdlerized by means of projective identification. In that case we must come to the question of love for the truth and its relation to the aesthetic level of experience of the primal objects.

The second piece of material, which takes us back to our poet, four months on, bears directly on this problem. Following the material reported earlier about the 'magnificent breasts' and his 'collection' of other men's women, we entered on a period of some turbulence both in analysis and his external life situation. A young protégé who was almost like an adopted son left the country to rejoin his estranged family, and the patient abandoned the job which was his financial mainstay owing to political differences. But I felt that the central disturbance was reflected in his analytic material, which pursued the theme of attacks on the breast shown in the trio of dreams introduced by the 'dead bodies in the mud'. The issue of jealousy of the next baby became unequivocal in his dreams, showing a savagery that quite astonished him. As a result a fairly deep split in his personality, consisting of the poet and lover of truth versus an ambitious, greedy and sly infantile aspect, declared itself openly, although it had been suspected earlier for historical reasons. Distrust of the analyst and of the analytic method introduced a certain reserve and tentativeness into his previously open and enthusiastic participation, as a certain loneliness and restless sense of inertia suffused his daily life.

Indecision about the future course of his work pushed him to accept an assignment for three weeks to Nicaragua, attracted by the money, the danger and the political turbulence. On return, after missing this period of analysis, he found himself able to write up his experience with a speed and vividness that

141

paralleled the enthusiasm and comradery which he had found and entered upon so wholeheartedly there. He had been particularly attracted by a woman, an American, who seemed to have made herself completely at home amidst the danger and confusion, quite completely 'gone native'.

Without any apparent diminution of his satisfaction with the analyst's work or reneging of his former conviction of the benefits that the two years of work had reaped for him, he decided that he had had enough help. The justification for this was a bit disingenuous, for, while he was now contemplating pursuing a career of free-lance roving journalism, he harked back to an earlier discussion in the analysis. At that time he had expressed some anxiety that the analytic resolution of infantile conflicts might adversely affect his poetic inspiration. I had agreed at that time that it was an issue about which my experience was too limited to express any contrary conviction. My private thought, which I have eventually shared with him, is that balking at the threshold of the depressive position (as I think he was contemplating), might certainly damp creative thought for reasons that the following material illustrates.

Shortly after his return from Nicaragua, in the midst of his pleasure at writing so well, with such ease, and at far greater length than he had expected, the following dream arrested his attention. In the dream *he was defecating but gold and silver coins were mixed up with his feces.* This rather surprised him for money-making had never been a passion. Yet he could see the implication: journalistic productivity that brought in the money was not the same as poetic inspiration, which certainly did not. Two weeks later an even more arresting dream appeared, in the context of his having made a definite decision to stop the analysis on the eve of his departure for his next, and far more protracted, journalistic venture. *There was a house, large but not particuarly grand, at the top of some monumental steps, like the Spanish Steps, and on a balcony high up were the surviving members of the family of a man who had committed suicide. The house was to be taken over and converted, perhaps to a pub or museum and the architect was explaining to him some of the problems of conversion. The patient himself was particularly concerned with the task that would confront them, of removing from the steps all the political slogans that had been daubed on to them. But the architect assured him that this was no problem, for they had a new method. This involved painting some substance over the daubings which, when it dried, enabled them to lift whole sheets of the paint off, revealing the stone beneath.* The patient commented that the pavements and walls in Nicaragua were daubed with slogans, one of them being 'A Nicaraguan is worth dying for.' I thought that our problem had to do with what was worth living for, and that political slogans, which are intended to make creative thought unnecessary, are the stuff of which the steps to mental suicide are paved. What impressed me most about the dream was the way in which the slogans which hide the truth of the enduring stone beneath, also hide the monumental beauty of the steps in development — that is, evolution rather than revolution.

In Chapter IX of *Studies in Extended Metapsychology* I described some clinical material which seemed to suggest that lies do not destroy the truth in the mind but only obscure it. This material is another example and would seem to be a tribute to the 'new method' of psycho-analytic inquiry, into language usage and dreams, which enable the lies to be 'lifted off'. But it is also a testimony to the Keatsian dictum, 'Beauty is truth, truth beauty'. Whether it is 'all ye know on earth and all ye need to know' is another matter. But I would agree that 'the great beauty of Poetry is, that it makes every thing every place interesting —' (letter to George and Georgiana Keats, September 1819).

This seemingly banal statement about poetry and the power of its aesthetic impact, that it makes everything interesting, I take to mean 'makes it food for thought'. This seems to me to be the nub of the matter, the core of my thesis. The most adequate description of 'passion' would seem to be that our emotions are engaged in such a way that love, hate and the yearning for understanding are all set in motion. The quantity or intensity can be disregarded. It is the consortium that is essential. Many objects and events arouse one or the other; we love this, hate that, wish to understand the other. Our passions are not engaged. Our interest is in abeyance; we wish to engage with the object of love, to avoid or destroy the object of hate, to master the object that challenges our understanding. But when we encounter something that engages our *interest*, when we see it as a fragment or instance or sample of the beauty of the world, we wish to ascertain its authenticity, to know it in depth. And at

143

that moment we encounter the 'heart of (its) mystery', along with the severe limitations in our capacities for knowledge. We enter upon the realms of science and art, the cathedral of the mind hidden in the forest of the world.

The emotional flavour of our passions, of awe and wonder, surely become jaded with time. I do not refer to the crushing of passion by the child's education in and out of the family, from which he has an opportunity of recovery in adolescence. I mean rather the filling-up of the apparatus of interest and questioning by the bombardment of explanation to which we are subjected, by science today as by religion in the past. The double-helix type of discovery dispels the 'cloud of unknowing'; fatigue and the yearning for comfort reach out for such explanatory morsels, without noticing that the little bit of nourishment they offer is accompanied by a strong dose of the lotus. Whereas to see with passionate eyes is to see the Poetry.

This is the solipsistic plight; its depth of loneliness fosters the urge for communication, the need to share, the hunger for intimacy, to say what can be said — and to show what cannot.

9 The Retreat from Aesthetic Conflict: Cynicism, Perversity and the Vulgarisation of Taste

Freud's discovery of the key to masochism, which he described so wonderfully in 'A Child is Being Beaten', awaited the recognition by Melanie Klein of the mechanism (phantasy) of projective identification to give it clear clinical application. The deviousness of the masochistic manoeuvre and its close connection with virginal anxieties leaves very little doubt that when in the fixed pattern (rather than its reversible form of sado-masochism), whether of sexual perversity or of more social and moral variants (or extrapolations), it is the masochist whose phantasy life calls the tune. By its nature, masochistic longing easily finds its partner, because brutality is so common a feature in character or so easily provoked. But more important than this ease of enactment, is the fact that the participation of the sadist does not require so complex a phantasy but lends itself to the simple acting out of the social processes of our hierarchic structures, based as they are on tyranny and submission, privilege and obedience.

The masochistic manoeuvre, then, involves a complicated process of splitting and projective identification, similar to that found in the hypochondriac and depressive states. The primal (infantile) phantasy is, as Freud discovered, that a (rival) child is being beaten (to death). In the enactment of this phantasy, through splitting and projective identification with the mother-containing-the-new-baby, the masochist enjoys (as observer) a double role, of both mother and baby. He/she, the observer, enjoys vicariously, as in a film, the spectacle of a mother submitting to a brutal sexual assault, ranging from rape to so-called love-making, in which the baby is destroyed (aborted, miscarried). The drama may be augmented in its interest by ambiguity in the motives of the mother, cf. to sacrifice one child to save the others (*Sophie's Choice*) or to save herself (*Mother Courage?*). Further entertaining complications can be introduced by the observer entering into the situation, offering him/herself

145

as victim, particularly as the baby (*A Tale of Two Cities*).

This much of the metapsychology of sado-masochism can be construed from the Kleinian model. Its conjunction with social processes, and in particular the hierarchic structure of Basic Assumption Groups, rests on Bion's work. But the theory of aesthetic conflict adds another facet: the new baby as aesthetic object. Not merely can it be seen to have the import of an aesthetic object, but the mother-baby unit may be suspected of playing the role of prototype of all aesthetic objects. How this can be, would bear further investigation; but at this point one can at least say from clinical experience that the economic role of sado-masochism within the total personality has the significance of vandalism. By destroying the prototype it is possible to destroy, at least temporarily, the capacity to apprehend beauty and to be impinged upon by aesthetic conflict. A young woman, married and with children, had entered analysis because of her inability to resolve the conflict over a deep split in her relationships to family and to a lover. Slim and waifish, intelligent, highly verbal, with a soft voice and pleasant Spanish accent, she displayed from the beginning a subtle and complex capacity to be pleasing. The material she brought was rich, she was thoughtful and attentive in response to interpretation, seemed to bear well the processes of de-idealization of herself which the early period of analysis involved, and generated an atmosphere of unaggressive, uninsistent erotism. The presenting conflict, of loving two men, soon dissolved into a far more complex configuration.

She had been born in a South American country with a brutally tyrannical regime, and her parents had emigrated for political reasons when she was eight years of age. Despite high intelligence, lack of interest made her a poor scholar in childhood, prone to be curled up with a book and her thumb. Although her family had not been touched directly by the Nazi holocaust, the similarity, and potentialities, of the regime of her native country seem to have been vivid to her in early childhood as part of the family culture. She had married early a man only slightly older, a loving and successful marriage among the bourgeois intelligentsia. But her own lack of education, career, personal status and intellectual achievement had begun to trouble her as soon as her first child was born. Her gift of tongues soon took her out into the world of left-wing politics connected with refugees from her native land, into an organization which seemed democratic and cultural in its revolutionary aims, but which she suspected of having a secret terrorist wing. She promptly found herself, to her amazement, having an affair with one of the leaders, which she soon broke off.

But it was not very long before she fell in love with another, former leader of the group, and commenced an affair which had lasted several years by the time she came to analysis. The clandestinity, the hairy bigness and violent sexuality of her lover marked this relationship so sharply from the tender child-oriented one with her husband that she felt very little conflict, particularly as the mores of the political group, headed by rather wealthy and upper-class people from her native country, quite encouraged such relations. Only the clandestinity, on which her lover insisted, seemed a bit at variance with this group ethos.

The early work in the analysis, particularly the investigation of her pleasing ways, yielded the first major stroke of de-idealization, for dreams revealed that her much admired social ease and flexibility was in fact the consequence of a very shallow, two-dimensional chameleon quality based on keen observation and automatic mimicry of social behaviour. The pliability with which she 'fitted in' to the analytic method and situation being thus instanced as shallow, we could discover more of her less conscious motives for coming to analysis. She expected that I would take a dim view of her unfaithfulness to her husband and the jeopardy to the family that it implied, but would very gently win her away from her lover. By what means? By becoming her third lover? No, by making her feel protected. Against what? Dreams gave the answer promptly. In a series of dreams she was confronted with political upheaval and chaos, unprotected by husband or father, in fear for her children, not for herself. The political group had somehow provided this sense of safety, that she was carrying the flags of both revolution and status quo and would be able to wave the appropriate one in times of danger. But she was discovering that she did not like or trust the people of the political group and in her dreams they only afforded her limited or grudging protection from the upheaval, like accommodation in a grubby attic room, unpleasantly reminiscent of the room of the clandestine rendezvous.

So clearly the analyst was not expected to introduce her into another grubby room of secret sexuality, but rather to educate her, belatedly, to take her as protégé in the fortified community of psycho-analysis. This was quite difficult to understand, for she knew very well that psycho-analysis had been an object of vicious attack by the regime in her native country and that many analysts had been forced to flee for the safety of their adolescent children. Nonetheless, in this atmosphere of safety which the analysis seemed to afford her temporarily, she found the courage to withdraw from the political group, despite pressure from the leaders. And it seemed that she was about to break with her lover, despite my insistence that it was only the infantile aspects of that relationship which came under scrutiny in the transference, and that I had no way of forming an opinion about the value of adult aspects, especially her apparent love for this man. Indeed the patient had brought such sparse material about the quality of that relationship and the sexual activity that I had very little means of defining even its infantile aspects.

The patient's dreams now became quite consistently anxious: chickens were in danger from a fox; her children were in danger; frightening men turned up at the door of her home. But for contrast she was also, in one dream, Sally Bowles, in Soho rather than Berlin, the Sally of *Cabaret*, vulgar and excited, rather than Isherwood's or Julie Harris's touching waif of *I am a Camera*. In the first session of the week she was rather irritable and anxious. She did not like the area in which my consulting room was located as it had unpleasant and degrading erotic connections with her first lover. She felt angry with her husband for suspecting nothing and with the analyst for not giving her clear-cut directions. She was going to meet her lover for the first time in some weeks and felt frightened of him in some vague way.

The following session she reported, with some anger, that her lover had raised the possibility of his getting Aids from her, but she had 'courageously' defended herself reminding him that she had had no other lover for some years, that her husband was completely faithful to her, and anyhow, the lover himself was the promiscuous one. It seemed quite in keeping with the 'Sally

Bowles' dream that she should defend herself like a whore who was being challenged to produce her medical certificate; but her lack of sense of degradation by the challenge and her satisfaction with having defended herself seemed quite mystifying, to me initially, but to herself as well once I had pointed it out to her. The dream and other material of the next session threw a sharp light on this question.

The patient entered the next session looking very anxious, saying that she was very shaken by a 20 year old daughter of a neighbour coming to her to confide that she was going to kill herself. Despite having taken all the necessary steps to contact the girl's parents and practitioner and to take away the pills the girls had with her, my patient still felt full of responsibility, that she should have stayed with the girl instead of coming to her session, as she would if one of her own children were ill. I suggested that, in keeping with recent dreams, we have better try to find out in what way her own babies were really in danger. She then told the following dream from the night before:

> she seemed to be on a deserted country road waiting for a bus, but rather frightened that the last bus had already departed. Then a bus did come along and stop, but did not open its doors. However when she rapped on the glass, the driver opened for her. Inside she found a slim, cream-coloured whippet that immediately cuddled up to her and that was comforting. Later she seemed to be at a farm, viewing a peaceful scene of cream-coloured cows and their calves although in fact looking more like deer than cows, quite beautiful. But up on an overlooking hill was a group of the nastiest of the political group's members and she felt threatened by them.

I suggested that the rapping for entry was connected with the 'courageous' way she had dealt with her lover's challenge about Aids in order to claim her right to exhibit her cream-coloured bottom, with its masochistic sign, 'whip it', to arouse him as her protector from the group and its evil designs against cow-mothers and their calf-babies. Confusion between her buttocks and mummy's breasts seemed implied by the cream-coloured aspect, claiming that by drawing away the enemy penis from the breasts to her bottom she was protecting the babies rather than enacting an attack upon them, as in her seduction of the lover to undertake a sadistic role. Thus the dream claimed that

149

she was behaving 'courageously' in the socio-political context ('Mother Courage'?) rather than masochistically in an intimate venue. The trouble seemed to be that she was doing both, and that the primitive social anxieties thus compounded and sanctified her perversity.

It is not, of course, immediately apparent that this involves a type of geographical confusion, because the psychic spaces involved are not very specifically defined by the material. Rather it is the confusion between the areas of social (casual, contractual, basic assumption) activities and that of intimate relations which stands out. But analytical experience tells us that these areas or modes of activity and relationships have their particular spatial reference, as was discussed in the earlier chapters on violence as a violation-of-private-spaces concept. It seems a cogent view that tyrannical social systems have a psychic reality reference to the internal mother's rectum, presided over by Milton's Fallen Angels under the slogan of perversity, 'Better to rule in Hell than serve in Heaven'. Entry into this space is represented in the dream by rapping on the door (anal masturbation) of the unexpected bus that appears when the last bus has already gone (when mummy and daddy have withdrawn for the night and the child feels unprotected she discovers her accommodating bottom). By contrast the mother's breast and genital areas are represented by the farm with its cows and calves, cream-coloured, and the implied but absent daddy-bull. This scene is said to be very beautiful, but note that the cows and calves look more deer-like than bovine. Has the aesthetic of cows and calves been tampered with? Have we in view rather the twee creatures of Bambi and Babycham, kiddy-porn, as I am inclined to call them? Cute, pretty, diminutized — and vulgarized!

This close relationship between perversity — that is, the caricaturing of the love relationship by sado-masochism — and pornography, has already been somewhat explored, in its social implications, in the dialogue with Adrian Stokes (see Addendum I). That statement, from the 1960's, prefigures the present exploration of aesthetic conflict but can now be amplified by the more precise conception of aesthetic object. The baby's aesthetic experience of the breast-feeding relationship would seem to bring into existence (in the manner described by Bion of an innate preconception mating so fully with realization that a conception is created) two objects of a combined nature: baby-and-breast, nipple-and-breast; the latter casting its shadow forward to eventuate in an image of a hidden and essentially mysterious Nuptial Chamber of the parental intercourse. It is an indispensable aspect of the conceptual machinery that this coitus should be shrouded, behind the veil of awe and wonder for the child, to be discovered in maturity through the workings of introjective identification in the context of a passionate (love-hate-knowing) relationship of one's own.

These three objects, baby-and-breast, breast-and-nipple, parental-couple-in-their-nuptial-chamber, have the extraordinary quality of being both concrete and symbolic, that is, serving as containers of ever-increasing meaning. The manner in which this abundance is gradually packed into these objects-as-symbols would seem to be a function of the myth-making capacity of the individual, augmented by the art-world. Fairy-tales, stories of cultural heroes and religious mythology are the traditional means, with their graphic, musical and dance modes of expression by which the individual imagination is augmented from the earliest days of childhood. In more recent times political ideologies and the mass media make their more dubious contributions.

The techniques by which the aesthetic of these objects is attacked by perversity are, in the present material, far from subtle in their graphic mode: the baby is diminutized and made fragile (the calves turned into the twee cream-coloured little deer which the patient described as 'fragile'), the breast is erotized by being separated from the nipple and equated with the buttocks (the cream-coloured whip-it) and the veil of privacy of the nuptial chamber is rent (procreation altered to trans-mission of venereal disease — Aids at present, as syphilis in the past). The verbal techniques are more subtle and the musical ones are beyond my capacity to explore.

Perhaps another example might serve to fill out this differen-tiation. A university student, good-looking and vain, supercili-ous in demeanour and uncertain in his sexual orientation, brought 'the most beautiful dream (he) had ever had'. It was connected with a pretty Japanese girl in his college whom he fancied. He was hopeful of making a relationship with her. In the dream:

151

he and the girl had been collected from the airport by her industrialist father and were being driven to the family home. They drove along a beautiful coastal cliff-side road, winding through coves and inlets. He noticed two large pipes which kept appearing above ground and then going beneath again, assuming they carried water and perhaps gas. But as they turned to drive up a valley he saw that the pipes came to an end and one was spewing forth brown sewage into the cove beneath. Further up this splendid valley he saw a Samurai castle but was told it was a power station disguised. He thought this a good idea. Then the country opened out into terraced paddy fields with natives in conical hats working, all bathed in golden light so that even the sky looked yellow. And finally they saw the family home, a huge modern structure on a hilltop, obviously extremely well architected with balconies and ribbon windows with flowing curtains. He was told that two families dwelt there and once inside he was turned over to the daughter of the other family to be shown about while his girlfriend changed. This other girl showed him the view of the beach where swimmers could be seen and she said he could bathe too if he'd brought his swim suit. But he had not and asked if he could buy one, although not at all keen on swimming. The girl said there were two types, one costing thousands of yen but a cheap khaki type worn by the police that cost only six dollars. When his girlfriend returned her hair was done in an extraordinary way, all in thin plaits tied round with white ribbon and pulled to one side, slightly Medusa-like.

The impression this made on me was of the glossy travel brochure and the patient agreed that it might be, as he had been into Thomas Cook's that day looking at them. I knew that he'd been studying nineteenth century poetry and was stuck by features referrable to Kublai Khan ('Alph the sacred river', i.e. the River Alpheus — pipes, and the 'pleasure dome') and he added the painting of Diana and Endymion on the cover of the Penguin *Keats*. The Medusa was perhaps also a reference to Caravaggio, whose work he greatly admires, partly for its perverse elements. He had in fact been impotent with his previous girlfriend, and was consciously averse to the female genital. All in all, pipes, power station, travel brochure glossiness, the yellow (urinous) sky and peasants to do all the work, the atmosphere of luxury, aristocracy and indolence, the repellant hair-do and the unwillingness to pay the price in yens (yearnings), preferring the cheap khaki of the police (fecal penis of perversity?), seemed all to catch the passivity and perversity in his character with which the analysis had been preoccupied and for which he sought treatment to begin with.

It was of special interest that after fighting the interpretation for a while he became silent and thoughtful, then became quite lyrical about Keats's Odes and about an exhibition of Claude landscapes he had recently seen. It all seemed a brilliant exposition of the way in which perversity seeps into the apprehension of beauty to corrupt the judgment and produce bad taste.

This vulgarization of taste can be contrasted with the type of blunting of sensibilities demonstrated by the lady of the 'dropped typewriter' dream. An austere orthodox education in a small community devoid of cultural opportunities would appear to have crushed the latent passionate nature, probably from a very early age, for she was the last of a large family born at a time when the parents' relationship had withdrawn into mutual silence. Her greedy and exploitive attitude was just as innocent as the naïveté with which she had for many years allowed herself to be exploited in the name of charity and good works. When the beauty of the world broke upon her, an astonishing and admirable blossoming took place, in her appearance, her interests, her social capabilities.

A more disturbing story from a man in middle age illustrates the corrupting inroads of cynicism and hypocrisy that perversity brings in its wake. He had come to analysis in desperation about the periodic outbreak of homosexual involvements, coupled with an inability to deepen a relationship with any woman since the failure of his brief marriage some fifteen years earlier. Although a prosperous businessman with his own firm, he harboured a secret yearning to throw it all up to train as a psychotherapist, hoping that the analysis could really effect sufficient change in his sexual and intimate life to make this possible. He had been the eldest of three boys of immigrant parents, the father a successful restauranteur and the mother a beautiful but submissive woman. The father had left the family when my patient was in puberty. Despite his bemoaning the lack of a strong and good father, the evidence of the analysis, in which his argumentativeness was the most prominent, and exhausting, item, strongly suggested that, as gang leader of the boys, he had driven his father out of the family and usurped his prerogatives.

It became gradually clear that his relationships with women, although completely asexual, were covertly cruel. Being rather handsome and charming, he repeatedly aroused the desires and expectations of the women he encountered, eventually to greet their urgent advances with kindly big-brother types of patronization and helpfulness. Mainly they were women who did not at all attract him, unmarried and of his own age. But that he was both intensely attracted to feminine beauty and frightened of such women came to light over 'the woman who glows in the dark', a patient of another therapist whom he regularly encountered at the consulting rooms. She was indeed an extraordinarily beautiful young woman, but so also was one of his new secretaries. As the Easter holiday approached this young woman, who had left his employ because of difficulties with an older member of staff, became the object of his big-brotherly attentions. But at the same time he had been contacted by a former homosexual companion who invited him to spend the holiday in Paris.

All attempts to demonstrate the evidence that acting out was both in progress and incipient brought his argumentativeness to a new pitch of talent and ingenuity. Just before leaving he heard the news that the wife of the brother of his friend in Paris was expecting a baby and also that his best friends in London were likewise expecting. These news filled him both with hope and with loneliness. He returned after the two week break triumphant that no homosexual activity had occurred, except in dreams, but saddened that the baby of the Paris couple had been stillborn. On his return he had taken the former secretary to dinner and had gone home to meet her family consisting of mother and two elder sisters, one married with two children. He also brought a dream which became the storm centre for the next three weeks' work.

In the dream *his former wife, Clara, had become married to some foreign man and already had two little girls and a new baby girl. But it was ill and Clara seemed to be drugged and indifferent, while her husband was unavailable. So the patient had to arrange everything to get the baby and Clara to the hospital. There the nurse was also so indifferent that he slapped her and showed her that the baby had purple welts all over the lower half of its body and was in a desperate state. Eventually the baby died, to everyone's relief, for it was suffering terribly.*

It seemed clear that there was a strong connection between the children of Clara in the dream and the former secretary, who was the youngest of three daughters. Also the slapping of the nurse made it certain that the purple welts implied battering, and had a link to the stillborn Parisian baby.

My interpretation of the dream and its context was that he had acted out, by tantalizing the former secretary, something that had the significance of battering a baby girl to death inside his analytic mummy-wife who 'glows in the dark'. This crime was covered by the hypocrisy of being the good shepherd who looks after mummy because daddy is unavailable during the holiday. This had an immediate explosive effect: argument, accusations, threats to leave the analysis and, that night, defiantly flamboyant dreams of fellatio with his hairdresser. For the next three weeks a struggle ensued, in the course of which he swung from persecuted accusations to arrogant boasting about his manliness, his genital, that his masturbation was a greater pleasure than any woman could afford him because no woman really appreciates the beauty of a man's penis, etc.

Into this atmosphere of combat a dream brought a ray of deeper understanding which was, in its turn, resisted for the next two months until shortly before the summer break.

In this dream he seemed to be leading his two brothers through a large department store with the intention of going out a rear door. The store seemed to be wedge-shaped, narrowing towards the back, where he found his free passage obstructed by three women, one trying on shoes, a second serving her and the third looking on. When the women ignored his request to move out of his way, he angrily grabbed the pair of shoes, stuffed them under his jumper and marched on. But a store detective stopped him. Then the scene in the dream changed. He was watching a ballerina, dancing on points, and was told that she used to be a man but had had a sex-change operation.

It seemed reasonable to link the points of the sex-changed ballerina with the shoes under the jumper. That he conceded. But he would not allow that he was misusing the department store as a shortcut and that he therefore had no right-of-way. I suggested that it implied using the analysis as a shortcut to

155

becoming a psychotherapist as equivalent to a sex change operation, by smash-and-grab methods, without any real change in his character. He had not expected to encounter a store-detective-daddy who would not be driven from the home by his argumentativeness. Nor, for that matter, had it occurred to him that a mummy who 'glowed in the dark' might be very difficult to dominate, even with his gang of little homosexual brothers. Clearly the analyst was meant to be like the hairdresser of his dream and join in his exaltation of his penis to the role of prototype aesthetic object. The underlying envy of women's compelling beauty is revealed in the sex-change part of the dream in which the shoes under the jumper clearly signify the points of the ballerina-breast as the true prototype, or, more correctly, if we link it with the 'battered little girl' dream, the breast-and-baby as combined aesthetic prototype.

The implication of this material for our understanding of the aesthetic conflict is very poignant. The parents making love in their Nuptial Chamber stand in relation to the baby-at-the-breast as noumenon to phenomenon, as the sun, that cannot be looked upon directly, does to the shadows on the cave wall, which can be.

But even granting that we are all in the same position, looking at the phenomena, with no prophet to gaze at the noumenon or talk directly with God, must we stand helpless before 'de gustibus'? I do not mean that we must find means for debate about aesthetic values. Nothing could be less profitable. But there must be means by which we can learn to defend ourselves against the external, but particularly the internal, forces that generate the vulgarization of taste. The problem is a very difficult one, for one would like to be able to rely on one's own judgment, to think for oneself, but a little introspective attention quickly reveals how dependent we tend to be on received values. We are slaves to fashion; we do look at the name on the frame before we really expose ourselves to the painting; we do read the critics, much as we despise their tyranny and sycophancy; we do have great difficulty distinguishing price from value, rarity from preciousness, antiquity from artistry. So powerful and subtle are the fears of being out-of-step and so attractive the coziness of snobbery in its myriad forms, that we shrink from the problem. Or else we deceive ourselves by the adolescent technique of equating opposition to fashion with independence of judgment.

There, of course, lies the whole burden of this book: the recognition of aesthetic conflict. To have aesthetic experiences we must first expose ourselves to ravishment by the external formal qualities of the object. Then we must grapple with our doubts and suspicions about its internal qualities. Since this conflict relates only to the mind of man and man's products, the great avenue of relief is to expose ourselves to the beauty of nature. Unless even in that area we are concerned to 'justify God's ways to men', we can look upon the volcano in eruption as a magnificent spectacle — from a safe distance. But even so we have to travel to the highest mountains, the open sea, the utter desert wastes to find nature untouched by the hand of man and his intentions and judgment. Some thousands of years of sylviculture, agriculture, horticulture and animal husbandry have surrounded us with modifications of nature, training her creatures to the will, use and taste of man. Even the virginity of the skies is deflowered by jet trails, when it is not obscured by smog. The bluest sky with the loveliest clouds may be tainted with radio-activity. There is no gainsaying it, we live our lives amidst man-shaped aesthetic and man-fashioned vulgarity. Censorship, government control, legislation, societies for the protection of this and that: these are all instruments of tyranny in the wrong hands. And where are the right hands? No, the artists must teach us how to protect ourselves from the vulgarizing influences and our mothers must help us to bear the conflict from its very inception.

Yet artists and mothers give ambiguous messages which we may use or misuse. A major factor in this balance of use/misuse has not been clearly indicated as yet, but it is surely close to the bone in everyone as a factor in turning away from the aesthetic experience. Pride, which cannot tolerate the aesthetic impact in the absence of reciprocity, can immediately call up cynical attacks on the object of aesthetic apprehension to reduce its force.

A woman in her late fifties, handsome in a rather masculine way, had come to analysis after a highly successful professional career, thinking to shift her interests on retirement, but also suffering from a recent bereavement. After a year we both

157

found ourselves puzzled by the waxing and waning of her enthusiasm and participation in the analysis. It did not seem to correspond to the infantile transference but more to the level of her intellectual and emotional engagement to psychoanalysis as a field of study and work. One evening she went to a public lecture on psychoanalysis and came to the next day's session in a state of enthralment, partly with the presentation by the speaker, but mainly by the glimpse she had caught of the beauty and grandeur of the psychoanalytical method and view of life. But the next session it was gone; one of her doldrums had set in. So the week passed but to the first session of the following week she brought a dream that opened the retreat to scrutiny.

In the dream *she was a Greek warrior of Iliad days complete with helmet, greaves and shield and part of an army that was secretly invading Great Britain, perhaps by parachute. But what was clear was that each soldier had to make his way secretly to Loch Lomond where a huge black box had been hidden long before containing all the supplies, weapons and ammunition they would need for their conquest.* She had never been to Loch Lomond, though she knew it was a famous beauty spot. She had visited Loch Marie, which is also her middle name. Perhaps there was some reference to Holy Loch where the Polaris submarines are based. Then she suddenly thought of a recent news story about the discovery that heroin was being smuggled into Great Britain in great quantities by tourists who swallowed amazingly large condoms full of the stuff, shown in a photo as black. I hardly needed to interpret the dream at this point, as the Trojan Horse technique for destroying the beauty of her experience of psychoanalysis was clearly revealed. The patient could promptly fill in the details.

Following the ecstatic session she reported, she had begun to feel humiliated at being one-of-the-crowd of worshippers and had consciously begun to rubbish the experience, the speaker, the method, the theories. Once it had started she was 'hooked' and could neither stop it nor recover.

10   Recovery of the Aesthetic Object

Surely it is a rare thing in the development of a child for the original passionate response to the beauty of the world and of the mother, her breast and her face as the objects of its passion (but also the symbols of the experience), to remain un-diminished. The various stations in development at which the sensibility to beauty and the engagement in the aesthetic conflict are partially, or sometimes totally, sacrificed can be arranged in a characteristic list: prolonged separations, physical illnesses, weaning, birth of the next baby, the advent of social experiences (crèche, school, etc.) To this list of experiences which have a certain traumatic impact we must add the great continual factor of the family culture. Every family is divided in its ethos to some extent between the task of helping children to develop their individuality and the intention of training them for obedience to the adaptational demands of the community at large. This pressure towards obedience, sanctified as it is in all sorts of irrefutable ways, offers the child a ready-made escape from feeling and thinking for himself. The most striking example is the loss of imagination and emotional vibrance in the latency period of adaptation to the requirements of school-type education.

Analytic experience seconds these pessimistic expectations; regardless of the absence of psychopathology or the excellence of character of patients or candidates, the blunting of sensibilities and the narrowing of the range of emotionality is demonstrated. In the process of their recovery the damping of responsiveness and joy becomes apparent even if invisible beforehand. In the course of the analysis of a large percentage of our patients, who have come to analysis for reasons of character rather than symptomatology of a debilitating sort, the recovery of aesthetic sensibilities is of a rather quiet nature, having a noticeable crescendo only at the theshold of the depressive position and during the weaning process. But in more ill patients or those in whom the denial of psychic reality has become very extensive and with whom acting out is so persistent in analysis (in which category we can safely include patients with strong addictive and perverse trends), the recovery of the aesthetic object and the experience of aesthetic conflict is far more abrupt, at times quite explosive. But, of course, it is these patients who show us the nature of the process most clearly, and by implication — in reverse, as it were — demonstrate how the original loss of sensibility took place.

The analytic process with such patients tends to come to a very turgid impasse at the theshold of the depressive position and to end either in mutual exhaustion, compromise or in mutual idealization of the undoubted advances. On the occasions when determination on both sides resolutely pushes beyond this impasse, the catastrophic situation against which the impasse had been ranged soon makes itself felt. The danger of suicide is too manifest to be denied its relation to the analytic process. Not so when the catastrophe takes a psychosomatic form. The mysteriousness of such events invites the analyst to deny the connection. For after all, we are sincerely intent on helping our patients to live, not on killing them with good intentions. I am going to report on the analysis of a young woman which I had the pleasure of hearing about on two successive occasions a year apart because it seems to illustrate all of these aspects: the overcoming of denial of psychic reality, the struggle with perverse sexual trends, and above all the crisis of seeking individual identity outside the 'dear octopus' of a rigidly bourgeois family culture. In the course of these developments the catastrophic change appears to be taking the form of a psychosomatic development of disseminated sclerosis and gives every promise of a tragic outcome.

This young woman came to analysis at the age of twenty-seven complaining of confusional states, difficulty in thinking, inability to relate to her child or her husband. She had married young 'without conviction', had a daughter soon after and in the subsequent years acquired first a sadistic lover and later a youthful 'cavaliere servente' to add to her sexual partnership with the husband with whom she stayed 'for convenience'. This configuration faithfully repeated the pattern of her childhood with two elder brothers and her father, where a fierce competition had reigned with her mother. Six years of analysis had wrought very considerable changes in her ability to think, to feel, to learn and to work as the analytic transference gradually expanded from one of blatant envious competition and acting out to a more ambivalent state. I will now report verbatim in translation the second presentation in September, 1987 with my commentary on each session. The analyst is Signora Giuditta Alberio of Novara, in Piemonte.

Introduction

It seems to me that during this intense and painful seventh year of analysis there has been a further evolution in our analytical relationship.

My patient's psychopathy, her continuous acting-out and her falsity seem to have toned down to make room for an intense analytical relation, marked by pain, desperation and hatred, paralleled by the development of a solid and sound relationship with the analyst.

In February, during some sessions in which she appears to be overwhelmed by very strong and primitive emotions, as if she was lacking an apparatus allowing her to modulate and filter anxiety, she was unable to remain reclining; she had to sit on the couch or crouch down on the little carpet nearby, flinging away in rage her wrist watch, which she then picked up, crawling on all fours.

She was upset by ideas of jealousy referring to her lover and to a sister-in-law that were almost delusional.

She had been complaining about motor troubles for some time: she loses her balance, she stumbles, one of her legs fails, she falls while running.

Around the end of February she was hospitalized for diagnostic checks; the results showed no evidence either of a brain tumor or a plaque sclerosis.

She was discharged from hospital after a diagnosis of functional disturbances. Even if diminished, however, her difficulties remained, and in June, following the advice of another neurologist who feared these are symptoms of a disseminated sclerosis, she was hospitalized once more for more specific tests (magnetic resonance, evoked potentials) that unfortunately confirmed the neurologist's fears.

The present material starts from the third session after the last discharge from hospital and includes the four last sessions prior to the start of the analyst's summer holiday.

Friday 26th June 1987

(Her face is twisted and drawn; since she is back from the hospital she comes to the sessions wearing very short shorts and a tee shirt, looking as if she was in her panties. She throws herself down on the couch.)

Patient: Do you know something? It seems to me that this girl (herself), so dependent, so fragile and neurotic, is in fact a little less so than other people, less than my family for instance, 'fuck', what a family, they have ruined me and are incapable of helping me.

(With a steadily growing fury, a tone of voice growing more and more acute and determined, sitting on the couch, she starts shouting, expressing a very violent rage against her people, particularly her mother, who apparently are reacting as if they were unconcerned about her illness.)

Patient: Even if mummy's face was twisted last Sunday and even if I was able to cry with her second brother, later on everything seemed to be running along just as usual.

Mummy was paying no attention when I talked to her, since she and Granny were watching 'Crystal Hell' on television; and besides Mummy worries about Granny's health, the health of an old thing, and called my doctor but asked nothing about her daughter's health. I say NOTHING! (shouting) How I would worry and ask to be informed if *my* daughter was ill! (and she goes on shrieking with unrestrained violence).

Analyst: (Only when she gives me a chance, I am able to remark, with great difficulty, on these experiences of hers as expressions of something that she wants to convey to me, just as if a part of herself was shouting her pain, her fear and her rage [the summer break is also getting near] at a mummy-analyst whom she fears is unconcerned, distant or likely to leave her alone.)

(She lay down once more: later on she will get up to take a handkerchief.)

Patient: Yes, terribly alone (her voice has got quieter), do

162

you see, I am afraid that you may refuse to put up with my rage and my anxiety, as everybody else is doing; do you see, as a reward for being strong, for going on working even while in pain, I would like to have a place where I could give up fighting, where people would understand how fear and pain are frightful . . . I am scared of progressive paralysis . . . oh, don't you understand how I found myself in a neurotic family; I have come to analysis to try and get out of it and now I find myself this way, I wish I had understood this earlier!

It is almost unbearable. Of course I am scared! I don't know whether I feel enraged about the summer break because I know that it is that way; in fact I feel grateful to you because you have always behaved well about this story and moreover you give me this moment in which I can pull everything out, even if I am not fondled nor have anybody close to me, at least I am allowed to talk.

And if I am thinking again of M (her lover) since yesterday . . . do you see I have a new dress, it is a beautiful one, my husband bought it for me; he now has a little more money. I too, since I am through with paying my share for my parent's house . . . now I shall have to save it for medical treatments.

I shall now go to G. where they have a specialized centre for plaque sclerosis.

What this disease does to you! It shrinks you, perhaps you become spastic. Of course, I might live from 25 to 30 years longer; I might become old; it is as if old age was quicker to come, do you see?

In short I would like to see M, I don't know whether he would be able to see me, they told me he is down-hearted, he is not well: he might represent life, as you said: he is vital . . . I have lost my battle and this time it wasn't the disease . . . you should know; you know if a disease is caused by a state of psychic illness, perhaps by a decrease of defences, perhaps you know.

If it is that way it means that I haven't been strong enough; I am desperate; frankly I am desperate and I am clinging to you. I am sorry to be heavy, but I don't know what to do about it. You must not leave me, you mustn't, please, don't leave me, think of what it means to be so disappointed in my

163

family which I always considered a protection. Think of my love which now is useless . . . everything is too big, too awful, don't leave me alone, don't leave me, let me come here . . .

Analyst: This fear was already present during the past sessions.

Patient: You too perhaps cannot stand a sick person, just as other people cannot, and, as I was telling my daughter, if a person is near you and is feeling ill one cannot help feeling guilty and run away.

Now that I am really ill I do my best to pretend I am alright, as I did when I went to the tavern and I drank a glass of wine and was cheerful, I was saying, now that I am so clever I will no longer go to hell . . . (it was a fantasy of hers about a pleasant hell, a prize for the wicked, as she used to tell M). It is as if I was paying, I don't know how, for this thing of avoiding going off my head, of going on joking, this thing of being very clever, and I expect the others to understand, and it is as if the others ignored it instead, welcoming my 'mature' behaviour . . . my head turns . . . you know that sclerosis causes psychic disorders? such as loss of memory and other things.

I ask you one thing, you wanted to help me to live, you wanted to help me to live longer . . . I have been through all that pain and anxiety and I got somewhat tired of all the things that suck you back . . .

Commentary

This session, the last of the penultimate week prior to the analyst's holiday, is as complete and dramatic as the first act of a Chekov play. Our heroine, dressed like a small child, may be dying or facing progressive incapacity. Or is it all part of her mental disorder, intrinsic to the analysis? Or is the analysis killing her instead of helping her to live better? She is in a rage with her family for their apparent indifference, with the analyst for persisting in her routine holiday plans, with her lover for his lack of availability, all unrelieved by her husband buying her a pretty dress. Her feeling is that the analysis has helped her to rise out of the torpid organization of her family and to become more feeling, but the result is that the culture of the family no longer cocoons her. She springs from the couch, but the analyst's intervention, which merely conveys that her communication/projection has been received and understood, calms the patient.

There follows a clear exposition of the pseudo-maturity upon which basis her social adjustment had been achieved and of the feeling of being cheated and betrayed by the family's intolerance of her infantile needs. A somewhat tentative gratitude to the analyst supervenes but is quickly brushed aside in favour of her relationship to husband, lover, doctors. Soon, however, it returns with a renewed and deeper expression of her dependence on the analyst, full of anxiety about being insupportable in her neediness. The 'cleverness' of her perverse relationship to her lover and the promise of a voluptuously pleasant afterlife in hell now seems just silly.

But the present burden is too much for her to bear alone and death without an afterlife would be a welcome release. Even for that she would need the analyst's support. Towards the end of the session, in counterpoint to the patient's desperation about her family, the analyst had reminded the patient (not in the record) that their relationship to one another is not based on cultural stereotype or ritual but on years of emotional experiences with one another; that they are in a sense in the same boat on a stormy sea, hoping for a haven. This metaphor of the analyst will have far reaching consequences in the following week.

Monday, 29th June
   Patient: Where did I read it? when you were telling me 'as if it did not have skin ... stomach' ... somewhere I read about a being with a new skin, grown in atrocious pains until the skin became stronger ...

Perhaps we were closer, as you told me before I went to the hospital; perhaps you can give me courage and strength helping me to die. Don't give me psychological support, forget about it, you know very well that dying may be something ... when I was suffering for M and was saying 'I would like sclerosis' ... now I would like to die, but my love has changed into an illness that doesn't cause death but causes decay ...

And I see my family for the first time, even if I am

165

exaggerating perhaps . . . where is that cocoon; that warmth, that little corner I always looked for; now I feel like running miles away from my family, of course if I die my daughter will still be there but I wouldn't be available to protect her, but one should not believe oneself to be King Kong.

You might unload me any moment: you may decide to go away, to go to a different country, to a different town, to unload me . . . anything may happen, I am distressed at the idea of being so dependent on you, of needing you so much . . .

Analyst: (remembering and succeeding in reporting what I am returning to her is very difficult; I believe I am talking to her of a reality in which we live and about which we know very little, also trying to return to her the sense of the time we spent together, of the work done which we are still carrying forward. I also talk of this dependence which also has the meaning of a link, with all the experiences that can spring out of it. I also summarize the pain and the drama of these moments as something that we are living together).

Patient: (She cries silently.) Here is why my people hated you so much, they talked about you in such a rage, with such a fear . . .

Analyst: (I collect this material too, as an aspect of what she may experience about me as her analyst, which goes together with other things, opposite in sign, as if we were in a stormy sea together where, however, the possibility of a haven also seems to be present.)

She nods and spends the last minutes in silence.

· Soon after she is gone the bell rings: she left her spectacles. She goes away smiling faintly.

Tuesday 30th June 1987
Patient: After all . . . I don't know . . . (she smiles) I came here with my daughter, to do some shopping for her last Friday afternoon and it was terribly heavy for me; L has gone to collect the clinical reports from the neurologist who perjured himself that everything is just as it was before i.e. that the foci in my brain are more focused to the left. I am ignorant but I have troubles with my left side, therefore I feel they are making a fool of me.

I wanted L to stay with me on Friday night but he went to see a horse show instead and I immediately phoned S (the cavaliere servente). I went out with him, showing the worst of myself, and I was quite staggered afterwards.

I then was to go to the seaside with L on Saturday, and I was very anxious because I was afraid he might not show up. Finally poor L arrived.

It was awful at the seaside, just as if I was an oldish woman who, when she isn't at home. . . . *the sea is beautiful at the Cinque Terre. One had to climb big rocks and there I was, clinging to them, I was afraid . . . the waves scared me . . .* poor L! I illtreated him . . . the motor-cycle was out of order, we had not been able to find a hotel room. I can't bear things that are not perfect and I make L pay for it then; later on we found a hotel room, with twin beds and I went into his bed. He was sleepy; then he said I was wet and it was terrible! L had never refused me before. It was awful! Even if later he looked for me and told me: 'come on, come here', and we made love.

In the morning something painful happened, I had not been sleeping well during the night. I always dream about my illness, about myself and my illness, but I don't remember my dreams . . .

I didn't like the place when we had breakfast; the brioche was tough: I threw it twice on the floor, and crushed it and L was upset . . . I was able to swim even if I couldn't stand the children, I was in a fit when they were near me; at the restaurant I felt hungry, but then I lost my appetite.

My anxiety about losing self-control is such that I don't accept imperfection, even if they are ordinary realities. In fact from now on I will grow old, and I will die and this is a reality, and yet my illness is terrible for me. And then the brioches and the faulty breakfast! The rage for my lost health vent itself against that breakfast.

The road along the sea shore was very beautiful but I was feeling anguished . . .

Here I am, unable to enjoy things because I always have my situation in mind as a nightmare.

Monday I went for a check to a Medical Centre specializing in the treatment of sclerosis; I went there with daddy and mummy. She was happy I had asked her to come; daddy had not gone to work and the previous time mummy had been feeling somewhat excluded when I asked to be hospitalized without telling her.

She was present during the medical visit, this doctor made an awful impression on me, a cool Nazi, chilly, like those people who take children they don't know in their arms and smother them with kisses and fondle them ... Ignoring all the documentation I brought him, perhaps because he is a presumptuous man or perhaps because he has great experience, he just gave a glimpse at the X-ray photos, which he said had been made by an important Medical Centre, and treated me in an odd way, hurting my feelings as well.

He then went away to find out whether I could get my visual potentials checked, which can usually be done without hospitalization, but he wanted me to be hospitalized for some time. I asked him why and he said: 'Well, this way you can see me for a while'.

I said 'I don't feel like it, also because I would prefer to do it after the end of the school', but he talked to me as if I was stupid ... 'Come on, you are a beautiful girl' ... he didn't tell me: 'you must do magnetic resonance again', I asked: 'but what additional tests?' but he didn't tell me; when I spoke of the old diagnosis, functional troubles, and of my psychological problems he said: 'Nonsense'.

It is a fact that my troubles have increased since the diagnosis. I believe I would be better able to face the situation if I was treated as an adult person.

Sclerosis seems to be a likely diagnosis, spots are on my left side, even if I have a hidden hope that they may be a consequence of the trauma to my neck in the car accident.

My mother mentioned that I was having analysis, but he wanted me to be hospitalized immediately. I maintained that I wanted to delay it one week at least and he said 'Yes, I know how fussy analysts are; they interpret it as a flight, but after so many years ...' and mummy: 'Yes, she was thoughtless and cheerful once, and that woman ruined her' ...

I must be told things clearly.

(Then she speaks of another neurologist who apparently treated her more respectfully).

(She goes on complaining about the new doctor) : I cannot

accept the idea of not being treated like a person, of being hospitalized without knowing what tests I am supposed to undergo.

Perhaps there is a conflict between him and the Hospital here and he was saying: 'Touch me, give me a kiss, smile ...' I realized how children must feel when someone they don't know comes and wants to take them in his arms at all costs; in any case I said desperately and furiously 'no, I don't want to be hospitalized'.

I felt better when I went back to work; a colleague suggested I should go see a pranotherapist and I welcomed the idea.

Well, you know, there is something about magic in me, even if I have never been to see mystics and forget horoscopes.

I don't believe in doctors and that one I didn't like at all; do you know what happened later? M phoned me and I will see him next Thursday if you will kindly let me have your bill tomorrow so I can pay it before your holiday. In fact, you know, this isn't a flight; I felt a bit angry with M since he didn't remember that I am still working, and besides I am a bit scared of my reactions now that I am ill. But I am still myself, with the same whims and with the anguish of having got worse.

Analyst: (I suggest we might dwell for a while on what she is bringing to this session, the idea of skipping next Thursday's session and, here and there, a rage creeping in towards me as her analyst)

Patient: Quite frankly, should I not come next Thursday; You can't help thinking that this is a flight ... you might ask: 'How often has M phoned you during this period of time?' and you might say that I should have suggested that he should come another day. In this sense, yes, it would be a flight. But it isn't a flight from you: it is a fear, a stupid fear, and there is also some rage because M didn't remember about my working hours, and a feeling of separation, perhaps connected to my illness.

I am in a fit of rage because he has not been present during this period of time.

Perhaps I am angry with you even if I am pleased with the

169

way you spoke, how you stepped in, the things you said . . .
But in fact I thought: 'Well, even if I skip one session, she will
be away two months (she yawns) perhaps the summer' . . . I
might also wish to punish you a little (she yawns again).

Analyst: (I tell her that there may be a transformation of an
experience so that it can be changed from a passive one into
an active one. I also review the rage material, aimed against
me as her analyst, against her doctor and his manners and
against tyrannical methods with children, as if she
experienced me as God Almighty who gives peremptory
terms like the dates of vacations. I add that there might also
be an effort to react to the dependence-link, a problem that
also emerged during the previous session, as if there was
some fear of the pain.)

Patient: (She listens to me, one hand on her tummy and the
other hand clinging to a back-cushion, with her arm inserted
between two such cushions; she is silent and after a while her
breathing gets heavy, as if she was fast asleep).

I just fell asleep . . . that alley at the seaside came to my
mind once more, I was being pursued by the old woman, but
I wasn't afraid since I knew I was here (this is an old
repetitive dream of hers) Yes, that goes back many years. I
was with my daughter . . . coming here is pleasant.

You hate M, you dislike him, I don't know (she tries to lift
both legs alternately) This one I can move alright, the other
one (the left one) isn't normal . . . do you understand? I want
to see him, if this thing did not exist . . . I am afraid not to be
as as I used to, I get scared, I get anxious . . .

Analyst: (I tell her she gives the impression as if there were
two things that cannot be together, perhaps as if there was a
daddy and a mummy . . . If you are with one of them you
take something away from the other and vice versa, I also
point to her old dream, with the frightful old woman: even if
she is a little less afraid because she feels she is here . . . a bit
as if she experienced me both as an old-dangerous-witch and
also as a reassuring-mother).

Patient: How sleepy . . . (she is still clinging to one cushion,
her arm stuck between two cushions) Why do you believe it
to be a flight? I am alright here, I am glad to come, of course
I would like to receive more, a lot more . . .

170

Analyst: (I tell her that the time is over and at the same time I think I have kept her here five minutes longer. I then realize that it is the right time instead).

Commentary:

The week-end having served as a rehearsal for the holiday break, the drama of ambivalence and the thrust towards integration commences. The patient's need for constant companionship in the face of the terror related to her impairment finds no satisfaction at the adult level because the anxieties are too primitive for either her daughter or her husband to respond to. But as an echo of the analyst's last comment on Friday, she is able to find an adequate representation in the rock to which she clings when the waves of the beautiful sea threaten to wash her away. From that point on the two levels enter into a fugue relation to one another in the material, the frantic need for sexual union either with L. or with M. which is as enragingly unsatisfactory as the stale brioche, alternating with the theme of the beauty of the sea; or the disappointingly shallow companionship of her parents, coupled with the infuriatingly patronizing behaviour of the new doctor, standing in apposition to her courageous defense of the analytic sessions in the face of the demand for immediate hospitalization. But gradually the hostility to the analyst begins to come forward, first through the patient's mother's mouth but then in the form of betrayal, the attractive magic of the pranotherapy (a grossly fraudulent healing technique with magnets and laying on of hands) and of the sexual relationship with M., for which she announces that she will miss her final session.

The patient feels correctly that the analyst is staggered by this treachery and begins to see that in fact the M. who disappoints her by his inattentiveness and the analyst who is going away have become emotively indistinguishable to her. The recognition of this eases her, she becomes sleepy and the analyst has her first opportunity to interpret the substance of her infantile rage and revenge. The infant clinging to the pillow breasts, like to the rock at the beautiful seaside asserts itself and she falls asleep, to dream her repetitive persecutory dream of the old woman, but unafraid, for she retains the awareness of being at

171

the analysis. This sequence makes it clear that M.'s penis and the old woman are coupled together in her mind as the torn-out nipple, which becomes the fecal penis of her sado-masochism, and the breast with a hole in it, with which she is identified when ravenous for sexual intercourse. Now the analyst can interpret the catastrophic anxiety about the reuniting of this violently split combined object, unable as yet to clarify the distinction between the persecution from the partial objects and the catastrophic anxiety towards the reunited combined object, the beautiful sea-analysis and the rock-pillow.

Wednesday, 1st July, 1987
During the following Wednesday session I am under the impression that I am just unable to organize the material that she is bringing, as if my mind refused to work, I believe I am not grasping enough of the charge of rage and contempt aimed at the analysis and at myself that she is expressing here through other people's words, even if perhaps I recover slightly towards the end.

I reproach myself for not having worked on this hypothetical skipping of next session and I feel very sorry when my patient finally says: 'I should like to pay your bill now because I am not going to come tomorrow'.

I tell her I haven't prepared her bill, I will give it to her tomorrow or, in case she does not come in September. I am left with this painful doubt until next day.

Commentary: It is of great interest to note the degree to which the analyst has been reduced to a state of paralysis by the patient's attack. One could almost say that the whole scene at the seaside has been reversed: the mother is now desperately clinging to her hopefulness and trust in the breast-analysis as she sees her beautiful analysis-baby in danger of being swept away by waves of rage and allies hostile to the analysis. She has refused to collude by preparing the bill in advance of the arranged ending for the holiday and indicates her hope of seeing the patient on the following day. But the analyst is left full of anxiety and misgivings about her work.

Thursday 2nd July, 1987
Patient: Well, I am here because dear M did not phone me

after all (angrily). At this point I take the liberty of telling you that he is a pig and a coward, he is a mean fellow, he doesn't know about my illness, without mentioning feelings and how he handles them. Some people have a pathological egocentricity, with such an indifference, such a hate, such a disdain, people ... I find no other way to explain the indifference after his phone call, 'I'll see you', he said. Perhaps I haven't been able to play the role of a girl like that, completely available. I told him I had an engagement next week and he asked me: 'What sort of an engagement?' as if I had implied a romantic engagement; and I said: 'No, I haven't forgotten you', I didn't mention my hospitalization. What does he know of the things that happen to me, of my life. I don't feel like having to look for further justifications as I did at other times ... but this time, frankly, he doesn't know of my illness. If he knew ... but what person can behave that way.

I too have behaved badly, despising L., my daughter and other people ...

Analyst: (I say that this material probably expresses a part of her who despises me as her analyst, as well as the analysis).

Patient: Yes, my dear, do you know? A thought was in my mind: if I had not come to analysis I wouldn't have fallen in love, as when I was imploring you, keep both me and M. in analysis, please ... this stupid love, perhaps I wouldn't have fallen in love with a stupid illness called love, which has become a bitch of an illness, this dirty love is like a rat that I throw away, this brown rat has infected me, this disgusting sclerosis ... sclerosis is here, the illness called love is here ... now I may feed on tender, light feelings. M. you are shit. If I had an opportunity to kill you I would do so.

Analyst: (I again relate this rage and hatred to myself)

Patient: Yes, I agree with you. Where do you think it comes from? Would you give me a picture of yourself, so that during the session I could hold it here (she waves her left hand as if she was holding a picture; she refers to the pranotherapy that she mentioned in the previous sessions) I must do the therapy with the picture of this one (referring to M.) with a machine aimed at me, at a certain time of a certain day and I shall recover, just as I believed in you and in your analysis.

It isn't your fault if I got sclerosis, OK, perhaps it is the consequence of the trauma. I feel disgusted. It isn't your fault even if I still think that if I had not been in love I would not have fallen ill or, as my little mummy or big mummy says, I was carefree and in good health once, even without love.

Perhaps it is your fault, or my fault, I shouldn't have come to analysis, it is true that I hate, I hate everybody, everywhere, as I was telling my colleagues: 'When you are a child, they teach you not to throw waste-paper around the place and I have a bagful of it, but when I am angry I spread it all around and would like to pee on the floor and do more that that ... you know, with all these negative things it seems to me I don't love anybody, not even M.

And now I shall go to the hospital; they will give me cortisone, I wanted to see him now; who knows in what a state I will be when I get out of hospital.

I would prefer accusing myself rather than feeling this way about him; there only is hatred and contempt in me and people realize how much hatred and contempt are hidden under my quiet behaviour ...

Analyst: (I say that just now M.'s figure and mine seem to be close to one another, with a rage as powerful as the waste-paper-pee she is spreading around, a rage for her illness and a rage against me as her analyst. I remind her of an image she had some sessions ago, an image of a child who beats the floor when he falls, as if she experienced the floor-analyst-analysis as something that makes her stumble, or as something that is full of traps-empty-areas-vacations, like a disappearing floor).

Patient: (She keeps silent for a long while, then she says in a quieter and somewhat sleepy tone of voice): How sleepy I have been feeling recently when I come here! incredibly sleepy ... can you imagine, last night I had a dream, but I forgot it ... In any case things were happening just as they do in a film, with somebody going to the electric chair and somebody being killed ... perhaps I was responsible and perhaps I had accused him ... I was responsible in some way, but I have forgotten ... it seemed strange to see it just as in film ... this electric chair, flashes of energy, how frightful, something extremely painful, undoubtedly it was my fault, I was responsible . . . M . . . I believe it was a man who was guilty and perhaps I had accused him; he had been found guilty and sentenced, perhaps his guilt wasn't so serious . . . the cemetery where my great grandparents and my grandfather are buried now comes to my mind . . . my grandfather was a badly dressed man, with trousers that hung down a little: perhaps my father . . . I remember when he came back from Switzerland wearing a plaster corset and looking like an old man: perhaps he too had been given a lumbar puncture . . .

But it is love that makes me hate so much, the desire that comes back, I have killed him on an electric chair because I would like to kill myself on the electric chair.

I am grateful to you for giving me a chance of loving and it is not your fault if I got sclerosis, I am talking nonsense . . . now you go away for a long time; you don't know what will happen this time. Last year I was happy. Yes I was fussy but . . .

This year you go away and this is right, but all the hatred and rage that I am feeling . . .

Analyst: (I refer to the dream and to the associations, without being clear in my mind about what I am going to say, but she stops me.)

Patient: (excitedly:) The dream has come back to my mind. Do you know why I had him sentenced? He is the husband of a woman with many children, *eight* of them, and she got old . . . and I had him sentenced because of a guilt connected to this woman with many children . . . but perhaps she had not had them with the man that I had sentenced since she had already been married once . . . please go on saying the things you were saying.

Analyst: (I ask what is her impression of all this . . .)

Patient: Well, I didn't think this woman was in a great rage [she yawns] and this amazed me, I don't know what the man had done, perhaps he had won her love, children can be conceived with the man one loves, perhaps I had the man she loved killed and the woman was also guilty and there was no room for the children . . .

Analyst: (I try to organize all of this material, the idea of a couple, in her dream and in her associations, a daddy who is

175

back after an absence looking old and deteriorated to her, the woman that got old in the dream, the children. I direct her towards experiencing an analyst-mummy coupled with a daddy during a period of vacation-separation from her; the electric chair as a simultaneous expression of a presence and of an attack to the link, the wires that carry the current of love.)

Patient: It is as if I experienced the link, the relationship, as something deadly, as if I experienced my relationship with you as well as my relationship with M as both springing from you, as something deadly that in the end destroyed me, as if this current with its power, its strength and its energy was all the power and strength of love that in the end destroys and incinerates.

Analyst: I say: 'Perhaps it is as if you experienced it that way'

Patient: I met your son yesterday, a handsome boy, a nice face, also your daughter. Congratulations, you brought them up well.

Commentary: Act four of our drama scintillates with passion; hatred of the fecal penis that is accused of seducing and abandoning her; hatred for the breast that is going away without her; welling up of love towards the analyst ('my dear') without being able to understand either the nature of the object of this love nor whether it is filling her with life or killing her; and a powerful drive to understand the mysterious processes that are going on in her body and mind and relationships. She seems convinced that the so-called 'falling-in-love' with M. was absolutely bound up with the analysis and her relationship with the analyst, and has been somehow involved in bringing about the sclerosis. It also is clearer to her that her 'quiet behaviour', that is, her docile adjustment to the culture of family and community, has hidden hatred and contempt. But the analyst suggests that she has not only hidden but also expressed these emotions towards the absent analyst-parents in an infantile manner.

This interpretation brings a return of the sleepy-baby of the Tuesday session and recall of the dream which clarifies the nature of the betrayal: that she has attacked the analytic family, with its quota of eight children-patients, by false testimony (lies), connected with masturbation orgasms (flashes of energy, the electric chair), against the father who takes mother away. When the fecal penis is recognized as the brown Nazi rat, it can be differentiated from father's and grandfather's genital which are good and give babies rather than killing them ('no room for the children' when the lies and attacks changed the parental love into a sado-masochistic perversion).

When this has been all formulated by the analyst, the patient is left still with the uncertainty in the face of the mysterious power of love, for while it seems to be killing her, it produces the well-brought-up children of the analyst whom she had met the previous day. The facile answer would be that she has not loved M. but has only had a perverse relationship to him as the fecal penis, and this is what is killing her, i.e. that her super-ego is punishing her for her betrayal of the combined object. This was in fact Melanie Klein's theory of psychosomatic illness, in which she failed to distinguish it from hypochondriasis.

The Bionic theory of psycho-somatic illness is quite different and greatly illuminates material such as this, while the theory of a punitive super-ego merely gives voice to the patient's own religious and moralistic phantasy and expectation, even in a sense her wish to be punished with death rather than to have to experience the powerful emotions of fear and love, hate and dependence, ignorance and the yearning to understand, life at the passionate level of aesthetic conflict, clinging to the rock, ravished by the beauty of the sea, terrified of being swept away. Swept away by what? The material says it clearly: swept away by the preference for mindlessness, cocooned in quiet submission to the demands of the culture of the family, seasoned by secret perversity.

11   Holding the Dream:
The Nature of Aesthetic Appreciation

(i) Aesthetic appreciation through symbolic congruence

the calm
And dead still water lay upon my mind
Even with a weight of pleasure, and the sky
Never before so beautiful, sank down
Into my heart, and held me like a dream.

In these lines from the *Prelude* Wordsworth captures the essence of aesthetic appreciation through symbolic congruence: the 'fitting' of the individual mind to the aesthetic object, in such a way that boundaries merge and yet the independent integrity of both partners in the drama — internal and external world — is affirmed and radiates significance. He does this without any selfconscious rhetoric relating to the 'pathetic fallacy'; no 'as if's' or personifications; it is simply described as a fact, that the mind at the bottom of the lake of consciousness is pressed upon by the weight of water reflecting the sky, in such a way that it both holds and is held by this ethereal expanse of light which has taken on a quality of weight and density — sinking 'down' (as if like a stone) yet in fact like a 'dream'. The alternation of down and up-movements, suggesting increase and decrease in density, confirms the sense of dissolving and reforming boundaries as mind seeks congruence in nature and through this, the experience of becoming known. Likewise, Adrian Stokes speaks of architecture as being a 'solid dream', in which 'directions and alternatives and the vague character of a weighty impress' are captured, held, integrated with 'full cognizance of space', until the 'changing surfaces, in-out, smooth-rough, light-dark, up-down, all manner of trustful absorption by space, are activated further than in a dream'. And as an extension of this, Stokes describes aesthetic response in general, as recalling and holding the 'feel' of a dream:

Appreciation is a mode of recognition: we recognise but we

178

cannot name, we cannot recall by an effort of will: the contents that reach us in the terms of aesthetic form have the 'feel' of a dream that is otherwise forgotten . . .

('The Luxury and Necessity of Painting', in *Three Essays*, 1961)

At the heart of aesthetic appreciation lies the problem of holding, recognising, the feel of the dream which is evoked between the dreamer and the aesthetic object (whatever form this may take). This is a diaphanous cloud of unknowing, which seems composed nevertheless of solid elements with shape and texture, awaiting capture into a symbolic correspondence. As Stokes says: 'Owing to the corporeal nature of the adult's inner objects, it seems that a dream can deposit a residue of sensations of shape, as does art the more general . . . perception of inner objects' (*Painting and the Inner World*, 1963). So, holding the dream has to do with a congruence or reciprocity between internal and external objects: with 'full cognizance of space'. And in the fields of art and literature, for example, the artist's experience as embodied in the art form, serves as a model for the aesthetic mentality: not just by providing an aesthetic object as a thing in itself, but also by exemplifying the process of symbol formation which is what will enable the viewer to hold the dream in his mind, under observation, until such time as it becomes meaningful.

In this chapter I want to focus on the implications of this for literary criticism: first by expanding the definition of 'symbolic congruence', with the help in particular of Adrian Stokes; then by exploring the apprehension of beauty in Wordsworth's sonnet 'On Westminster Bridge'.

In academic literary culture in recent years, so strong has been the grip of the softhumanist mentality — upholding the polarity between thought and feeling, reason and intuition — that any attempt to undermine its supremacy and to investigate the aesthetic foundation of creative thought is doomed to make one feel like Sisyphus pushing his stone up the hill. The only popular alternative at present seems to be the recurrent mechanistic one of linguistic behaviourism, in the form of structuralism and pseudo-Freudian interpretation. And inspected more closely, this turns out not even to be an alternative, but

179

merely another version of the same thing, only presented under the aegis of prep-school verbal trickery, rather than that of complacent liberal maturity. Altogether the prevailing academic view of art seems to be one in which oral or anal gratification, ineffectively checked by conscious efforts at didactic morality or reasonableness, is displayed (acted out) under the pressure of social adaptation. There is on the whole no concept of psychic change.

Among the false or anti-aesthetic aproaches to what should properly be seen as an aesthetic concern, one may include such things as: the notion of art's 'incompleteness', as if its social function were to titivate the intellect of the cultured bourgeoisie in order to complete itself; the notion of the critic (or the 'normal' aspect of an artist) imposing some 'secondary process' on art's 'primary process' to keep it in order; all criticism based on the phantasy of uncovering the 'secrets of the unconscious' (thereby employing no distinction between secrecy and mystery); and all criticism which shows no awareness of the distinction between sign-systems and symbolic forms (so that the art-symbol is talked about as if it were merely a manifestation of society's basic assumptions).

Yet the critic who *is* aware of these distinctions, who has a grasp of the aesthetic quality of the material he is handling, and tries to approach it in an aesthetic manner, is hampered by the weight of the stone he is pushing — not just in terms of convincing others, but owing to the task itself; shouldering 'the burden of the mystery'. In effect, he has a task analogous to that of the artist, in trying to evolve a language which is capable of containing the implications and reverberations of an emotional experience — yet probably without the degree of talent for discovering and expressing mental life through symbolic forms, which is the artist's most essential characteristic. In aesthetic criticism, therefore, he is heavily dependent on using a faculty of receptive congruence to the formal structures evolved by the artist for the containing of 'meaning' or 'artistic import'. He is dealing with the same mysterious phenomena, the life of the mind in process; yet owing to his smaller stature is under perhaps even greater pressure not to call infantile omnipotence to his aid, not to penetrate intrusively the mystery of the aesthetic object and explain it away by providing (even implicitly) the ultimate interpretation. No critic can attain the same felicity of expression as the artist who is his subject and guide. Yet without certain qualities he would be incapable of doing his job. From the aesthetic critic we are entitled to expect, therefore, some ability to tolerate the uncertainty of the cloud of unknowing aroused by confrontation with the aesthetic object, without irritable reaching after fact and reason; some capacity to look steadily at the subject until eventually a pattern emerges. That is, we expect the concern with 'knowing' to dominate the inevitable academic background of 'knowing about'. We also expect some means of verbal expression which, however inadequate it may be, is nonetheless in intention geared towards receiving the inherent expressiveness of the art-symbol, rather than towards superimposing the critic's preconceptions. Above all, though most elusive to define or locate, we expect from the critic who is genuinely involved in the aesthetic mentality, some overriding sense that his encounter with art constitutes one of his life's formative experiences: that it is, to use Bion's terms, a species of 'identifying with the evolution of O' — 'O' being the 'absolute essence' or 'central feature' of an emotional situation, translated by Bion and others as equivalent to 'the state of being in love'. The network of identifications into which the viewer is drawn by the invisible tensions and forces materialising in aesthetic forms, activates the heart of passionate experience, the source of the world's meaningfulness. The structure of this experience, if not its intense daring, is the same for the viewer or critic as for the artist who was 'the first that ever burst/ Into that silent sea' (in Coleridge's phrase). So the aesthetic critic's prime responsibility in holding the dream for the reader, is to show by example how it is possible to think *with* the book, rather than showing what to think *about* it. To do this he has to avoid both intrusive curiosity (converting the aesthetic object into a secret), and also, buttressing himself through judgement and evaluation (as if he were self-elected guardian of the object).

The language of aesthetic criticism, should therefore, by means of its own deep-laid metaphor, image a goal of generating new realms of meaning through exploration and discovery, based on passionate congruence between the forms of the inner self and those of the aesthetic object. Commitment should be to a process rather than to an interpretation: to the vale of soul-

181

making, the evolution of O, the 'vision of a former world and a future' (Byron's definition of poetry). The aesthetic critic, by contrast with the solely academic critic, needs to respond to what Stokes calls the 'envelopment' or 'incantatory' factor in art, rather than standing guard over the external qualities of the object as a museum piece. As in that archetypal model for aesthetic criticism, Keats's 'Ode on a Grecian Urn', he must revere the object's inviolate world-of-its-own, yet at the same time allow its sculptured contours to melt and mingle with his own state of mind, together with the anxiety, excitement and confusion entailed as it 'pipes to the spirit ditties of no tone'. This transcendental music, this penumbra of significance beyond the lexical connotations of words, begins to impinge on the observer as he ceases to be a mere observer. He becomes a partaker, and also the one who is being observed. Feeling himself drawn in to the aesthetic object, and responding to the psychic tensions captured by its formal qualities, his own inner mental structure is inevitably modified. This drawing-in aspect of aesthetic experience is described by Adrian Stokes in *The Invitation in Art*, as 'a vehemence beyond an identification with realised structure, that largely lies . . . in a work's suggestion of a process in train, of transcending stress, with which we may immerse ourselves'. While at the same time, Stokes continues, 'under the spell of this enveloping pull, the object's otherness, and its representation of otherness, are the more poignantly grasped':

> The great work of art is surrounded by silence. It remains palpably 'out there', yet none the less enwraps us; we do not so much absorb as become ourselves absorbed.

The two modes or rather aspects of aesthetic response — incorporation and envelopment, observing and being observed, holding and being held — are complementary and mutually enriching. Unless the viewer or critic can respond to the 'incantation' of art, there is no sense of *self*-exploration. And if there is no self-exploration, then neither is there full appreciation of the objective qualities of the art-symbol. 'Knowing' as opposed to 'knowing about' can never be objective in the academic sense; yet it is clear that the kind of subjectivity which is required by an aesthetic response, is very different and in fact antithetical to what is usually meant by the term 'self-expression', since it is rigorously tied to the formal structure of the object. It is in fact, as Emily Bronte said, 'when the eye begins to see and the ear begins to hear'. The Urn, archetype of the mother's body — being the subject of our primary aesthetic experience — does not yield the *meaning* of its message 'Beauty is truth, truth beauty' to the viewer who has not committed his *self* for observation and exploration. Those words may mean nothing, and may mean everything, depending on the character of the viewer's progression through the rest of the poem; they materialise on the surface of the Urn at the end of the poem, as if emerging from within and only now becoming readable. To the conscientious critic who has painstakingly laboured through to this point, they appear like a slap in the face from the poet, who tells him that his entire mode of evaluation has been inadequate. In order to read the Urn, or to read a poem on the Urn, it is necessary to find a mode of procedure which can take account of the aesthetic object's infiltration of and — in effect — *attack* upon the viewer's own established ego-structure, so that it re-forms from the vertices of 'love, hate and knowledge' in response to the recognition of 'Beauty'. 'The import of an art symbol', writes Susanne Langer, 'cannot be built up like the meaning of a discourse, but must be seen in toto first':

> Artistic import, unlike verbal meaning, can only be exhibited, not demonstrated, to anyone to whom the art symbol is not lucid ... [The articulation of the art symbol] may be traced, but it can never be constructed by a process of synthesis of elements, because no such elements exist outside it.
>
> *(Feeling and Form, 1953)*

The problem is how to know that which, however concrete, is ineffable — in such a way that we are discovering ourselves at the same time, and responding to the invitation in art. Our immediate reaction to a great work of literature may be one of amazement, awe, disturbance; we may intuitively see its truth, yet not recognise this new experience. Yet our desire to 'know' the work better may be an ambivalent one, a type of self-defence, if it is based on explaining-away, unearthing secrets,

183

diagnosing the psychopathology of its author — even perhaps the apparently harmless scholarly pursuit of establishing sources and references. And the usual way we read, a species of daydreaming, is no less an indulgence in preconception than is the more systematic procedure of academic interpretation. Nevertheless the work of art does demand for us to know it, in a more essential sense; it exists for the use of mankind, to awaken and give shape to our need to be known and to know ourselves. We confront the work of art; an emotional experience occurs, which needs to be integrated within the mind in the form of a reciprocal symbol, such that its meaning may become known; 'but first a container must be found to hold the experience' (Bion, Meltzer). Then in the interaction between the mind of the viewer and the artist's mental process as embodied in the art form, a new emotional event germinates. The meaning of the art-symbol crosses beyond art's material boundaries, into that desolate no-man's land where as Keats said 'the sedge is withered from the lake/ And no birds sing': the 'undiscovered country, from whose bourn/ No traveller returns'. This is the area in which aesthetic criticism operates.

Tolstoy uses the image of a field of battle, as yet untouched by contending forces, its boundaries quivering in anticipation of some strange transformation, to describe the threshold of knowledge:

> One step beyond that line, which is like the bourne dividing the living from the dead, lies the Unknown of suffering and death. And what is there? Who is there? There beyond that field, beyond that tree, that roof gleaming in the sun? No one knows, but who does not long to know? You fear to cross that line, yet you long to cross it; and you know that sooner or later it will have to be crossed and you will find out what lies there on the other side of the line, just as you will inevitably have to learn what lies the other side of death.
>
> (*War and Peace*, tr. R. Edmonds.)

This is what Bion calls the 'caesura' between commensal worlds, which comes to vibrate with meaning as a 'discovery' is heralded, and the idea of a mutually penetrating 'common sense' takes shape. The importance is paramount of being able to construct a space where 'it' can happen, by means of a struggle both active and passive, a relationship with some inspirational power experienced as outside the self. Without some underlying spatial metaphor – Urn or battlefield – to give internal objects a chance to achieve symbolisation, the dreamer or viewer or critic may feel overwhelmed by the cloud of unknowing, and unable to hold its meaning or be held by its meaningfulness. Like Tolstoy's battlefield shaped between its opposing armies, Milton makes a dual approach to the 'void and formless infinite'. The formless space is defined by two reciprocal movements: on the one hand, by holy Light investing the 'rising world of waters dark and deep', and on the other, by the flight of the poet's soul 'through utter and through middle darkness'. The soul is seeking a return to the place where light gave the world meaning and safety ('Thee I revisit safe'); but light no longer seems to give the secure (and familiar) form of Nature's 'book of knowledge fair' to the formless infinite. In fact all form is lost in space, until another area for light's operation is discovered as its rays are forcefully reflected in the direction of the unknown: 'Shine inward, and the mind through all her powers irradiate'. From this confrontation between the self and a higher power in the realms of infinite space, the poet forges a new container for meaning — the world of the mind: a world which he now has the higher power's aid in observing.

Our aesthetic reception of poetry has to be modelled on the poet's own struggle for symbolic form; poets and artists are, inevitably, among our main guides to aesthetic experience. Yet even with the poet as guide (as the poet has holy Light, or the Muse), the process of working towards a symbolic congruence is so difficult that one is tempted to lapse into hopelessness about the point of it all, and thence into complacency. The gap between the poet's experience and our own might seem so vast (when we try to take it seriously), that we prefer to relegate it to the spheres of romance and daydream; we find that astronomical conjectures are not relevant to our late 20th century selves who are in the adulthood of mankind's evolution and don't have to depend (like Milton) on imagination and a glimpse through Galileo's telescope, to discover the mysteries of space; such flights of fancy can have no bearing on grown-up thought and reason. The temptations to demean or recoil from aesthetic experience are strong, especially when we don't know

185

what to do with it. Yet the universal infant within everyone would not regard as remote or meaningless the experience of flying through utter and middle darkness, or of the 'universal blank' at the withdrawal of the 'human face divine', or of food for the soul as well as the body when 'eyes' are 'planted inward', mist is dispersed, and the mind expanded and fulfilled. Adrian Stokes describes mental life as 'a laying out of strength within, in rivalry as it were, with the instantaneous world of space':

> For all the blaring echoes, there are many cries to which we are normally untuned. Yet so vast is emotion, we come to feel that cries from the heart rebound to us from the astronomical distances of the universe.
>
> *(Inside Out, 1947)*

Milton's space, prophetic though it was of later scientific discoveries, is first and foremost a field for 'tuning in' to the ineffable qualities of emotional life, those 'ditties of no tone'. It dramatises what Tolstoy calls the 'bourne between the living and the dead'; what Stokes calls the 'line of equivalence between emotion and the outer world':

> By means of expression, his perennial activity, the mind of man vies with the world in outwardness: deeper things come forward. An expressive token of all expressiveness, the face of the stone is made to show through the stone; and in the evening light there is a moment when mind seems to become extension, stands revealed in the eyes.
>
> *(Venice, 1945)*

Along this line of equivalence, between classical and romantic zones, or 'carving' and 'enveloping' modes of contact between self and object, the dream is evoked and contained; the drama of the inner world finds its symbolic form. The infant-soul's interaction with the body-spaces of the world-mother con-stitutes the formation of Mind — a sort of 'extension' of the solid object in the changing light: the inside emerging outside, the outside sinking in and holding like a dream. Donald Meltzer stresses the primordial quality and centrality of the aesthetic sense, beginning with the baby at the breast or even earlier, and being what separates 'protomental' activity (nominative,

externally factual, quantitative) from true 'mental' experience
— symbolic and qualitative, carrying meaning in the sense of
imaginative import. Aesthetic congruence, under the aegis of
the Mother/Muse, is the source and foundation of all developmental thought-processes, of essential 'knowing' above and
beyond 'knowing about'; based on simultaneously exploring
and being explored. Responding to the aesthetic object's
incantation, and incorporating its function of observing our
internal processes, we enter the world of coming-to-knowledge.
In Bion's words: 'What is to be sought is an activity that is both
the restoration of god (the Mother) and the evolution of god
(the formless, infinite, ineffable)' (*Attention and Interpretation*,
1970). The reason why we need a clearer grasp of what aesthetic
experience is, through recognising and evaluating it, is not
therefore to swell the numbers of artists or musicians or
psychoanalysts, but to locate and develop that aspect of our
mental life which governs the meaningfulness of our attitudes
and relationships in other spheres.

(ii) Beneficence in Space — Stokes on Turner

To focus again on the particular field of aesthetic experience
which is aesthetic criticism: I want now to take some extracts
from Stokes's essay on Turner*, this time not primarily for
their theory of art, but rather as a model for the kind of criticism
which does not merely interpret, but translates from one
symbolic mode into another, in answer to the 'deep-laid symbol
of form', and which offers a container for the 'feel of a dream
that is otherwise forgotten'. We are looking for an approach to
the body of art — the Urn — which expresses a congruence with
the tensions and directives of its underlying Idea, its commanding form: an approach which is the opposite of reductive,
and which in a sense partakes of the art-symbol's integrity and
echoes its world-of-its-own. On one level, Stokes gives a
'Kleinian interpretation' of art; but it is not one which is
founded principally on categorising art's phantasy contents,
still less on the evaluation of psychopathology (which he

*In *Painting and the Inner World*, Tavistock, 1963

187

regarded as a sad travesty of the 'transcendent' or 'effervescent' or 'widely significant' psychoanalytic spirit). Nor does he rely solely on the other critical favourite, on tracing the motif of 'reparation' — the Kleinian restatement of the traditional theme of innocence beyond experience — though he is indeed continuously aware of the rhythm of attack and reparation, and the artist's anxiety at confrontation with a blank sheet of paper where the first step in creation is violation. But Stokes's major stance for investigation is his architectural sense of worlds within worlds, of three-dimensional structures, spatial volumes and lines of force, which he recognises as dramatising psychic tensions. In particular he focuses on the resonance between inside and outside, where the dual function of envelopment and incorporation — the essence of aesthetic appreciation — takes place. Thus he describes simultaneously both the reconstitution of the 'independent, self-sufficient, outside good object', and our relationship with it as it evolves through 'contemplating and following out' its formal network of directions: the way in which we become 'in touch with a process that seems to be happening on our looking, a process to which we are joined as if to an alternation of part-objects'.

How then does Stokes work his way to a symbolic congruence with the aesthetic object, and with the creativity of the artist, in 'The Art of Turner'? His image of Turner's 'beginnings' — drawn from sketches and the underlay of paintings — is, like Tolstoy's battlefield, the simplest statement of the existence of two opposing or contrary forces, in this case sea and sky which cover the entire scope of the picture's surface and will contain the drama which emerges within it:

> One element assaults the other in the simple, zoned beginnings. Concentrating upon sky with land or sea, the artist was under compulsion to record faithfully and repeatedly a stark intercourse, then to reconcile, then to interpose, perhaps with a rainbow.

This general statement about a typical late Turner canvas concludes with a touch of local colour, the motif of the rainbow, brought in from a specific painting, and heralding the resolution of the drama like an emblem of what artist and critic know must be if the picture is to become a world-of-its-own, though its particular tensions ('reconciling, interposing') are unknown and have yet to take sensuous shape. In the course of reviewing and considering in general terms the evolution of Turner's individual genius, the particular inside-out drama between the painter and the canvas, Stokes remembers sketches which suggest 'the carver's elicitation upon the stone's surface of a prevalent form attributed to the block', or which 'suggest messages that have appeared from within a wall upon its surface' — that is, the sudden appearance or discovery in visual terms of the inside of an object externalised, manifesting itself through patterning on a sensuous surface in response to the artist's observation rather than through creation ex nihilo. The mystical, abstract expanse of sea and sky becomes peopled from within, as internal objects take the stage, and a few sketchy hieroglyphics suddenly become meaningful and establish the appropriateness of their existence. At the same time the viewer has a sense of illumination as it appears that these 'messages', although part of the object's self-sufficiency, have some quality of radiating outwards and inviting the viewer's participation, just as the Grecian Urn speaks, tantalisingly, despite its classical aloofness. Through looking steadily at the object, a pattern emerges. Yet the pattern itself is not explanatory but disturbing, at this early stage of aesthetic response.

Stokes's most intense struggle with Turner occurs in this area, over the 'primitive and aggressive compulsions' which he sees operating throughout his work, and which have an uncomfortable effect on the viewer, demanding an empathic subjective identification, being swept along with the artist in what is feared may lead to 'ferocity and consequent despair'.

Stokes notes, almost with surprise (as if this observation ran counter to the expected moral diagnosis of a 'Kleinian interpretation') that this 'compulsively unitary, forcing side of Turner's art' does not impair but rather enriches his 'lyrical vein':

In many supremely lyrical works, a linking, a co-ordination, an integration, of different degrees of compulsion and different tendencies of the mind were achieved. In the last great period, not only is the world washed clean by light, but humidity is sucked from water, the core of fire from flame, leaving an iridescence through which we witness an object's

189

ceremonious identity: whereupon space and light envelop them and us, cement the world under the aegis of a boat at dawn between Cumaean headlands, or a yacht that gains the coast.

Together with Turner's whirlpool of fire and water we experience beneficence in space.

The original 'stark intercourse' between sea and sky is no longer a straightforward attack, but a mutual incorporation of qualities: light, like rain, washes the sky downwards, while the sea's humidity is sucked upwards like a column of fire. The resulting 'iridescence' both enhances the 'ceremonious identity' of a pictorial object, and draws in the viewer, whose tiny exploring soul becomes symbolised by the boat which is protected, set in perspective, by the vast masses of coast and headlands (enveloping light and mother earth); the boat is both insignificant in stature and yet central to the composition, cementing the world in its passage. This 'beneficence in space' is a far richer 'reconciliation' than the overtly symbolic statement of the rainbow. In subsequent paragraphs, Stokes then examines further Turner's 'envelopmental' explorations over the picture's surface and within the picture's illusion of three-dimensional depths and recesses. He describes Turner's characteristic flat figures or messages patterning these underlying spatial volumes: the 'salmon-like siblings' 'glued on banks and bases' or 'flitting about the declivities and rises of an encompassing breast'. These messages of *form* then become reinforced by the descriptions of *motifs* in the paintings for which Stokes has now found a language capable of containing the emotional quality of these marks and colours: such as the massive *Temeraire* 'full of distance from the funnelled infant steamboat by which it is tugged, to which it is closely attached'.

In the midst of this intense concentration on the process of finding a containing, descriptive language congruent to the artist's own symbolic explorations, Stokes inserts his image of the artist at work — confronting the ineffable via the canvas, through what he calls 'embracing conceptions':

We can take it that in the act of painting, even his vast distances were pressed up against the visionary eye like the breast upon the mouth: at the same time it was he who fed the infant picture. In these embracing conceptions, no wonder that figures glue themselves on banks and bases, variegated figures, salmon-like dully flashing films of colour, perhaps floating beneath a cloud — like architecture, perhaps pressed to the ground like the catch in baskets upon a quay, glistening at dawn.

For the artist, the 'line of equivalence' between self and object, classic-romantic, carving and modelling values, is felt and its resonance accepted; resulting in 'embracing conceptions', a mutual feeding between eye and picture.

Meanwhile the critic's identification with the artist, which has moved him to insert a picture of the artist at this point, and which followed on the relinquishment of sitting-in-judgement and the acceptance of art's 'invitation', now gives him a firmer grasp of the workings of the 'deep-laid symbol of form' and its supremacy over overt symbolic linkages. He returns to the battlefield between sea and sky with which he began: to the 'tension, the counterpoint, the bringing together of storm with sun, the good with the bad'. In one particular painting, *The Wreck Buoy*, he now finds 'more significant . . . as deep-laid symbol':

> The high, lit, sail-tops, ghostly against a sky that falls in curtains of rain, cleave to the rainbow's half-circle tri-angularly, in contrast with foreground water, wastes rich in light flanked by darker mounds of sea, that topple over towards the spectator yet seem at the back to climb up to the boats and to the falling sky. The meeting of these movements occurs near the centre of the canvas from where one has the sense of extracting the heart of so vertiginous, so desert, yet so various a scene, in terms of the rose-red jib on the nearer sailing boat: at either side verticals incline outwards and thereby stress that centre. Awareness of a centre in great space will favour a rencontre of contrary factors in whatever sense.

In a passage such as this, it is clear that the critic's achievement is to follow the artist's movements, not in the literal or technical sense of how he painted it, but in the abstract or essential sense of finding a pulse in common, and thinking *with* the aesthetic object. This is possible because he has immersed himself in the artist's struggle to achieve formal integrity, and has evolved a descriptive language of his own, to meet the corresponding struggle of his own relationship. Making contact with the deep-laid symbol of form, and fastening himself on to the drama between warring forces which traverse 'great space', he ultimately comes like the artist to the awareness of a 'centre' — here the rose-red jib at the heart of a 'various' scene, like the boat which 'cements' the world. The lines of tension direct inwards and the governing centre radiates outwards. Instead of the frightening feeling of loss of identity and of objects in the normal pictorial sense, which alienated Turner's first viewers, the viewer here — through a 'containing' mode of criticism — has his self held and reinforced even in the midst of Turner's fiery whirlpools, in the midst of awesome 'great space'; like Milton in the formless infinite. He is both inside and outside the picture; space and light 'envelop them and us'; 'wastes rich in light ... topple towards the spectator' then climb upwards again, governed by the heart of the picture imaged in the red jib, which is at the same time experienced as the viewer's heart or his umbilical link with the art-symbol.

In Stokes's conclusion:

> Accepting his sublimity, and entertaining thus a merging experience, the spectator shrinks as a complete or separate entity but regains himself as he absorbs the stable self-inclusiveness of the art object.

This drama of identifications is what the aesthetic critic can exemplify for.the viewer: being drawn inside the art-object in such a way that its and his own independent integrity is established. In this way, not only does the final shape of the work of art become known, but also the developmental thrust of its author's mind becomes introjected. This is the experience of 'beneficence in space'. For a symbolic relationship, in aesthetic appreciation, is not the perspective of one thing upon another, nor a reference through one thing to another thing beyond and apart from it which is supposed to be the 'real' subject; rather it is a two-way exploration, governed by a congruence. Art does not veil its inner mystery as if it were a secret treasure which has to be rifled; on the contrary, the mystery speaks through its objective, sensuous form; but it can only be observed by the viewer who has also surrendered his own inner self for observation; and this particular ingredient is one which no amount of academic training *in itself* can develop, substitute or fake, and which certain aspects of academic training even tend to discourage. Under the intense scrutiny of the art-object, the aesthetic critic has to marshal whatever descriptive devices he has in his power, to 'answer' the emotional pressure from the artist which may be bearing down on him overwhelmingly. His main hope of salvation, as it were, is that if he can keep looking steadily at the phenomena, then eventually a pattern will emerge from within, provided he can keep at arm's length what Stokes calls the 'greedy, prehensile and controlling act of vision', the temptation to superimpose a familiar interpretation from without, which acts as a barrier against 'embracing conceptions'.

(iii) On Westminster Bridge

It is clear, then, that criticism cannot get to the heart of art's emotionality, cannot become 'aesthetic', unless it can expand from being simply a 'discursive' talking-about procedure, into becoming a 'presentational' form in itself, which however faintly or awkwardly, manifests some sort of symbolic congruence to the formal structure of the art-object. The very fact that literature, unlike art, is already composed of words, is liable to put an additional obstacle in the way of the literary critic's attempt to achieve an aesthetic orientation. Whenever his competence wavers, he will be tempted to treat its verbal fabric not as an art-symbol, but as ordinary communicative discourse. As Susanne Langer writes:

> The reason why literature is a standard academic pursuit lies in the fact that one can treat it as something else than art. Since its normal material is language, and language is, after all, the medium of discourse, it is always possible to look at a literary work as ... a piece of discursive symbolism functioning in the usual communicative way.
>
> (*Feeling and Form*, 1953)

The unaesthetic orientation includes not only treating the art-symbol as merely the communication of the author's didactic opinions, but also, treating it as a manifestation of generalised social discourse, for the communication of society's basic assumptions (as in behaviourist criticism). In both cases the verbal fabric is treated as a notational rather than a symbolic system. However, literary criticism can also profit from literature's being a verbal medium, since the poet's own words can form a major part of its response; the very feature which can make literary criticism boring, reductive, 'untrue', also offers itself as the critic's most hopeful opportunity for bettering his own faculty of expression. Literary criticism is of course complicated by the fact that most literary genres are capacious enough to contain different aspects of their author's mental activity; poetry can co-exist with propaganda. Our present intention is to concentrate on the poetry, on literature's presentational symbolism; and to use Stokes's 'spatial' model for defining and reciprocating the rhythms of psychic process which are evolved by the art-symbol, as a basis for approaching Wordsworth's sonnet, 'On Westminster Bridge'. We will also invoke the aid of the nearly-lost discipline of 'practical criticism' which (like baby-observation in analytic training) is always in danger of being ejected from the academic syllabus for the very reason that it focusses on that most intractable and confusing problem: namely, *what exactly is happening inside* the aesthetic object.

'Westminster Bridge' is chosen partly because in its fourteen lines, it does not have the chance to be both poetry and propaganda (like *The Prelude*), and what it is is poetry; there is nothing irrelevant to distract from our subject; and because it is perhaps the purest, most quintessential expression of Wordsworth's poetic genius, of the infant-soul feeding and being fed by the world-mother. Of all poets, Wordsworth's genius is the hardest to define, being the least easily circumscribed by analysis of poetic rhetoric and diction; it is difficult to say what distinguishes his poetry from prose, apart from a world of feeling; he is different from all other poets, and yet the most 'natural', essential and therefore universal of them all. Academic criticism tends to find itself at a loss before this essential, ineffable poetic quality; it doesn't know what to do with it, so veers off instead into extraneous considerations about ideology etc., based on viewing poetry as discourse, and often defiantly taking what tradition and intuition tell us are Wordsworth's worst poems, or the worst parts of his better ones, as being the most representative and full of significance. We are taking 'Westminster Bridge', therefore, as a kind of primal act of poetry:

> Earth has not anything to show more fair:
> Dull would he be of soul who could pass by
> A sight so touching in its majesty:
> This City now doth like a garment wear
> The beauty of the morning; silent, bare,
> Ships, towers, domes, theatres, and temples lie
> Open unto the fields, and to the sky;
> All bright and glittering in the smokeless air.
> Never did sun more beautifully steep
> In his first splendour valley, rock, or hill;
> Ne'er saw I, never felt, a calm so deep!
> The river glideth at his own sweet will:
> Dear God! the very houses seem asleep;
> And all that mighty heart is lying still!

How is it that this succession of ordinary words, adding up to the commonplace sentiment 'what a beautiful morning', induce in us a sense of amazement, even of dramatic action though patently nothing happens, resulting in the experience of 'beneficence in space'? The poem progresses from a sense of great space, with the entirety of earth's surface open to a view as from a great height, to the concrete yet invisible 'mighty heart' which belongs both to the City which, laid asleep in body, becomes a living soul, and to the poet whose blood-motion is suspended as the gliding of the river takes over as symbolic of the 'spirit that rolls through all things'. The first line, with its emphatic irregular rhythm spacing out every syllable, establishes the expanse of our vision, and the key verb 'show' which governs the action of the first (larger) half of the sonnet, weaving between a falling, onwards-moving rhyme ('pass by, majesty, temples lie') and a more emphatic rhyme which delays and resonates ('fair – bare – air'), as earth's beauty is stage by stage revealed or shown. The poem's second line establishes the viewer's presence in this process, passive though it is: 'Dull

195

would he be of soul'; the line's fluid movement, in contrast with the first, suggests the soul passing by until it is arrested by the 'sight so touching', in a way which implicitly endows 'touch' with its literal sensuous significance not merely its sentimental one; the viewer's progress pauses as the line comes to rest in the word 'majesty'. The half-rhyme which then links 'majesty – this city – the beauty' indicates the ceremonious identity of the object, the city flanked by the abstractions bearing on it. The one simile in the poem, 'like a garment', adds to the impression of obeisance paid the city, while at the same time, like diaphanous clothing, serving to accentuate the form of the body beneath it: thus the words 'a garment wear' are underlined, literally, by 'silent, bare', and immediately there follows a cluster of body-like shapes – ships, towers, domes, theatres, temples, – which suddenly emerge as it were through the mist, and 'lie/Open', embedded once again in the sense of a vast expanse both lateral and vertical, the fields and the sky. At this point, all the small alternating movements and contrasts which led to the discovery of the majestic city as in sculpture the inner shape appears on the surface of a stone, culminate in the joyous line 'All bright and glittering in the smokeless air'. The solidity of the temples which so firmly 'lie' in their place, melts upwards into the sky and gives the air its new iridescence, its blandness pierced by the little sharp sounds 'bright and glittering', suggesting the quivering of images in atmospheric shimmer. 'Smokeless' is not paraphraseable by 'pure', since the image of the smoke associated with the working of the buildings is in a sense present but vanished; its absence disturbing and making alive the air, so reinforcing the garment of beauty which both conceals and displays.

Following the classical (Petrarchan) sonnet pattern, the poem pivots after this point, into a new rhyme-scheme and a new orientation – the sun, I, and God. In response to the invitation of earth's 'show' in the first part, the image of the sun appears with its governing verb 'steep' – 'Never did sun more beautifully steep/In his first splendour . . .'

'Earth' and 'sun' (not 'the earth' or 'the sun') are like goddess and god; and 'his first splendour' carries the sense of the beginning of time, just as the garment of beauty carries the sense of 'trailing clouds of glory', the soul entering the world

from its first home. A vapour of ghostly life separates the city
from its usual existence. Then 'valley, rock and hill' emerge
into the picture – not this time discovered from within the
stone but painted by one stroke of sunlight: lit from without, not
glittering upwards from within. The two modes of sunlighting
are complementary, and the cluster of solid shapes which
appears in nature's rock and hill, is structurally congruent in
the poem to the first cluster of ships, towers, domes; as if the
landscape's skeleton were revealed, less for the sake of contrast,
than to underline the shape of the city's 'silent, bare' flesh. In
this poem, for perhaps the only time, Wordsworth works on his
customary moral antithesis between country and city (representing good and bad values, beautiful and ugly), and achieves an
integration between opposing principles. The man-made
temples and domes are not parodies but rather civilisation's
homage to valley, rock and hill, whose elemental forms – it
now appears – still lie within and support the structures which
echo them. Through a sudden inspiration — the steep sunlight
– the city and nature are seen to be part of the same enveloping
structure, the earth; they become together the scaffolding on
which the apprehension of beauty is hung; and the flatly
emphatic idea of the 'fair earth' stated in the first line, opens out
three-dimensionally to the poet's vision. The city's beauty
exists both in opposition to the ugliness, noise or confusion of its
mighty heart underneath, which is temporarily suspended, and
also *because* of it:

Ne'er saw I, never felt, a calm so deep!
The river glideth at his own sweet will:

As if in response to the new fluidity and contact between
different planes of the aesthetic object – the inside showing
itself outside, and the outside shining inwards – there now
occurs a fusion between the external world and the poet's mind.
The sun's emphatic, directed radiance, governed by the strong
verb 'steep', carries its all-seeing gaze rhythmically on into the
depths of the poet, to rest in 'a calm so deep'. As in the lines
from the *Prelude*, when the sky 'sank down/ Into my heart, and
held me like a dream', nature both penetrates and envelops.
Now, the 'calm so deep' describes not only the poet's recep-
tivity, but also a shift in the poem's line of force, from the

197

horizontal expansiveness connected with surveying the scene from a wide angle and distance, down to the river flowing below the bridge, and further, below its surface to its invisible depths. The deep calm expresses the vertical dimension of Wordsworth's mysticism, the depth without the tumult of the soul.

At the same time, the opening of this linear passage or channel for communication between mind and nature, releases the river from the overall scene's spellbound stillness, and it becomes the only moving object in the poem, gliding 'at his own sweet will'. The river, flowing along the boundary between both vertical and horizontal zones, guarding, infusing life, like the spirit that rolls through all things and is felt along the blood, moves with a will of 'his' own (like another god). It is perhaps because of this freedom of ongoing processes, that the poem – in contrast with 'held me like a dream' in the *Prelude* – ends with a sense of awesome anticipation, rather than of supreme security:

> Dear God! The very houses seem asleep;
> And all that mighty heart is lying still!

The juxtaposition between sleeping houses and gliding river invites an involuntary exclamation to God not just of wonder but of fear; further implications of the 'majesty' which first touched the passer-by and made him into a poet, are implicit in the word 'mighty': implications of unknown power, coiled up as in a spring and only temporarily lying still. The moving river testifies to the heart's governing, pumping function, and to the reserves of power carried with ease. It is almost as if, owing to the increased dimensionality and complexity of spatial correspondences evoked during the poem, Wordsworth has brought the apprehension of beauty to a point at which the tumult of the soul can begin.

On Westminster Bridge, therefore, we observe a sort of transcendence of everyday existence which is founded on suspended movement, the heartbeat of a deeper pulsation. No sound has been made, yet the silence emanating from the city is of the intensified, abstract 'ditties of no tone' type, piping to the spirit. It is a model of reality which allows for extensions of itself, reverberations, owing to its quality of primal poetic experience, containing embryonically the process of further poetic experience. Yet we cannot even see the 'unmoving' movement, the areas of dramatic tension, without employing some such model as Stokes's of the interpenetration of self and architectural object, i.e. which describes formal relationships, classes and correspondences. Otherwise interpretation of the poem's content alone, can only lead to something like: 'Wordsworth says that the city is beautiful for once, but only because it appears dead, and as much like the country as possible'.

Aesthetic analysis should help to confirm not dispel our intuitive 'first impression' that the 'truth' in such a poem, far from depending on splitting processes and denials of reality, tells us 'all we know and all we need to know' about the most fundamental process in the life of the mind. Wordsworth's rocks and towers become Starbuck's 'teeth-tiered sharks', as the poet stands on the bridge and gazes down into the gilded sea which contains love, hate and death: 'I love deep down and do believe'. As experience achieved, the poem epitomizes the aesthetic conflict contained. But at the same time, as a true aesthetic object with infrasensual roots in 'a former world and a future', it embodies the warning that experience is about to begin — by implication, our own experience of poetry and its 'cannibal ways'.

12   The Shadows in the Cave and the
Writing on the Wall

Sitting in a consulting room some two thousand hours a year watching the shadows on the wall of one's mind, would certainly seem an ascetic and fanatical thing to do were it not for the intimate companionship with the patients. There can be no illusion of being able to look into the mind of the other person, but the situation and method does certainly encourage and develop an ability to look into one's own, and an interest in the events found there. But occasionally an essentially unpleasant event occurs; instead of pictures, one's dreams of the patient's dreams, writing appears, as on a word processor. This is unpleasant because it seems to carry an imperative that drags one to the typewriter to record the experience. And in time a book accumulates and must be rewritten and assembled to look like a unified, scholarly, respectable opus. Such is my resentment of these two types of confinement that have overtaken an outdoor boyhood, that I feel at the end of each book I should be entitled to please myself. And this of course means to say what I mean, which in turn implies to make a fool of oneself, to embarrass one's friends and give one's enemies a good tooth-hold on the hamstrings. I remember how Adrian Stokes begged me to change the silly phrase 'sermons to siblings'. And I heard that Winnicott, at a scientific meeting, held up a copy of *The Psychoanalytical Process* to praise it, adding that of course the last chapter was complete nonsense.

I know Mrs. Harris Williams will forgive me for dragging her along in this dubious tradition. But up to this point the book has been saying what psycho-analysis means by aesthetic conflict. I will, despite the cries of anguish from friends and the slavering of enemies, proceed now to say what I mean. It will be embarrassingly personal, of course, so the reader is forgiven if he prefers to skip over to the addendum.

Melville's dissection of the heart of man confronted by the mystery of nature, and by implication the mystery of woman as prototype of the world, has gripped me since adolescence. It has become more meaningful with each reading, a decade at a time. The tripartite structure is striking and has become more significant to me since grasping Bion's ideas. Ahab, Starbuck and Stubb: the whale, the sea and the sharks: Queequeg, Tashtego and Dagoo. And like Horatio, Ishmael — the observer and recorder of the story. But there is another observer and, in a sense, recorder: poor Pip who 'jumped out of the boat' and lost his mind, like Ophelia. I see Ahab now as embodying the forces of minus LHK, the tyrant, philistine, the believer in punishing with the lance and rewarding with the gold guinea. It seems right to say that he has not emotions but is being consumed by obsession and a delusion of god-like prerogative. Yes, consumed seems the right word, for he is destroying his own capacity to feel and think as he destroys the sextant because the instrument cannot tell him where the whale is at that moment. Starbuck I see as the artist-scientist who sees that the beauty of the outside hides an inner mystery which includes the teeth-tiered shark and the kidnapping cannibal ways as integral to the truth, the beauty and the goodness of the whole. Stubb is the sensualist who lives on the surface of the world and has forgotten his mother's womb. His timeless and two dimensional jollity has an enduring quality that binds him to the tribal mentality of the three harpooneers.

For myself it has been the horse which has been the symbol since early childhood and I will talk of the love and fear of horses, since it is that bit less close to the bone than woman, psycho-analysis or art, as symbols of the World. My passion was generously indulged by my ordinary beautiful parents from about the age of seven, with riding lessons in Central Park and summers at a ranch in Arizona. But being a city boy I never owned my own horse until the age of fifty. In the name of the children I indulged myself then, carving a paddock out of a woodland, building a stable, finding the local farrier and a good vet. Then it was love at first sight. I bought Syllabus from a beautiful Kay Kendallish young woman who found her too strong and lively. She was anglo-arab, bright chestnut, standing fifteen hands two inches, with a grand eye, splendid tail carriage and heavenly gaits. She had been well schooled, with a soft mouth, very responsive to the leg, and nimble as a polo pony. Her first foal, by a seventeen hands flat-racer named Highboy, became known as 'Dear Girl' and is still, at age 19, my favourite. Her beautiful mother died in pain from a twisted gut three months after her fourth foal, appropriately named Tristan, who withered away and would not be consoled. So much for teeth-tiered sharks and kidnapping ways.

Now a well-bred and well schooled (I will not say trained or broken) horse is a huge and powerful creature. With slow and careful schooling she loses her childish ways by the age of five and becomes a mature and sensible friend. Intelligent, with a sense of humour, she has a mind of her own and will not develop vices unless confined in boredom. But she must be feared as well as loved, for it is clear that she can kill with a kick, throw you off at will, hurt you with a bite. But being deeply kind, willing and patient, she seems loving and eager to give pleasure. Yet she will not be mastered. Any brutality of handling brings out a latent slyness which makes her truly dangerous. She does not love people as she does other horses and will happily be naughty and hard to catch to show off to the others, the other girls, I am prone to say.

The horse 'seems loving' but 'does not love people as she loves other horses'. That is the crux of the matter. It is not possible, in the full passion of response to the aesthetic of the horse, to imagine that horses apprehend human beings as aesthetic objects. Perhaps they do. Humans may be the gods of their religion and not the yahoos that Swift suggests. But it cannot seem likely to a lover of horses. Dogs? Yes, a lover of dogs can imagine that dogs worship people and long to be human. But not horses! Why? The size has a great deal to do with this lack of a sense of aesthetic reciprocity. The magnitude, the power of the horse mobilizes an infantile component, both of awe and of fear. And a discernible hatred is kindled likewise when we see that they are not attracted to us. If we call or whistle, they come, sometimes at a trot, more often at their own sweet walk, and we know from their nuzzling that it is not caresses but food they want. The disparity in attraction is hurtful, yet they want to please and are responsive to our love. We must forgive them their nature. Yes, it is other horses they love. They will not mourn our passing as a dog will, but they will grieve over the disappearance of a weaned or dead foal. They can grieve, but not for us. They die and we grieve. It is

202

unjust, and we hate this inequality of attachment and attraction. But we are no longer babies; we can bear it, and must, if we are to continue to be sensible of their beauty and mystery. We can evade the conflict by anthropomorphising, but that is a child's fiction and not the fruit of thinking about the emotional experience of loving a horse. It is projective identi-fication. Worse still, we may evade the conflict by adhesive identification, by becoming 'horsey' people, jolly riders, like Stubb.

The more favourable outcome of this love is more mysterious, an introjective identification by which we may attain some of the horse's virtues of patience, kindness, wil-lingness to work. 'Who best Bear his milde yoak, they serve him best', as Milton said; in fact we discover that we must 'stand and wait' if we are ever to be visited by the Muse and to carry the burden of inspiration. We are allowed to comfort ourselves only with humour, while we wait. A famous Jewish joke depicts a phone call between a helpless young woman and her Jewish mother who is ready to do anything to assist, until she suddenly realizes she has the wrong number and it is not her daughter she is talking to. The young woman whines, 'Does that mean you're not coming?'

'A naked man on a naked horse is a fine spectacle; I had no idea how well the two animals suited each other' wrote Charles Darwin in the *Voyage of HMS Beagle*. So much for making a 'fine spectacle' of myself. We must now move closer to the bone, where the impersonal language of science enables us to speak with lessened selfconsciousness of things closest to the heart: of woman, psycho-analysis and art. This book has two authors because the two sciences of psycho-analysis and art, or in this case, literary criticism, are so intertwined with one another when approached from a descriptive vertex. If it behoves us, as I think it does, to eschew metaphysics and approach the problem of Truth, in its inseparable relationship to Goodness and Beauty, as a psychological problem, we realize immediately that we are speaking of a mental function, Truth-fulness. There can be little doubt, that beyond the requirements of correct logic and the employment of precise linguistic usage as sine qua non, the foundation of truthfulness resides in the quality of observation. It was, for instance, a revolutionary step in

203

psycho-analytic education when Esther Bick initiated infant observation as the primary move in the education of child psychotherapists. In Martha Harris's hands this became the Observation Course, a two year education in observation and recording and discussion as a prelude to the clinical training in the techniques of psycho-analytic child psychotherapy.

This book is not ostensibly about methods of observation, but is instead a contribution to the Model of the Mind for use in analytic consulting rooms. But in another, and more important sense, it is not meant, and such models in general are not meant, for importation. They are intended as a vade-mecum, as a guide to the discovery of the model that the individual analyst is in fact using. And of course, the hope is always that through such discovery he will be enabled to extend and develop his own model further. It is very important to grasp this in order to see clearly in what way a model is not a theory. Of course the main factor is that it has no explanatory power because in psychoanalysis we are working in a non-causal system, where events are factors in a field and everything is symbolic of meaning, metaphorical. For this reason it is essential that models be used for discovery and not as rules or guides to action. If the practice of psycho-analysis is an art, as I firmly believe, and its findings are those of a descriptive science, it is essential that it be done by individuals who can think for themselves. This means loneliness, uncertainty and an inescapable sense of incipient persecution by the group — the people who think alike and can say 'we' instead of 'I'.

Thus, in a wider sense, the book is about methods of observation, for it is not possible to make observations and find a language for transformation without there being a Model of the World in the back of the mind. The process of discovery of new phenomena is completely dependent on the explicit and conscious use of a model in order to recognize the emergence into one's awareness of phenomena which cannot be described by the existing model. The evolution of the science is of this inductive-deductive spiral nature, that novel phenomena require an extension of the model, and this extension opens to view other phenomena which not only could not be described before, but could not even be recognized.

But, as observation forms the foundation of truthfulness as an artist-scientist, truthfulness is itself a mental function which has its own foundation. The heart of the matter of this book lies in this area: the exploration of the foundation of truthfulness in our relation to the world. Its contention is clear: that this relation , if it is to implement the creative potentialities residing in the structure of the mind, with its basis in 'thy will, not mine', must be a passionate one. Here Wilfred Bion's great formulation of the emotional links, of their origin in the impulses to love, to hate and to know our objects, and ourselves, rescues us from the impotence of quantitative modes of thought about emotions. It enables us to see that passion is not a matter of intensity, but rather of integration of these three impulses when confronted with the impact of objects, and, again, of ourselves. Yes, I have a passion for horses, but it does not figure in my life with the magnitude that it did as a child. I am not ready to risk my life for a horse.

The implication, however, is that one's prime aesthetic objects do make this demand: that one dedicates one's life, and in that way risks it, for their sake. It only becomes clear that 'dedicate' and 'risk' are indissolubly bound together when the aesthetic conflict and its inevitability are recognized. For we may be deceived in our objects. The ravishment we experience owing to their external formal qualities may hide from us their interior-mental ones. When our capacity to observe evidence of the objects' interiority is not obscured, our capacity to think about these manifestations may be paralyzed. When we are able to observe and think, our judgment may nonetheless be diverted by prejudice, hope, or the gambler's predicament — inability to leave a game where we have already risked and lost so much.

These are the conflicts which drive us back to the group, to adaptation in preference to growth. And in so doing we open the barriers of our private world of relation to our aesthetic objects: external ones and, even more important, the internal ones. A person is a fool if he does so, but he is a greater fool, in the Shakespearean sense, when he does not. The inevitable outcome, except perhaps for the very few greatest of creative minds, is compromise. For courage in the face of one's enemies is a relatively simple matter compared to courage in the face of one's passionate attachments.

205

Addendum 1
Concerning the Social Basis of Art (1963)*

MELTZER:

You have asked me to amplify what I said in our conversations that followed your paper *Painting and the Inner World* (similar to Part I of this book), read to the Imago Group.

As a practising psycho-analyst I shall draw from clinical and theoretical knowledge the implications of Melanie Klein's discoveries, with the aim of adding to what has already been written by Dr. Segal and yourself. On that foundation I shall try to extend understanding of the relationship between the artist and his viewer: hence, more widely, my concern, in this dialogue with you, will be the social value of art from the psycho-analytic angle. But first I shall want to comment on art as therapy for the artist, especially in regard to one of the themes of your paper.

Freud, and other writers following his lead, considered artistic creativity to be a part of mental functioning very closely related to dream formation. They have explained the manner in which artistic creativity, like the dream, is taken up with a working over in the unconscious of the residues of daily experiences, particularly those of the repressed unconscious. The Kleinian approach to art has tended to emphasize a more systematic self-therapeutic process of working over and working through the basic infantile conflicts that go on in the depths in relation to internal objects. The most constructive part of this process attempts to build a firmer passage from the paranoid-schizoid to the depressive position by way of internal object relations, consolidating, stabilizing the internal world.

STOKES:

Before you go on, I think you must supply an account of what is meant by the paranoid-schizoid and the depressive positions.

*Reprinted from *Painting and The Inner World* — Adrian Stokes, Tavistock, London, 1963

MELTZER:

Since later on in this dialogue some implications will be drawn from Melanie Klein's formulation of the two positions, I shall restrict myself at this point to a brief differentiation between the concept of *position* and the other, more clearly developmental, concepts of *phase* and *primacy*, formulated by Freud.

Freud conceived his meta-psychology to have four aspects, topographic, genetic, dynamic and economic. Among the genetic phenomena he discovered developmental sequences that seemed to be biologically based (though open to environmental modification), centred on the shifting of primacy between erogenous zones, oral, anal, phallic and genital, as the libidinal organization of the infant and child developed. The discovery of the focal office of the Oedipus complex directed attention to *phases* of development, pre-oedipal, the period of oedipal conflict dominance, latency, puberty, adolescence, maturity, climacteric and senescence.

Melanie Klein's formulation of two *positions* does not conflict with these concepts. The emphasis lies with the organization of the self, together with the value systems involved in object relations. The formulation is only secondarily genetic in its reference, since progress from the paranoid-schizoid to the depressive position (or regressions in the opposite direction) fluctuate throughout the course of life: the transition is never complete.

The essence of the transition is twofold: on the one hand there is the struggle towards integration of self and objects, especially internal objects, whereby splitting and exclusively part-object relations are overcome in favour of integration of the self and of whole-object relations characterized by the separate and self-contained qualities imputed to objects. The transition requires as well a shift in values from the pre-occupation with *comfort, gratification and omnipotence* characteristic of the paranoid-schizoid organization, to the central theme of *concern* for the safety and freedom of the good objects, particularly again, internal ones, and especially the mother, her breasts, her babies and her relationship to the father.

While this shift in value systems has a link with Freud's distinction of primary and secondary process in mental functioning, it is by no means synonymous with it. Another item of importance, however, presents an identity of concept, though the form is expanded. Freud's categories of anxiety and guilt find expression in Kleinian theory with the conception of two spectra of mental pain, the persecutory anxieties of the paranoid-schizoid position and the depressive anxieties such as guilt, shame, remorse, longing etc.

Now you will recall that in conversation, talking about your concept of a minimum object, we found ourselves involved in a discussion that turned out to be an investigation of the difference between what might be called 'safety' in one's internal relationships as against 'security'. I put forward to you something that I think is inherent in Mrs. Klein's work. There is no such thing as safety in object relationships to be found in the quality of the object itself. In contrast to processes characteristic of the schizoid position in which idealization, for instance, attempts to remove the object from the realm of interpersonal processes, subject to envy and jealousy, or where the splitting mechanisms attempt to reduce an object to a point where the impulse to attack it and fragment it further, is diminished; in contrast to these mechanisms of the paranoid-schizoid position, the very heart of the depressive position is the realization that security can only be achieved through responsibility. Responsibility entails integration, that is, accepting responsibility for psychical reality, for the impulsivity and effects and attitudes, for all the different parts of the self *vis-á-vis* internal and external objects. Inherent in the concept of the depressive position is the realization that the drive towards integration is experienced as love for an object, that is, as the experience of cherishing the welfare of an object obove one's own comfort. It is also implicit in these theories that, for an object to be loved, it must be unique and it must have qualities of beauty and goodness which are able to evoke in the self the feelings of love and devotion. The corresponding inner object that undergoes a development parallel with the self's integration, achieves those qualities as it becomes fully human in complexity. Thus it demands a life of its own, freedom, liberty of action, and the right of growth and development. In relation to such an object the feeling of love arises; the impulse, the desire, is aroused to take responsibility for all those parts of the self that are antagonistic and dangerous to the object. In essence this is the basis of the drive towards integration, towards the integrating of the various parts of the self. It perhaps is also important to mention that love for the truth becomes very strongly allied to the capacities to appreciate the beauty and the goodness of the object, since manic defences, and through them the danger of regression to the paranoid-schizoid position, have their foundations in an attack on the truth.

I think that, in so far as the creative process is an entirely private one, we have learned from Dr. Segal and yourself that we should think of the artist to be representing in his art work, as through his dreams, the continuous process of the relationships to his internal objects, including all the vicissitudes of attack and reparation. But if we say that the artist performs acts of reparation through his creativity we must recognize that in the creative process itself, phases of attack and phases of reparation exist in some sort of rhythmical relationship. This implies that the artist, at any one moment of time in the creative process, finds his objects to be in a certain state of integration or fragmentation; he consequently experiences a relative state of integration or fragmentation within the infantile components of his ego in relation to his objects. It must be recognized that this process necessarily involves great anxiety. In referring to anxiety we must remember that we have in mind the whole range of persecutory and depressive anxieties.

STOKES:

You are going on to speak of the role of projective identification in regard to art. Before you begin, I would like to comment on what you have said about the plain projective character. My paper, the context for this discussion, is concerned with the ordinary projection of inner objects (though I had something to say as well about the strong projection into us of haunting shapes). You accepted it as our point of departure for this discussion, with one important exception, in the matter of what I called 'a minimum object', a phrase by which I drew attention to the bare, generalized, sometimes almost geometric, and in general, ideal, place on which much art-work takes place. In the interests of the fight for integration, characteristic of the depressive position, about which, in accordance with Hanna Segal's formulation, we entirely agree that it provides the *mis-*

209

en-scène for aesthetic creation, you object strongly to a mechanism in art, as seen by me, that forges safety for the object. You have just said, very notably: 'There is no such thing as safety in object relationships to be found in the quality of the object itself. In contrast with processes characteristic of the paranoid-schizoid position in which idealization, for instance, attempts to remove the object from the realm of inter-personal processes, subject to envy and jealousy, or in which the splitting mechanisms attempt to reduce an object to a point where the impulse to attack it and fragment it further is diminished; in contrast with these mechanisms of the paranoid-schizoid position, the very heart of the depressive position is the realization that security can only be achieved through responsibility', i.e. for 'all the different parts of the self *vis-à-vis* internal and external objects.'

I am very far from wanting to quarrel with that statement, as you know. But you have gone on to say that art mirrors the *struggle* for integration and for an integrated object; and that there are alternations of integrated and unintegrated states in the very process of making art. No one can doubt for a moment that a trend towards idealization characterizes much of the greatest art (nor the aggressive projections against which idealization is one defence). I think that a large part of the reassurance provided by art exists in the service won from paranoid-schizoid mechanisms — the transition is never complete, you have said — for what is, overall, a triumph of integration on the depressive level. Even in the best integrated people, something, at least, of the earlier mechanisms remains active, in satisfactions as well as in the conflicts. Indeed the primitive identifications, with an oral basis, that tie society, are always particularly to the fore. The fact that you are going on to speak of the relevance to art of the primitive mechanism of projective identification among others, makes me chary of cutting any ground from under foot in the matter of early mechanisms and the production of art. Now, in *Envy and Gratitude* Melanie Klein wrote that it is not always possible to distinguish absolutely between the good and the idealized breast. Someone has said that art brings together the real and the perfect. This is not primarily a question of sugaring the pill of reality as Freud, I think, suggested the role of form to be in clothing the artist's day-dream, since to this element of invitation as he saw it, we attribute a far more fundamental part in the chemistry of the pill. All the same, art can easily be debased into a sugar-coated product that usually has great popularity among those who are hostile to art for whatever reason.

MELTZER:

I think Mrs. Klein was stressing the fact that only by knowing the genesis of an object can we be certain of its value. The clinical material that I shall present will demonstrate it. First, as you have indicated, I want to talk about the concept of projective identification. This is an essential concept of Melanie Klein's work, very different from the earlier Freudian concept of a projection concerned primarily with ideas, impulses, affects and attitudes. Mrs. Klein's concept defines the mental process by which very concretely portions of the self and internal objects are projected into objects in the outer or the inner world. She emphasized both the normal and pathological uses of projective identification, stressing what she called 'excessive' projective identification, excessive in so far as it was primarily sadistic and destructive in intent, or excessive in so far as it was so dedicated to the search for freedom from anxiety and pain as to interfere with the normal working through of conflicts. Bion, on the other hand, has described, particularly in his recent Congress paper, the role of projective identification in communication; he has brought this concept to the fore as the mechanism of primitive *preverbal* communication. However, since we are talking about art, we mustn't restrict this aspect to *non-verbal* modes of communication. Projective identification plays a part in *verbal* communication also where it transcends the syntactic mechanisms for transmitting information, information, that is, in the mathematical sense. What is communicated by this mechanism is the *state of mind* of the projector. Individuals vary greatly in their capacity to use this technique, likewise in their sensitivity to its reception. On the other hand, a strong tendency to use projective identification for very aggressive purposes seems always to be coupled with an increased vulnerability in the face of its aggressive use by others.

If we understand projective identification in this way, we can recognize that the artist during the creative process, when

211

confronted with the anxieties inherent in the flux of relationships to internal objects, at any moment may be impelled by the pain within him to seek relief through projective identification in the sense Mrs. Klein spoke of as 'excessive', that is, excessive in terms of the sadistic and destructive intent of projecting it into other people, due to the complications of the guilt involved, or excessive in the sense of endangering the on-going nature of his own dynamic process. On the other hand we must recognize that the impulse to communicate through projective identification, plays a central part in the normal relation to external objects in the depressive position, implementing the desire, as Bion has stressed, to be understood by objects in the outside world, especially where they are closely linked with the primal good objects of the inner world. It plays an important role also in the relationship to siblings, embodied in the depressive concern for all the mother's babies. I shall come back to this aspect later. What I want to emphasize at this point is that the social impulse involved in artistic creativity — this includes the exhibiting of creations — derives in the first place from the pressure towards projective identification. In constructing a theory of art we must therefore consider the theoretical possibility of what I will call at this point *good* and *evil* art in terms of the motivation behind, not the basic creative process, but behind the exhibiting of the artistic product. In order to avoid muddle in language later on, to use *good* in this sense would mean that we would, in talking about what is ordinarily spoken of as good or bad art, need to change our terms to *successful* and *unsuccessful* art.

At this point I want to introduce two bits of clinical material from children that illustrate the impulse towards artistic pro-ductivity derived from the need to use projective identification. One of them is an example of the need to project a destroyed object, and the other is an example of the need to project a destructive part of the self. The first material is from a little girl who was four at the time. In her analysis she was very much preoccupied with her greedy relationship to the breast, following the birth of a sibling who was being breast-fed. During the session I have in mind, she made out of plasticine a little hot-cross bun which had many times been recognized as linked with the approaching Easter holiday. As soon as I interpreted to her the connection between this good breast, the hot-cross bun breast, and the anxiety about my going away at Easter, she began to stab and mutilate the little plasticine bun. In the midst of it she stopped, her whole mood changed from vicious attacking to one of smiling benevolence, and she pointed to the box in which her crayons were kept. This box had, on its outside, pictures of animals. She pointed to one of them and said, 'Oh, what a precious little robin redbreast.' You can perhaps see that she was attempting to project this mutilated breast by presenting it in a hypocritically idealized form for me to take in, as though it were something good and beautiful.

STOKES:

I find your interpretation relevant to a danger in the situation of art. It illumines artefacts we call pretty or prettified in a derogatory sense. In so far as such artefacts may without exaggeration be called nauseating, it is to be explained in the manner you have interpreted the 'precious little robin red-breast', a clear gain for understanding, especially in regard to the sugar-coated product that deceives the Philistines: or is it that they would like art to be thus debased? I think they are trying to share the pleasures of art in the sickly and contradictory context of denial.

MELTZER:

The experience of nausea, as a mental or physical reaction, illustrates the concreteness with which projective identification works. The second bit of material is derived from a five-year-old boy who in the transference situation, following the weekend, was extremely preoccupied with my children at home and expressed his attacks upon them, representing the attacks on the babies inside the mother's body, by taking the crayons out of his box and breaking the points off. He crushed up these points, verbalizing his vicious attacks on these babies and mashing them up, saying he was making faeces out of them.

At this point the viciousness of his demeanour changed. There was first a moment of anxiety, and then he began to smile, became rather elated, and went over to the tap. He got a little water which he poured on the table, and stirred the bits of crayons which are a type that tends to dissolve in water, making a water colour.

After he had mixed the water and the colours, smiling, and in somewhat of a manic way, he went to his drawer and took out a block of wood and dipped this into the coloured mixture, which was now muddy brown. He then went over to the wall and verbalized that he was printing pictures. Each time he made a muddy smear on the wall he would stand back and admire it, confabulating to it that it was a picture of gates, that it was a picture of trees, there were houses and so forth.

I think that you can see what had happened in this play. During his symbolic attacks on my children, very concrete mutilation was being done to his internal mother's babies. He had suddenly become confronted with an excessively painful situation inside himself, particularly the painful responsibility of depressive feelings connected with the attack, as I knew from previous material. In his exhibiting the process of turning these faeces, derived from attacks on the babies into paints and then into paintings that I was expected to admire, he was inviting me, by demonstrating the process, to relish, and thereby to wish to emulate, the omnipotence of his creativity. By this means also, of course, he meant to project into me that part of himself that tortured mother by making her watch her babies being killed.

STOKES:

A connection between faeces and paints, between the omnipotent use of faeces and of paint, has often been remarked. You suggest one way that the artist may be rid of his faeces in so far as they contain something bad, while at the same time they provide the means of omnipotence, and even sometimes of good communication.

MELTZER:

Yes; it illustrates the point I referred to earlier when I said that Mrs. Klein had shown that only by knowing the genesis of an object can we be certain of its value. This is perhaps one reason why retrospective shows of an artist's painting are more convincing and reassuring then a single example of his work.

Having now discussed projective identification in both its destructive aspect, and its constructive aspects as an instrument for communication of a primitive and concrete sort, I think we are in a position to examine the psychology of the person who views art. (Of course we are not restricting ourselves to the viewing of visual art only.) I am talking about people who view art as an important, and perhaps even central, part of their inner-life processes. I am therefore excluding the people who view art from more peripheral motivations. It will perhaps be useful to indicate that, in so far as contemplating art is a form of intercourse between viewer and artist, it has an exact parallel in the sexual relationships between individuals. We would want to distinguish here between events in which sexual relationships are casual regarding choice of partner, being in this sense a direct extension of the masturbation process. (By this I don't mean to imply necessarily that it is an extremely harmful or sadistic matter.) In contrast, there are those events of sexual intercourse in which contact with the other person's inner world is central. Here, of course, we would have to distinguish between acts of love and acts of sadism, again in the latter case not necessarily implying that these acts of sadism would have to be carried out in objectively perverse ways. In acts of love we know very well that processes both of projecting love and good objects, as well as of introjecting from the love-partner, are going on. In a similar way, in a destructive intercourse the projecting of bad parts of the self and of the destroyed objects, as well as the masochistic submission of one's self to this form of abuse are enacted. There is a parallel, then, in the intercourse between the artist and the viewer: the artistic production itself is a very concrete representation of what is transported. I think that the viewer we have in mind is not at all at play: while his social relationship to his companions may be part of his play life, towards art he is *at work*, exposing himself to a situation of intensely primitive (oral) introjection through his eyes or ears or sense of touch. That is, he enters a gallery with the aim of carrying out an infantile introjection, with the hope, in its constructive aspects, of obtaining something in the nature of a reconstructed object. Conversely, in a masochistic sense, a viewer may be going to expose himself to the experience of having projected into him a very destroyed object or a very bad part of the self of the artist. This aspect of masochism I have discussed a bit in my paper on Tyranny.

I would like to illustrate this with clinical material from the same little boy that I've spoken of in regard to the printing on the wall. At a point in his treatment when he was in extremely close touch with me as a good mother who was feeding him the analysis, he was standing by the table, leaning against me, with his thumb in his mouth, after having asked me to draw for him a diagram of the analysis and the sessions he would be having until Christmas. During the time he was leaning against me, he was looking at the wall opposite and said, 'Oh, it's so shiny, like a television screen!' And he said, 'Oh, I can see fishes swimming around.' At this point he took his thumb out of his mouth and commented that it was quite shiny too, that he could see in it the reflection of the light bulb that was over my head. He then very carefully, keeping his eye on this shiny spot on his thumb, put it back in his mouth and said, 'I've got it.' What I want to bring out in this material is that this little boy was having an intense experience of sucking on the breast, and you can see that sucking on the breast was accompanied by a particularly vivid experience of feeling able to look inside the mummy's body and to see all her little fish-babies restored, swimming about — it is implied — quite happily free from his usual attacking impulses. That is the kind of breast and breast-mother he felt himself to be introjecting at this point, represented by the shiny spot reflecting the light bulb that he put into his mouth and sucked upon. I am suggesting to you that the viewing of art is an expression particularly linked to this component of the breast situation, that is, the feeling of looking and listening to the events going on inside the mother, of seeing either the intactness of her inner world, or conversely, of seeing the destruction that has been wrought there. It means an experience of allowing, in the first case, the introjecting of this goodness and intactness and, in the second case, exposing oneself to having destruction projected into one.

STOKES:

I think you could say that because an evocation of the breast relationship and of the relationship to the mother herself are built into formal presentation as a perennial basis, we are induced, far more strongly than we would otherwise be, to contemplate the detailed reflections of the process of the inner life that a work of art may contain.

What you have said about the oral introjection performed by the viewer points particularly to the enveloping action of a work of art and to the breast relationship from which it derives. The work of art is basically a reconstruction not only of the whole and independent object but of the part-object, the beneficent breast. I refer once more to the general, the formal, value rather than to the impact, thereby magnified, of a subject-matter that may be negative, that may invite, as you suggest a masochistic state of mind. I would only add, in part; that even in such a case the post-depressive co-ordination altogether necessary, we are agreed, to the creating of art, will have been affirmed, transmitted, however indirectly. To put it another way; when a discernment of inner states, however horrific, however dispensable by means of a sadistic projection, is stabilized in terms of aesthetic oppositions and balances and other aspects of form, some co-ordination, some bringing together will have occured at the expense of denial; and this bringing together will have required, at the fount, the shadow of a reconstructed whole-object and part-object whose presence can at least be glimpsed in the very existence of an aesthetic result. Thus, a painting that represents violence, disintegration, provided it be a good painting, of the full calibre of art, should remain not at all unpleasant to live with, day in day out. Earlier on, you have distinguished between 'the creativity, the projection of it' and 'the exhibiting of the artistic product.' I am not so willing to separate as entirely as you do for some instances, all the motivations in these two activities.

To avoid misunderstanding, I think we should remark that the fact that many people are disgusted or outraged by a new departure in art, does not necessarily have a predominant bearing on the intentions, conscious or otherwise, of the artist. In my paper I discussed the dislike of art from the point of view of the fear aroused by so vivid a comment upon psychical reality. Maybe, though, this is important in putting the artist on his mettle.

As to sexual intercourse as a process identical in its method with relationship to the art-object, while endorsing the interchanges between viewer and picture that you suggest, I would like to add that the relationship exists, as does the parallel, only because of the essential otherness, the character of self-subsistent entity, the complement to the breast relationship, that has been created.

217

MELTZER:

We are agreed that the successful work of art is compelling; it induces a process in us, an experience whereby the viewer's integration is called upon in the depressive position to restrain his attacking impulses, for the sake of a good introjection; it means allowing the good object to make a good kind of projection into one's inner world. It requires judgement to distinguish the good from the bad processes of sadism in the artist; and masochism in himself, the viewer. I think it follows, therefore, that the experience of viewing art can be extremely taxing and extremely hazardous, but that the art-world, as an institution within our culture, provides a medium for people to carry out this introjective process in an atmosphere of relative external safety, corresponding to the safety of the little infant in the relative restraint of the mother's arms. When one walks into an art gallery, one is surrounded by other people and there are guards and so on; all this constitutes a continual external support to one's internal safeguards against attacking the pieces of art that are exhibited there. Similarly at a concert. It is well known that, in contrast to this safe viewing of art, at times of revolution or warfare, pillaging includes a wholesale destruction of everything of artistic value. There are instances when people of extremely unbalanced mental state have attacked priceless works of art in galleries.

I want now to discuss the implications as regards the social motivation in the artist for producing and exhibiting good works of art. I presume that this social motivation is present from the beginning of his artistic development but that it becomes stronger and stronger as his maturity as an artist is achieved, maturity not only of mastery over his materials but particularly of the sense of stabilization through his artistic activity and other processes in his social and internal life, of his relationship to his own primal good objects in his inner world. I have said earlier that it is necessary for a theoretical approach to recognize the possibility of evil motivation in the exhibiting of art, that is, either as a means of projecting the persecutory or depressive anxieties connected with destroyed objects into viewers or, worse, as a means of corrupting and attacking their internal relationships. But I have also stressed that the motivation for exhibiting good works of art is derived from two sources: first of all from the desire to be understood and appreciated by others, as an important element for reinforcing the capacity to carry on with painful struggle toward the depressive position; and second, I have implied that there comes a point of stabilization in the inner world when that element of the depressive position that has to do with feelings of concern for 'all the mother's babies' becomes very dominant. At this point, I believe, the impulse to exhibit works of art, representing the artist's progress in working through his depressive conflicts, begins to take a form that could rightly be called the impulse to *sermonize*. In this sense every work of art, from such a period of an artist's life, has the function of a *sermon to siblings*, a sermon which is not only intended to show what has been accomplished by this brother but is also intended to project into the siblings both the restored object as well as to project those capacities for the bearing of depressive pains which have been achieved by the artist in his own development. Seen from the spectator's angle, the viewing, and the yearning to view, the work of masters would not only derive from the relationship to the product of art as representing the mother's body and the contents of her body; it also represents the relationship to the artist as an older sibling from whom this kind of encouragement and help in achieving a sufficient devotion and reverence for the parent is sought.

STOKES:

You have now carried further your contribution on the role of projective identification. It brings me a feeling of light, first in regard to a matter that has been of particular importance. Things made by man please and depress the aesthete through a mode far more intimate than in his contemplation of Nature. You explain it by introducing the projective identifications of which the viewer of art is the recipient. I wish there had been the occasion for you to re-introduce here from your Tyranny paper your conception of the smugness remaining in the projector of evil, and that you had brought it to bear in connection with a remark you made to me about the effect on us of much Victorian architecture.

As to sermonizing to siblings, I cannot refrain from mentioning that I found long ago that I could provide no other word then 'brotherliness' to denote an interplay of equal, non-

219

empathic, forms in some of the greatest painting.

In applying psycho-analysis to the social value of art, to the manner of communication and to the role it plays in the calculations and satisfactions of the artist himself, you make a new beginning. It is from your angle, I think, that what appears to be the slavery of the artist will be most fruitfully approached, an aspect, I have pointed out elsewhere, entirely ignored by psycho-analysis. I mean the subjection of the artist to his time, and therefore to the art of his time, inasmuch as art must reflect typical concatetations of experience, of endeavour, in the milieu in which the artist and his public live; otherwise the artist's achievement of form seems to be nearly always without urgency or power. This cultural expression of significant dispositions both perennial and topical (underlying the creation of significant form) that may completely change the emotional bent, as well as the style, of art, will have entailed a novel psychical emphasis. Since we aesthetes are inclined to agree that the creator's prime social task is to help his siblings with their conflicts in a contemporary setting, identifying stress and the resolving of it with accentuations appropriate to a particular environment, just as each individual on his own is bound to do; since the artist's attainment of aesthetic value is understood to be inseparable from what is both subservience and leadership, we realize at once the penetration of your approach.

I fear that this may sound as if I thought a painter's work must include sociological comment. Of course it is not so. He is concerned with value in the inside and outside world, the value of landscape, say, to himself and to his contemporaries, a value that sometimes entails resuscitation of a discarded aesthetic tradition as he looks with new eyes, conditioned by current ideas, not only at Nature but at the art of the past. This application of the inner world to outside situations accords with the sensuous condition of art and especially with some degree of naturalism.

MELTZER:

I believe that the question you are raising now is one we must attempt to deal with if this present paper is to make a contribution, for, as I have said to you privately, all that we have been discussing up to this point has been either stated or adumbrated by yourself and Dr. Segal. Because of the concreteness of the splitting within the early ego, during the reintegration process of the depressive position the different fragments of the self hold a relationship to one another as siblings. It is characteristic, as seen in the analytic process, that the reappearance of a formerly widely-split-off part of the self, and its renewed availability for integration within the sphere of the primal good objects, are experienced by the already-integrated parts of the self as a 'new baby' situation. The resistance to the admission of this little stranger to the family of the integrated self derives from the spectrum of anxieties and jealousies characteristic of the birth of a sibling. But against these resistances is balanced the pull of the good objects, the determination of the parent figures to nurture *all* their children, regardless of qualities, hopeful of enriching the impoverished, and pacifying the rabid.

Such is the painful struggle in psychical reality towards integration of the split-off parts of the self and towards embracing *all the mother's and father's babies*. Progress in psychical reality is accompanied by modifications in attitudes and behaviour in external reality. Idealization of the in-group, and its corresponding paranoia, diminish. Guilt-laden feelings of responsibility, mixed always with contempt, give way to more genuine concern and respect for the potentialities of others.

But where progress is considerable — and I think this is often experienced by people in analysis — a very painful disequilibrium comes to pass, where the internal sibling-parts of the self improve, and the security and happiness of the primal good objects correspondingly improve, far in excess of what can be seen to be going on between siblings and mother earth in the external world. Also it becomes evident, as processes of reparation are more firmly established in psychical reality, that its corresponding process in the external world is very partial, limited by the frailty of the human body and its limited power of rejuvenation, extrapolating to zero at death. Further, the laws of psychical reality differ considerably from the laws of external reality where non-human agencies, structuralized as 'fate', play with human affairs, ten tragedies to every farce.

The agonizing problem thus becomes: How to live with a relatively harmonious inner world enriched by the bounty and beauty of one's good objects, in an outside world that mirrors its beauty but not its harmony, *about which one can no longer remain unconcerned?* This, I suggest, is the task from which the mature, exhibiting artist does not flee, but, to borrow Hanna Segal's words, with his 'cautionary tales', he sets about 'repairing the whole world.' It implies that an artist must sermonize his siblings as they exist *at that moment*: that the formal and emotive configuration of his works must be derived not only from the influence exerted upon him by his culture and fellow artists, but also by the force of his *concern* with the present and future of the whole world. In order to grasp the courage that this requires of such an artist, it is necessary to realize that every act of violence which he sees go unpunished and, above all, smugly un-repented, every cruel stroke of fate in the external world, threatens his internal harmony because of the pain and rage stirred. Thus, concern for the outside world increases the temptation to renew the old splitting and projection of bad parts of the self. The pull of the monastery becomes tremendous as a bulwark against the danger of regression.

STOKES:
Perhaps another time we shall construct our version of the artist as hero, with comment upon the growing cult that helps to inspire the present furore for art, especially the acclaim of Gauguin and Van Gogh.

You leave it to me to take up your distinction of good and evil art in the sense that a work of art is either predominantly reassuring or corrupting to its audience, as opposed to good and bad art aesthetically considered. As you know, while I agree with your formulation of reassuring and corruptive projective identifications ceaselessly transmitted through art — evaluatory criticism is inseparable from acts of correct appreciation — I trust more in the fact that a projection cannot be regarded as art unless some degree of an integrative blend of emotion, typical of the depressive position as you have defined it, shall thereby be communicated. Provided that it is deeply understood, I cannot view any true work of art to be predominantly corrupting in its many aftermaths. Perhaps I am the more ready to value very greatly what you have said about the social importance of projective identification since I have already considered other primitive mechanisms, though subject to the depressive position, to be embodied in art.

You emphasize you are concerned only with the social aspect, not with the aesthetic aspect on which we are agreed. But consider for a moment what Mario Praz has called in his famous book of that name, *The Romantic Agony*, consider the nineteenth century intertwining themes of satanism, sadism, masochism, homosexuality, of Medusa, Salome and the Gioconda smile, of the ruthless and fatal woman, *La Belle Dame sans Merci*, common to Flaubert and to the pre-Raphaelites, or of the Faustian Byronic man; an ethos to frame the savagery of Delacroix, the sudden ambivalence of Berlioz, the perversity of Baudelaire, great artists who were impelled to magnify at arm's length that which, in themselves as in the world, was untoward. By means of uneasy juxtapositions through their art, of beauty and despair or squalor, they sustained acrid versions of the integrative process. On the other hand, the celebrations of sadism — De Sade himself is the key, said Sainte-Beuve, to the literature of that time — and of masochism in which so many artists joined, did not do them, not to speak of their public, much good. It seems that self-destruction in some cases was the mode of liberation from cruel Victorian smugness. The first theme of all was the one of masochism. We need to integrate Swinburne's obsession with flagellation not only with his public school experiences but, more widely, with the cruelly smug Victorian culture to which he truthfully responded, in so far as his obsession inspired very considerable poems; we need to bring into relation with the milieu what Praz described as 'the lustful pleasure in contamination' that characterized so many romantics and decadents; Baudelaire's confessed aim of seeking beauty in evil; Lautréamont's concentration upon evil to make, as he felt, the reader desire good. As well as a dire creative synthesis often of the utmost beauty and courage, in all such cases one is likely as well to detect a straightforward element of bad projective identification.

A considerable amount of the romantic agony survives today. A mitigation, I feel, is due to Freud, though he has inspired further manifestations. Seen from the angle of art, Freud largely took over from artists the mere ventilation of specific perversions. It is well worth mentioning that a scientific discovery about the psyche could somewhat modify the central position of an artistic subject-matter. It shows in this case that, unlike the perennial reaching after violence in newspaper, popular novel and film, on which so many people have the necessity to feed, sensationalism in art includes as well an attempt at description, at understanding, hence at integration. I am inclined to think that artists, more than any other class perhaps, tend to find themselves unresponsive to daily sensationalism not widely symbolic, owing to the gratuitous quality, owing to a lack of reality or connection. It is significant, however, that it should be generally felt that art alone justifies a presentation of what otherwise would be unacceptable; art is felt to be a constructive if desperate or daring comment, though the artist may also be projecting into us the aggression by which he and his objects are threatened. What you have said about the depressive devotion to truth and the connection with beauty, is most relevant here. But if, in this extravagant process, we, as spectators, find ourselves to be losers, then we say that those particular paintings are no good; no good, as far as a simple judgement of acceptance or dismissal is concerned, in your sense and in aesthetic sense as well, since there is no aesthetic value without co-ordination, or, put negatively, without an overall lack of gratuitousness. Of course people will vary in their estimations of what is gratuitous: the more experienced in art usually find the less experienced to be timid, narrow about the channels through which they gain a positive meaning: similarly — at any rate to some extent — psycho-analysts may find others to be incorrigibly blind to the pathetic, even, at times, constructive, aspects of delinquency. It is remarkable, surely, that though cultural situations alter, no considerable achievement in art ceases to have relevance. The urgency of bringing together, of making one thing out of what is diverse, remains unique just because the material varies yet continues to give echo, to make itself felt and thereby to encourage us, even in those instances where we have reason to deplore emotional ingredients on display.

MELTZER:

This view of the artist, that he mobilizes powerful psychological equipment and that he exerts a great influence on his culture seems tacitly accepted; it is evidenced by the reverence (dead) artists receive, by local and national pride based on their creativity. But of course the more open attitude toward (living) artists is very different. Where grudging admiration is given to their craftmanship, their characters are condemned: where the social and political importance of their work is not sneered at as the mere embellishment of history, the state or patrons may attempt to exploit and control them: where they are not beggared and neglected, they are treated as pets or *enfants terribles*. To sum it up psycho-analytically, until they become 'masters' they are treated as new babies at the breast, by a world full of siblings who, while deriving hope from the new baby's existence and performance, cannot control their envy and jealousy.

Now, the aspects of psychical reality acted out through the socio-*economic* structure of society, are in part related psycho-analytically with the impulses to master and exploit the breasts and body of the bad, deserting and begrudging mother, fickle and selective in the granting of her favours, united to the powerful and punitive father. Flux in these aspects of group life, with ever-accelerating tempo, is constantly induced by technological advance (note, I speak of the application of knowledge, not of advances in knowledge itself, i.e. of technology, not of science). The phantasy of plundering this bad mother's body, of tyrannizing over her inner babies, is the driving force, I believe, behind economic aggression.

Juxtaposed to this unstable situation, constantly stirred by technological advance, there exists the socio-*aesthetic* life of people, presided over by the art-world. Here the internal reality of the good, or, as you point out, often idealized mother and her breasts, united to the good, creative and reparative father and his penis, find expression, reminding the children of the bounty of life and the relative insignificance of the differences in nature's gifts when compared with the great expanse of biological equality in the human life-cycle. The art-world is the institutionalization of the social forces towards integration. Earlier I have spoken, for the purpose of exemplification, of the viewing of art as if it were something limited to museums, concert halls and libraries. In fact the art-world monopolizes expression of the beauty and goodness of psychical reality, the craving for which no riches of external nature can gratify. In nature we can find reflected the beauty we already contain. But art helps us to regain what we have lost.

225

REFERENCES

BION, W. R. *Thinking* (unpublished).

BURKE, E. *A Philosophical Enquiry into the Origin of our Ideas of the Sublime and Beautiful* (ed. J. T. Boulton, London 1958).

KLEIN, M. *Envy and Gratitude* (London, 1957).

MELTZER, D. *The Interpretation of Tyranny* (unpublished).

MONEY-KYRLE, R. E. *Man's Picture of his World* (London, 1961).

PRAZ, M. *The Romantic Agony* (London, 1933).

READ, H. 'Beauty and the Beast'. *Eranos-Jahrbuch,* xxx (Zürish, 1962).

SEGAL, H. 'A Psycho-Analytical Approach to Aesthetics' (*Int. J. Psycho-Anal.,* 1952).

Addendum II

This chapter, had it been possible to write it earlier, would have rightly belonged in *Studies in Extended Metapsychology* since its main focus is on the operation of Alpha-function, its failures and their clinical consequences. However the clinical material has a thrust in another direction which suits it well to the present volume, namely on the close relationship between aesthetic and erotic impact.

Mindlessness: Failure and Reversal of Alpha-function as a Model for Relating Psychosomatics, Hyperactivity and Hallucinosis

By naming the mysterious function of symbol-formation and leaving it 'empty', alpha-function, as essentially unobservable, Bion has laid the groundwork of a model which divides the functioning of the mind into two great areas. While these have a certain resemblance to Freud's distinction between systems conscious and unconscious, and thus between primary and secondary mental processes, it has a different emphasis. It stresses the movement from disorder to order rather than from excitation to quiescence. Freud's model, under the later structural theory, envisages the ego's role as being directed towards the evacuation of excitation within the boundaries acceptable to superego and external world authorities. In Bion's model the self, with the aid of primal internal objects (the thinking breast), seeks to bind the emotional experience through alpha function, to create thereby the symbols which make dream-thoughts possible as the foundation for rational thinking processes, including the transformation into language. Memory, as a constructive process (Schilder), is thus made available as a mental function, contrasting with recall as a neurophysiological one (computer function).

But Bion's model goes further in its complexity and provides us with a basis for describing and relating a wide range of phenomena which, taken together, may reasonably be described as mindless, protomental (*Experiences in Groups*) or soma-psychotic (*A Memoir of the Future*). By adding to the concept Beta-elements the puzzling one of Beta-elements-with-traces-of-ego-and-superego (products of the reversal of alpha-function) he has constructed a model which allows for a wide differentation of degrees of fragmentation. In this paper I will try to differentiate three different levels of fragmentation of the emotional experience and the different modes of evacuation from the mental apparatus to which they lend themselves.

228

In order to make these distinctions it is necessary first of all to consider a model for representing the process by which symbols are formed which will contain implicitly an indication of their powerful charge of meaning. Along with Freud I am inclined to think of the central operation in the formation of symbols as one of condensation, much as a set of chessmen is both a condensation of and a symbolic representation of a feudal society. The process of condensation operates on the myth of the emotional experience in the same manner as a set of chessmen stand in symbolic relation to Gawain and the Green Knight, Morte d'Arthur, etc. In the mythic stage of recording an emotional experience, as in many dicursive dreams, the meaning is still open to many interpretations. But as the condensation proceeds, and finally results in a highly condensed symbol, say the Queen in chess, the meaning is now 'contained', no longer open to multiple interpretation. It must now be 'read' or understood, grasped. Thus a symbol may be said to be 'close to the bone' of mental pain, for it pin-points the zone of conflict.

This process of boiling-down can be followed with some precision in many analyses; as an area of transference conflict gradually moves in its progress towards clarification, the dreams move from discursive towards condensation, until the meaning of the conflict becomes unequivocal — or so the analyst thinks. That is, he thinks he grasps it in its unambiguous statement of the dream image, but he may be mistaken. Correct or not in his grasp, the meaning is all there, stripped of evasion and modification, even of modulation, with regard to the mental pain implicit. Its transformation into the language of interpretation always introduces a new dimension of woolliness, but it is the best we can do in the interest of reaching some measure of agreement. Perhaps this agreement is not even essential, as the meaning is now 'there' and must be comprehended in the patient's unconscious.

At this point of maximum condensation, when, in the Gestalt sense, the 'closure' takes place, the pain bites. But it casts its shadow before, and this may be seen as the penumbra of pain which mobilizes the forces against the truth, against emotional experiences — and against beauty and goodness — the forces of minus L,H, and K. They are the forces which reverse the process of alpha-function and cannibalize the evolving symbol.

Using this model we may, grossly, distinguish three different units of emotional experience which are made available for evacuation instead of thought, memory, judgement, action. First would be the raw sense data, rejected as material for alpha-function, namely what Bion calls beta elements. Second we could describe varying stages in the condensation of the discursive myth; and finally we could expect to find fragments of the formed symbol, attacked and dismembered. The first of these, the raw sense data might be conceived in terms of per-ceptual processes, already organized as percepts in the sense of gestalten, both of objects of external and internal sense, and perhaps glistening with an aura of incipient significance endowed them by the organ of attention, separated out from the general bombardment of sense data. We could imagine that such stimuli, organised only minimally, could be shunted, for evacuation, directly into the innervation of the organs.

The second category, fragmented mythic constructions, bits of stories about emotional experiences, could not be directly shunted. Because they contain a narrative structure, as fallen columns of a temple contain architectural qualities, they would lend themselves to evacuation through quasi-social actions. This is the significance of Bion's category of 'Beta Screen' as a designation for compulsive meaningless speech. We can add to this a similar beta-screen of action, as seen in the hyperactive child. I will shortly give an example. It was Bion's intuition that the counterpart of the beta-screen in action was discernible in the mindless conformity of the basic assumption group mem-ber. To generalize the description in a more usable form, clini-cally speaking, we could describe this form of evacuation under the heading of automatic obedience/disobedience.

In the third category of phenomena of evacuation of frag-mented, cannibalized symbols we would want to include the whole range of phenomena called hallucination: both normal, in the sense of incidental, and pathological, in the sense of an organized defensive posture. This would include Bion's catagory of Transformations in Hallucinosis as an aspect of character. I would also wish to include in this category the phenomena associated with hypnogogic drugs and thus link it to the phenomenology of addiction. One can easily see that this makes immediate sense of the sequence of events of withdrawal symptoms, commencing with hyperactivity and eventuating in unbearable psychosomatic phenomena.

To illustrate this thesis it might be useful to relate a case history which I heard in December, 1987 at the Instituto di Neuropsichiatria Infantile at Calambrone di Pisa described by the staff under Prof. Pietro Pfanner. As these are not my own observations and are limited in detail, they can only serve as the basis for an impression, not a demonstration. But the story is very vivid and adds clinical body to the skeletal language of theory.

During her second, unwanted pregnancy, a woman of thirty-three found herself in dread of having a girl child. Coming from a rural, strongly patriarchal family clan, she had rebelled against the restrictions of education and gone to university. There, however, in the context of her first sexual experience, her capacity to learn had failed her so she married her lover and in due time bore a boy child, after 'as long a delay as possible'. But the second pregnancy filled her with anxiety and she insisted on the husband throwing up his job in the city to return to her home village where she had confidence in the doctors of the regional hospital. She had also by this time severely renounced her sexuality, became bullimic and very rigid in her personality generally. The birth of the baby brought her a new experience, related closely to her attachment to her own mother and grandmother. She found the baby exquisitely beautiful with 'fantastic colouring, rosy cheeks and blue eyes.' Feeding the baby at the breast was both an intensely aesthetic and erotic experience. But it was interrupted, under medical advice, at four months when the baby developed seizures which were diagnosed by EEG as typical of the West Type of Epilepsy. The consequence was tragic, for the baby seemed to deteriorate rapidly in mental response, lost her beauty and became for the mother an object of obsessive rumination. Although psychologically unsophisticated, she interpreted everything in the child's behaviour both as modified fits and as having erotic phantasy content, mainly related to childbirth.

Steroid therapy soon brought the major fits under control, leaving only episodes of behaviour construed as 'absences' or petit mal. Also the EEG improved. But her mental development did not. By the age of three she was still mute, dull, hyperactive, inattentive, alternately clinging and rejecting of attentions, untrained for sphincter control. Psychotherapy was undertaken at that point and has continued once per week until her present age of seven, using a non-interpretive play technique. Progress has been slow but steady. Although the report of the two sessions, six weeks apart, are rather long, any attempt to abstract them further would fail to capture the quality of the child's evolution in each session, which is so revealing of her general personality development.

Session of 3/11/1987

C., accompanied by her mother, comes noisily into the department corridor. She's all wrapped up in a big jacket, a scarf and a hat that almost completely hide her face. She runs towards me and throws herself, *legs outspread*, into my arms. I have difficulty in holding onto her, bending over with my knees bent, and, smiling, in this funny position, we go into the room, the door of which she herself opens. She gets down immediately and in a decisive voice, she 'orders' me to take off her scarf. While I'm doing it she starts to count, 'three, four, five . . . brava!' Then I help her take off her hat and coat. She looks around, goes to sit down on the mattress and picks up the Little Red Riding Hood doll. It is a cloth puppet, made up of a single trunk with the face of Little Red Riding Hood, on which the faces of the wolf, the hunter and the grandmother are sewn, separately and one on top of the other at the level of her neck. She lingers over the face of Little Red Riding Hood. She looks at it carefully, turns to me and says, 'little girl?' I too am sitting on the mattress and I reply in the affirmative. Other questions follow every time that, in glancing repeatedly at the faces on the puppet, her attention is attracted either by the grandmother, who she calls 'donnina' (little woman), or by the wolf, whose eyes and teeth she points out to me without saying anything. After a while she suddenly gets up and, saying 'watch me, I'll show you!'; she opens with some difficulty, the cupboard opposite the mattress. She pulls out a wind-up, apple money-box, from which the head of a worm 'money-eater' appears when a button is pushed. 'Mummy, granny, Julia! I'll show you!' she says, coming back to sit on the mattress. She's very amused by this toy; she makes it work, she looks at it from near and far, she tries to keep the worm's head out by squeezing it hard between her fingers. While she's doing this, she adds, 'What does mummy tell you? No, you mustn't do that! What does the worm tell you?' She looks at me, laughs, leaves the worm and, pointing imprecisely with her finger into the open cupboard, she asks me, 'Will you give me that? Will you give it to me?' I tell her that I don't know what she wants, and she says, 'That, the magazine, not the doll, the magazine'. I get up and give her her favourite magazine. It's a catalogue — not a recent one — of Chicco toy products. For many sessions C. has enjoyed flicking through it and making comments on it with me. I sit down again near her, and she, casually flicking through, is attracted by a fish-thermometer, a white one, differentiated from another smaller yellow one. She looks at it with interest; she calls it, 'oh fish! ... is it a fish? ...' then, continuing to leaf through, she lingers over some rubber rattles, from among which appears the head of a child who is winking. Looking at it close-up, she says, 'is he winking? who is doing it? oh, boy! are you winking? ... where is Caia? where's Marco? I don't want mummy any more'.

Speaking these last sentences, C. becomes pale; the intonation becomes whining, the expression empty, and the muscle tone seems to slacken. She stays like that — torpid, almost amimic, but above all pale — for some seconds, and then recovers, turns to me, and suddenly she squeezes my neck tightly with her arms, and presses her chin against my forehead. It's difficult for me to look at her, but I notice that she has got her colour back and is calm. I say to her, 'C., how strong you are!' ... She gets up quickly, laughing, *goes to the mirror*, looks at herself quickly, and then turns round, and runs towards me, and, saying, 'I'll show you!' she throws herself on top of me, hugging me tightly, and again pressing her chin against my face.

I say to her, 'stronger and stronger, eh!' and then I add that in five minutes I will take her to her mother. She detaches herself and says, 'What's your name? I don't want Julia any more; I don't want you any more ... I don't want mummy! ... What does Grandma tell you? No! you mustn't do it!' She finishes this kind of rigmarole with, 'Give me that!' and points to the worm, which I hand her, and which she immediately starts to make work again. 'Watch me! I'll show you eh! Oh worm! is he winking?'

'C., we must go, you must get dressed again too'. She gets up quietly and lets me cover her up to take her back to her mother. Outside my room, when we are about to reach the social assistant's room where her mother is being interviewed, we meet a stranger to whom C. says hello twice. Having got no reply to her 'Good morning . . . good morning!' she turns to me and adds, 'is he winking?' and I, smiling at her, say 'he didn't say hello to you, eh!'

Discussion: The nature of Carla's relationship with Julia, the therapist, is immediately declared in its hyperactive, skin-to-skin erotic quality upon reunion, accompanied by tyrannical control, at the same time praising herself for learning to parrot one-two-three. While fascinated by the doll, she grasps nothing of the relationship implied by the interchangeable faces and is equally interested in the mechanics of the money-eating worm, which she tries to control. Rapid movement of interests, typical of hyperactivity, is reflected also in the interchangeable names 'mummy-granny-Julia' or 'mummy' and 'worm' being equally attached to the rhetorical question, the answer to which is 'You mustn't do that!' But the mode of relationship through rhetorical questioning then settles down with her catalogue of children's toys and equippage. She is closer and calmer and in a learning posture of mind until disturbed by the picture of a winking boy, linked to her brother.

This is a very dramatic moment and the first indication of seeing meaning, that the boy is winking at an unrepresented mother. This brings a sudden automatic rejection of the mother and some sort of psychomotor collapse for a few seconds. Is it an 'absence'? It would seem to be a somatic expression of jealousy, perhaps paranoidal, and the item of 'winking' returns at the end both towards the worm and towards the stranger who does not reply to her greetings. Upon recovery from this collapse Carla's aggressive and erotic reunion with Julia reappears, only to be followed by automatic expressions, confused in their object, as soon as the approach of the ending of the session is announced.

Sitting of 10/12/1987

Seeing me in the corridor, C. tells me, 'I don't want you!' but at the same time runs into my arms, provoking her mother's ironic comment about the sudden changes of mood of her daughter. While we are going into the room, C. shows me her shoes, 'I have shoes, look at me!', and repeats the sentence in front of the mirror too, where she has gone in a hurry, and where she repeatedly looks at her feet inside a pair of yellow suede bootees. I answer that they are beautiful shoes, and she, ready and peremptory, says, 'Yes!'

In the mirror, she has seen the rubber Bamby on the floor behind her, and she turns round to pick it up. She cradles it, 'Oh, Bamby!', then, jumping heavily onto the mattress and sitting down, she says, 'Ibò' and begins to squeeze its head tightly and to bend its neck, while her face takes on a sneering expression. She drops it suddenly and immediately takes the Little Red Riding Hood. She looks for the wolf. 'Where is the wolf?' she asks, even though she has found it without any difficulty. 'Oh wolf! where are your teeth? You mustn't do it, eh! What does the wolf tell you? . . . You mustn't hurt!' Then she turns to me — seated nearby on the mattress — with a fleeting glance, and, with another 'Ibò', she jumps agilely to her feet; she gets down on all fours, . . . she goes hurriedly to the mirror, imitating the sound of a dog, and looks at her position with a smile and an almost-satisfied expression. She turns to me and asks me to give her the worm. I get up and open the cupboard and hand it to her as I turn round, but she already has a rubber dwarf in her hands, which she has taken from a low table and which she makes squeak. She stops moving around on all fours, sits down again on the mattress, leaves the dwarf, and starts to press the button to make the worm come out. 'My eye hurts . . . will it eat my finger?' she says, putting her forefinger between the worm's teeth. 'Oh worm! you are eating my hand'; she looks at me, 'you mustn't eat my hand! you mustn't do it! Where's Caia!' She says all this without stopping the worm from biting her finger. 'Where's grandad? At work! Where's daddy? I don't want daddy! I don't want him any more! Where's Carlina?' She pronounces these sentences all in the same way, in the same monotone, almost mechanically, alternating questions and exclamations. Then she gets up and, on all fours, goes towards the open cupboard.

It's only now that I notice that the soles of her shoes are

different. One is higher than the other, but in particular the footprints would be different in width and shape due to the different designs. As soon as I realize this difference, it comes to my mind that C. has in many previous sittings 'recycled' and 'made her own' many things, among them the clothes of her brother, who is older than her but with much the same build. So I tell her that only now have I noticed the difference in the shoes and that I have realized a little late what she wanted to communicate to me when she came into the room, but that I still find her shoes pretty. She answers 'Yes' with the same stoniness as before, takes her Chicco catalogue, goes back to the mattress on all fours, comes up beside me, and hands me the catalogue, letting me flick through it from the beginning between our knees.

She describes the first picture, 'He's holding the dummy'; the second, 'A child with his mummy?', ignoring the attentive presence of the father, who is looking at the child. Then, contextually, she says at every picture, 'Is he taking the feeding bottle? Is he walking on all fours? Is he washing himself? 'Is he phoning?' I continue to leaf slowly through the catalogue, but she stops talking. There is quite a long silence, during which I let the pages turn and she watches attentively without commenting. At the end of the magazine C. has her head resting on my shoulder and, when I say, 'It's finished, shall we start again?' she lifts her head and takes the catalogue on her knees, letting the pages pass quickly through her fingers. For a moment she stops at the page on which there are the frog-rattles and the child who winks, but then suddenly she gets up and goes to get the big ball with transparent segments, which is not far away from us. She's about to kick it when she leaves it and goes to the smaller ball placed among the other toys on a little table beside her feet.

She says to me, 'Julia, watch me! I'll show you, eh! Let's play!' I get up from the mattress, and, moving away towards the window in the wall opposite, I urge her to throw the ball. 'Scoglio' (= rock, cliff) she cries, sending me the ball, which, in my turn, I pass back to her, playing like this, between her little cries, which accompany our passes, between her occasional 'Scoglio', and a lot of light-heartedness, for an undefined length of time. It's the first time that C. has used the word 'Scoglio'; I think that she wants to propose to me a game that she has probably already played, but I don't know where; but, above all, I think about how the word 'Scoglio' may be indicative, and not at all casual, for both of us.

We play until C., perhaps tired, stops to sit down and pick up the Bamby again; 'Oh, Bamby! Where's Bamby? Where's daddy? At work? Where's mummy?' There are five minutes to go to the end of the sitting and I tell her so. Indifferent to what I tell her, she continues to play around with the Bamby. She makes it squeak by pressing its head, and she moves it towards the Little Red Riding Hood, repeating, 'Oh, Bamby!', which comes out wrong, however, due to a contemporaneous burp and fart. I look at her, amused, as I go up to her and, holding out my arms, tell her that I must put her clothes back on. C., in her turn, stretches out her arms, but slides down onto the mattress and, resisting me, says, 'I don't want mummy! I don't want her any more', first in a whining tone, then almost crying. I try to calm her down and manage to get her to her feet, while she, staring at the lamp on the ceiling with a sad expression, says 'Where is the light?' I dress her and we go out of the room to rejoin her mother.

Discussion: This session, six weeks later, shows a distinct forward movement in Carla's symbol formation. Along with the hyperactivity and shifting attention following the aggressive-erotic reunion, as she shifts from shoes to mirror to Bambi, there is acknowledgement of the intention to hurt Julia, the Bambi, Red Riding Hood, and she identifies herself with the wolf and his teeth. She then becomes the wolf or a dog, makes the rubber dwarf squeak, as in pain. Then, with a feat of symbol formation, her eye, her finger and, by implication, the penises of brother, father and grandfather are all menaced by the teeth of the worm. It is a moment of enlightenment about her aggressive impulses yet all announced in a monotone, still on all fours as a dog.

It is at this moment, with the child on all fours, that the therapist is able to correct the conventional response she had initially made to Clara's demonstration of her boots, recognizing them as different sizes, obviously one belonging to her brother. This is done without interpretation of the symbolic representation of her identification with her brother, as in the bitten-finger-penis episode of the earlier session. Nonetheless, the consequence of this attentiveness is immediate contact and a return to the catalogue scrutinizing. But it is different this time. Instead of the mere naming of items and questioning for confirmation, Carla sees the meaning of the pictures and describes them confidently: 'He's holding the dummy', 'A child with his mummy', etc. Its natural termination is for Carla to cuddle up to Julia, head on her shoulder. Perhaps she is again disturbed by a picture of a child winking for the breast-contact becomes more aggressive in the football play, is reversed briefly with the Bambi but she clearly resists the ending of the session, becomes depressed and asks, 'Where is the light?', while staring at the ceiling lamp.

Conclusion: A case study such as Carla's cannot of course be more than illustrative of the ideas put forward in this paper, being second-hand material and very incomplete in its data. The formulation which I am suggesting traces the child's evolution in three stages, the last of which has not yet been reported. It seems likely that the breast-feeding situation was a very emotive and erotic experience for the mother, during which she projected onto (into) the child the totality of her renounced feminine sexuality. Under those conditions the feeding situation may have assumed the passion of a coitus between nipple and mouth which bombarded the baby with erotic excitement. Thus bombarded with stimuli, while at the same time lacking a maternal thinking breast that could receive and relieve the child of this turbulence, her recourse was to psychosomatic evacuation through seizures. The lack of an essential introjection of a reflective mother impeded severely the development of her personality.

Once the severe seizures were relieved by medical attention and medication, now no longer bombarded by the erotic breast-feeding but rather the object of obsessive, dolorous attention which saw 'absences' and sexual significance in everything the child did (or could not do), the evolving mentality of Clara could not find a consistent object relationship to support symbolic expressions of her emotional experiences through play. She became hyperactive, inattentive, alternately clinging and rejecting of contact, untrainable and ineducable. Psychotherapy of child and mother have slowly wrought an improvement in this situation, the most advanced position by age seven being shown in the second session.

But during this period of psychotherapy Clara has begun to be able to attend school, though hardly containable in the classroom and able to learn only by rote. Still, she is sociable, if somewhat exciteable, with the other children who seem to like her as she is pretty, lively and cheerful. However, her mother reports that as a regular feature she returns exhausted from school, lies down on her bed, begins to hyperventilate and soon commences a form of seizure that resembles either a coitus or childbirth or both combined. This would seem to represent the third stage in Clara's efforts to avoid being overwhelmed with stimuli and emotions about which she still has a very limited capacity to dream, think, play, communicate. Whether one prefers to call it a self-induced seizure, a state of auto-hypnosis or a state of transformation in hallucinosis, its abreactive and evacuative significance is strongly suggested.

Summary: In designating as Alpha-function the first move of the mental apparatus to encompass the complexity and turbulence of emotional experiences, Bion has mapped the shoreline of a vast territory of unconscious mental life. And in his assertion that he meant it to be an 'empty' concept he implied his belief that it was a territory impenetratable to observation, beyond the limits of introspection, and thus the 'heart of the mystery' of man's move beyond the dictates of homeostasis.

In this model of the mind the locus of alpha-function is the combined internal object, in its primal form the breast-and-nipple, the nuptial chamber of Keats's *Maiden Thought*. One could jokingly imagine that the 'prohibition' against intrusive voyeurism into this mystery and privacy would operate in the reverse of the fridge: if you open the door, the internal light goes out. This is a gentler view of these god-like objects than Oedipus' self-blinding would suggest.

If we accept these limits on direct observation, we are still not powerless to construe from the evidence of its failures? This paper represents a move in that direction. The story of this child's impeded development, coupled with analytical experiences of the evolution of the transference as seen in the play

239

sequences tells a compelling story about the processes of symbol creation. Much of it has been adumbrated in the various chapters of *Studies in Extended Metapsychology*. But listening to the material about Clara suddenly brought it all together. As will be seen, it all looks very ordinary on first reading, but thanks to the incipient terror of having to interest, I might add entertain, a seminar of a hundred people, the mind works at an unusual level, as facing death is said 'to greatly clarify the mind'. At no point in my work of the past fifteen years, trying to comprehend the products of Bion's genius, have I been so struck by the penetrating power of the conceptual tools he has made available to us. As in a vision I felt that at last I had a grasp on the seemingly incomprehensible series of clinical phenomena: psychosomatics – hyperactivity – beta screen – basic assumption mentality – hallucination – delusion formation – addiction – received ideas – creative thought.

Afterword[1]

By Maria Rhode

> The absence of the vocabulary of aesthetics in the literature of psychoanalysis, at least in its theoretical vocabulary, is nowhere more stunningly illustrated than in Melanie Klein's *Narrative of a Child Analysis*. The terse and even harsh language of her theories, and their preponderant concern with the phenomenology of the paranoid-schizoid position, stands in astonishing contrast to the emotional, and certainly at times passionate, climate of her relationship to Richard and of his overwhelming preoccupation with the vulnerability of the world to Hitler's destructiveness and his own. (p. 25)

Readers of the *Journal of Child Psychotherapy* will find no difficulty in recognising the area of experience alluded to in this quotation from *The Apprehension of Beauty* by Donald Meltzer and Meg Harris Williams. Theoretical formulations can often seem to fall painfully short of encompassing the reality of analytic experience, however useful, productive or indeed beautiful the theory in itself may seem to be. This is not in any way to diminish the importance of theory. As the authors point out elsewhere in this book, within the psychoanalytic method dwells the theory by which it is practised, much as the inner world of the mother is felt to be located behind the surface

[1] Reprint of Maria Rhode's review of *The Apprehension of Beauty* in the *Journal of Child Psychotherapy* (1989), vol. 15, pp. 115–18.

she presents to view: and they suggest that much of the mistrust evoked by theory may indeed be of a similar nature to that evoked by the mother's hidden aspects, and which is a main strand of what they term "Aesthetic Conflict". Still, from the time when Freud considered the problem of the "choice of neurosis", the particular humanity of individuals has often been felt to elude theoretical statement. More recently Bion, in his formulation of O as the essentially unknowable, the noumenon, and his distinction between "knowing" and "knowing about", has developed the idea of this elusiveness, in regard to the transference relationship in particular. One of the aspects of the present book that seems to me especially important is the way in which words denoting fundamental human emotions and concepts—truth, beauty, awe, wonder, joy—are reinstated in a central theoretical position.

Earlier studies of autistic children had led to the idea that at least some of these appeared to have been particularly sensitive to the emotional impact of their mother's beauty, and to have reacted in various defensive ways in order to evade the conflicts associated with this impact (*Explorations in Autism* (1975) by Donald Meltzer, John Bremner, Shirley Hoxter, Doreen Weddell and Isca Wittenberg). In the present book, the notion of Aesthetic Conflict is developed and discussed from many different aspects, as the sub-title makes clear.

Aesthetic Conflict is the conflict between the ravishment which the baby is felt to experience in the presence of the mother's outside, of the formal qualities of breast and face, and his mistrust of her inner world. It "can be most precisely stated in terms of the aesthetic impact of the outside of the 'beautiful' mother, available to the senses, and the enigmatic inside which must be construed by creative imagination". Beauty, a property of the "ordinary beautiful devoted mother", is thought of as a quality having the power to elicit a passionate response (passionate in the sense of involving all three of Bion's L, H and K links); and the capacity for this response is thought of as an innate property of the human mind of the "ordinary beautiful baby" through some people may "react violently from it". In many ways this conflict resembles that over the absent object, but it is essential to recognise that the authors think of the Aesthetic Conflict as concerning the *present* object: "it is the human condition".

The lover is naked as Othello to the whisperings of Iago, but is rescued by the quest for knowledge, the K-link, the desire to know rather than to possess the object of desire. The K-link points to the value of desire itself as the stimulus to knowledge, not merely as a yearning for gratification and control over the object. *Desire makes it possible, even essential, to give the object its freedom.* (p. 27; original italics).

One consequence of this formulation is that Melanie Klein's chronological scheme of the paranoid-schizoid position being succeeded by the depressive position is no longer tenable. Instead, conflict concerning the present object is held to precede conflict over the absent object, and "the period of maximal beatification between mother and baby arises very early, soon to be clouded by varying degrees of postpartum depression in the mother and ... the baby's reaction against the aesthetic impact". The use of the image of the infant retreating into the cave in reaction against the dazzle of the sunrise may be seen as the most explicit statement of a Platonist current in analytic thought that begins with Melanie Klein's idea, in *Envy and Gratitude*, that the inborn capacity for love is a precondition of a good feeding experience, and is developed in Bion's theory of innate pre-conceptions.

Evidence for these formulations is adduced throughout the book both from the clinical material of patients in widely varying states of development and from the works of poets and other imaginative writers. The mutual enrichment that is possible between analysis and literature is evident in the integration of the two authors' contributions. Passages from the poets are quoted as being particularly felicitous expressions—indeed embodiments—of crucial experiences in the realm of thought which can also be encountered in analysis: as manifestations of that inspiration which, in its reliance on the creativity of the internal parents, goes beyond the "useful productivity" in which received knowledge is appropriately applied. At the same time, we are given examples of the encounter between the critic and the work of art which embody the features of engagement with an aesthetic object; and many of the formulations concerning the task of the critic are directly applicable to the analytic situation.

Perhaps the central concept is that of the mystery of private spaces, a mystery which the authors repeatedly contrast with secrecy: secrecy being to do with the projection of curiosity and feelings of exclusion, and with the stimulation of the intrusive curiosity that culminates in violence. The sense of mystery and wonder inspired by the idea of the mother's inner world and the parents' "nuptial chamber" can be at best unevenly sustained: oscillations between the sense of awe and intrusiveness, between knowledge as exploration and knowledge as control, between Bion's "knowing" and "knowing about", are traced in the attitude of Hamlet just as in that of a little girl patient who was severely damaged at birth. Violence, both mental and physical, is seen as an extreme form of the impulse to violate the privacy of the parents' "nuptial chamber"; and the impulse to do violence to the baby that is the issue of this nuptial chamber provides the link with the perversions.

One of the ways in which the aesthetic impact of the mother, with its challenge to pride and envy, is felt to be made more bearable, and the impaginative relation to her private spaces therefore more tolerable, is delineated in the chapter "On Aesthetic Reciprocity". Here it is shown how a mother's failure to experience anything about her damaged little girl as beautiful was linked to the child's mechanical, intrusive and controlling "knowledge about" the parental intercourse, while the apprehension of its mystery could evolve through the therapist's acknowledgement of the child's genuine drive towards exploration and enquiry. Thus it is emphasized that the baby's initial response to the mother is to do with what it can perceive, while that aspect of "babyishness" that elicits the mother's aesthetic response is not to do with the baby's formal qualities, but with its potential for development. (This links with observations of some of the possible consequences when there has not been adequate containment of the conflicting responses to the object: for instance, psychosomatic symptoms when this impact can no longer be evaded ("the recovery of the aesthetic object"), or the avoidance of thought and meaning in favour of sensory experience that Frances Tustin has described in autistic children.) As one of the authors has said elsewhere, the development of an analysis is furthered if the analyst can keep in mind that he is "presiding over a process of great beauty".

This mental attitude, and the potentiality for symbolization and the apprehension of meaning that it generates, is also what characterizes the critic who engages with a work of art in such a way that he is himself open to transformation. In Meg Harris Williams' words,

> We expect from the critic who is genuinely involved in the aesthetic mentality, some overriding sense that his encounter with art constitutes one of life's formative experiences: that is, to use Bion's terms, a species of identifying with the evolution of "O"—O being the "absolute essence" or "central feature" of an emotional situation, translated by Bion and others as equivalent to "the state of being in love". (p. 181)

"Commitment should be to a process rather than an interpretation": the language of aesthetic criticism should be such as to make it possible to generate "new realms of meaning through exploration and discovery, based on passionate congruence between the forms of the inner self and those of the aesthetic object". Form and verbal imagery are seen as essential manifestations of the symbolic activity by means of which the emotional experience embodied in the work of art is contained, rather than as some kind of clothing which may be removed or analysed away in order that a secret meaning may be "got at". Meg Harris Williams quotes extensively from the work of Adrian Stokes to show how a psychoanalytic criticism may be based on a spatial model in which the viewer both incorporates and is enveloped by the work of art, and is impinged upon both by its surface and by its depths. Such a mode of criticism involves "thinking with" the work of art rather than "thinking about" it: tracing the formal qualities of its composition in such a way that meaningful resonances are set up within the critic, who then seeks to find a symbolic form that may convey these to the reader. The work of art "does not yield the *meaning* of its message, 'Beauty is truth, truth beauty', to the viewer who has not committed his *self* for observation and exploration". Williams shows that such an approach is equally fruitful with poetry as with visual works of art. The careful attention of "practical criticism" to the quality of the words and their sounds in "On Westminster Bridge" evokes an image of the evolving relation between the poet and the scene he is contemplating that is truly analytically meaningful in the terms of this book, though very far from being a "categorisation of art's phantasy contents". The relevance of such a position to the analytic situation—particularly to such issues as the difference between "explaining" and "explaining away"—perhaps hardly needs further comment.

An approach to the poem that merely involved a "translation" of its "central underlying idea" would, as Williams suggests, lead merely to some conclusions as: "Wordsworth says the city is beautiful for once, but only because it appears dead, and as much like the country as possible". Instead, she shows how, for the reader "thinking with" the poem, by the end of it "the city's beauty exists both in opposition to the ugliness, noise or confusion of its mighty heart underneath ... and also *because* of it". The greatness of the work of art consists in encompassing this conflict, indeed in embodying it. Similarly, in the dream of a poet reported at the beginning of the book, the patient "was seeming to shift his perception of beauty from the idealised good object to the struggle itself, thus including the malign and random, along with the good, as participants in the drama, and thus in his love of the world."

Maria Rhode
Professor of Child Psychotherapy,
Tavistock Clinic/University of East London

INDEX